The Bass
Fisherman's
Bible

The Bass Fisherman's Bible

Third Edition

ERWIN A. BAUER

Revised by Mark Hicks

DOUBLEDAY

NEW YORK   LONDON   TORONTO   SYDNEY   AUCKLAND

PUBLISHED BY DOUBLEDAY,

a division of Bantam Doubleday Dell Publishing Group, Inc.,
666 Fifth Avenue, New York, New York 10103

DOUBLEDAY, **Outdoor Bible,** and the portrayal of
an anchor with a dolphin are trademarks of Doubleday,
a division of Bantam Doubleday Dell Publishing Group, Inc.

Library of Congress Cataloging-in-Publication Data

Bauer, Erwin A.
    The bass fisherman's bible / Erwin A. Bauer. — 3rd ed. /
revised by Mark Hicks.
        p.   cm.
    ISBN 0-385-24690-0
    1. Black bass fishing. 2. Bass fishing. I. Hicks, Mark,
1948–   . II. Title.
SH681.B34 1989   88-39504
799.1′758—dc19   CIP

ISBN 0-385-24690-0

Illustrations by Frank A. Scalish unless otherwise noted

BOOK DESIGN BY PATRICE FODERO

10 9 8 7 6 5

Contents

Chapter 1

The Black Bass "Family"

It probably was a warm and beguiling day in June when Dr. James Henshall, a Cincinnati physician, snuffed out the gas light in his office for the last time and hurried to a nearby livery stable for his buggy. That was over eighty years ago. He carried an umbrella, to conceal a fly rod, and his black valise contained a reel, hooks, and rooster hackles rather than a stethoscope and other tools of his trade. He was starting on a fishing trip from which he never returned.

For several decades Doc Henshall traveled up and down the Ohio Valley, fishing with an enthusiasm that was uncommon in his time. Sport fishing around the turn of the century was confined almost entirely to eastern trout and salmon, but this pioneering doctor had "discovered" another fish—the black bass—which was abundant in local waters.

Henshall not only caught bass wholesale with hook and line, but he also devised new and better tackle to take them. He studied their habits and their physiology with a scientist's eyes and skills. He seined, netted, collected, autopsied; he kept valuable records, meanwhile swatting mosquitoes, losing sleep, and sometimes falling into chilly rivers. He wandered down into Kentucky's bluegrass country and later north through Michigan. During the periods when he returned to Cincinnati, he wrote about his experiences, and with his frequently reprinted *Book of the Black Bass* became the father of bass fishing as American fishermen know it today. He was the bass fisherman's Boone and Audubon rolled into one.

Henshall claimed that "inch for inch and pound for pound" the bass was the gamest fish of all. There's much room for argument there because, with times and transportation methods being what they were, Henshall never really knew such fish as the dolphin or the dorado, the tarpon or the bonefish, or even the western steelhead. But still he had a point. All characteristics considered, the black basses easily rank among the great game fishes in the world today, just as they did in Henshall's day.

Of the twenty-five thousand or so species of fish now living on earth, none arouse more interest among American anglers than *Micropterus salmoides*, the largemouth black bass, or *Micropterus dolomieu*, the smallmouth black bass. By sheer weight of numbers, and by the extent of their range and availability, the two black basses are easily the most popular game fishes in the United States.

Bass are easy to catch, but not too easy, which is a distinct asset. They are strong and fast and pretty fair jumpers. But best of all they are the most widely distributed freshwater game species

1

in the Western Hemisphere and, except perhaps
for the brown or rainbow trout, in the whole world.

A wandering angler nowadays can stow bass fishing tackle in his car and hit the highways optimis-
tically. No matter where he is going, and often no
matter when, he can probably put the tackle to
good use. Except for Alaska, there is no state in
the Union where an angler cannot find bass and no
month during the year when, somewhere on the
map, they will not be striking.

Bass fishing wasn't always this convenient. For
Henshall it was a day's trip to the next county and
a week just to West Kentucky. Now turnpikes, toll
roads, new automobiles, bass boats on trailers,
modern outboard motors, and assorted flying machines from pontoon-equipped Cubs to giant
Boeing jets place any fishing hole within one day's
reach of almost any sportsman anywhere.

Early records are so incomplete that no two fishery authorities agree on the exact original ranges
of the basses. But all that really matters, generally,
is that largemouths were natives of the Southeast,
the Midwest, and the fringes of the Great Lakes.
Smallmouths shared certain sections of the Midwest and lived in all the Great Lakes except Superior. A lesser-known relative, the spotted bass,
existed in certain streams of the Ohio and lower
Mississippi drainage areas. Curiously, spotted bass
weren't even identified as separate species until
the late 1920s. None of the three types existed in
the western half of the United States, or specifically
west of 100° West Longitude, which runs from near
Laredo, Texas, to Pierre, South Dakota. But no
matter where you find them today, bass aren't
really bass at all. Instead they are sunfish, the largest members of a purely North American family
that includes crappies, bluegills, warmouths, shell-
crackers, punkinseeds, rock bass, Sacramento
perch, and more than a dozen other smaller sun-
fishes. The only true freshwater bass are the white
and yellow bass, but common names are not too
important, as we will see.

The Largemouth Bass

The largemouth bass, *Micropterus salmoides*, is the
most adaptable and widely distributed of the clan.
They are still plentiful in nearly all of their original
haunts, and they have thrived wherever humans
have seen fit to relocate them. Once it seemed that

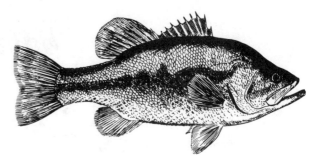

Largemouth bass.

largemouths would never again be as abundant as
in pre-Henshall times, when commercial netting
for them was possible. For example, in the 1880s
the commercial catch in just one place (largemouths
and smallmouths together in southwestern Lake
Erie) ran to 599,000 pounds a year. Modern out-
doorsmen are surprised to learn that largemouths
were also netted in such old Ohio canal reservoirs
as Buckeye, St. Marys, and Indian Lakes, as well
as in many southern sloughs. But changing habitats
and the gradual introduction of carp (which de-
voured vegetation and completely changed the
ecology of watersheds), which began in 1880, have
made such concentrations impossible. Just the
same, while cold-water trout and salmon have suffered from the impact of civilization, bass have
adapted to it.

Largemouths thrive today in all the water-supply
reservoirs of the East and Midwest. Fishermen find
them behind the high hydroelectric dams of the
South and in the giant desert reservoirs of the
West. Bigmouths have found almost two million
new homes in farm ponds across our landscape—
just as they have become naturalized in tepid Texas
"water tanks," in *resacas* of the Rio Grande, and
in old mill ponds of New England. They've even
occupied many a trout pond where they are completely unwelcome and eventually must be poi-
soned out. They like the slow rivers, clear or
slightly roily, of the Mississippi watershed as well
as the rum-colored "jungle" streams of Florida; and
they've found northern flood-control reservoirs as
suitable as the swamps, sloughs, oxbows, and bayous of Dixie. They grow firm and strong in pine-
and birch-rimmed lakes as far north as southern
Canada. And they grow stronger still in brackish
tidal waters at many points along the Atlantic sea-

A largemouth bass in its natural environment: the deep, dark water near the bottom of a lake.

board. Of course, they have invaded California in a big way and were carried over the Pacific to Hawaii as early as 1897.

The Smallmouth Bass

Smallmouths, *Micropterus dolomieu*, have not been quite so adaptable as their more numerous, more tolerant cousins, and that is easy to explain. There are fewer suitable waters without vegetation and without earth bottoms. Generally smallmouths need cool moving streams where the oxygen content is high, or cool rockbound lakes where there is a "current," or where the wind gives a wave action something like the tumbling of a stream.

Milton B. Trautman, whose book *Fishes of Ohio* is one of the finest volumes on fish ever compiled, has pretty well pinpointed the requirements of river smallmouths. The largest populations occur in streams that consist of about 40 percent riffles flowing over clean gravel, boulder, or bedrock bottom; where the pools have a noticeable current; where there is considerable water willow; and where the stream drops from four to twenty-five

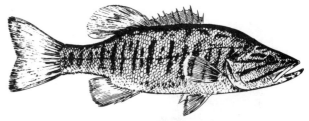

Smallmouth bass.

feet per mile. The last can be determined for any stream by consulting a topographic map.

Today, smallmouths are at home in Maine and New Brunswick as well as in the four lower Great Lakes. They are the fish of Kentucky's moonshine country, of those lonely Ozark waterways still unimpounded, and of eastern rivers like the upper Potomac, the Shenandoah, the Susquehanna, and the Delaware. They grow fat, bronze-colored, and wild in many lakes across southern Canada. Smallmouths have also adapted to some of the larger and deeper southern reservoirs in the United States, such as Dale Hollow in Kentucky, and more recently to a limited number of waters throughout the West and Northwest.

Almost every largemouth bass is an exciting jumper when hooked.

Spotted Bass.

The Spotted Bass

The spotted or Kentucky bass, *Micropterus punctulatus*, has nine rows of scales between the lateral line and the forepart of the dorsal fin. The upper jaw does not extend beyond a vertical line projected through the eye, and most individuals have a large black (or dark) spot on the point of the gill cover. A spotted bass also has a small patch of teeth on the tongue. Neither the smallmouth nor the largemouth has these teeth.

Distribution

Any history of bass distribution would be fascinating, and would sound almost fictional. Actually it has been so haphazard a process and so unplanned that to compile an accurate history is impossible. For example, one early unofficial shipment of smallmouths was carried across the Virginia mountains in the tender of a Chesapeake and Ohio coal train. Many years ago the state of Ohio, as well as neighboring states (Pennsylvania, Indiana, New York), operated a railway "fish car" that transported bass from Lake Erie to streams statewide. More than once, in the early years of this widespread fish transplanting, a local politician won an election when he just happened to show up at the same moment a load of fish arrived to stock his constituents' lake. Bass were stocked by accident in Nebraska when a train was wrecked while crossing the Elkhorn River, and the fish, en route to new homes in California, escaped on the spot.

Every smallmouth bass is also likely to make at least one thrilling leap when hooked.

Bass have been transported by hand, in milk cans by game wardens, on farm tractors, and via canal barge. Eastern states have traded bass eggs to western states for wild turkeys, and there even is a record of shipping bass to Mexico in exchange for quail. In recent years aerated tank trucks have been doing the job, but among the newest innovations is to ship them in polyethylene bags into which enough oxygen has been pumped to last for a week.

Largemouths have even become global travelers. The first shipment of five hundred went to Mexico in 1898; now the fishing is great in many large irrigation reservoirs south of the border. In 1915, Cuba and Puerto Rico were first stocked, and today the fishing in Cuba ranks with the best anywhere (see Chapter 16). New lakes in Brazil have been stocked since 1926, and largemouths have also been naturalized in Colombia, Costa Rica, Ecuador, Guatemala, Honduras, and Panama. However, not all of these releases have been wise because the bass have all but eliminated some valuable native fishes and birds.

Fish swapping has always been a popular practice, and for a long time bass have been traded or given to twenty European countries, the releases being at least mildly successful in Britain, Czechoslovakia, France, Hungary, Italy, Poland, Spain, and the Soviet Union. Bass have gone to a dozen African countries, but appear to thrive best in South Africa and Lake Naivasha, Kenya, where the author has had great luck with them. Largemouths are also alive and well in some waters of the Philippines and Japan, where angling is the only legal means to take them. Elsewhere the introduced bass may be harvested by any method.

Bass have as many names and nicknames as there are regions in the country. The largemouth is also commonly called bigmouth and even widemouth. In the South it is a trout or a green trout. Elsewhere you may hear linesides, jumper, Oswego, or green bass. Almost everywhere, but especially in the South, very heavy largemouths are known as "hawgs." It is not true, though, as one angler told his mother-in-law, that largemouths are the females of the breed, and smallmouths the males.

Smallmouths have fewer names, bronzeback being the most popular since it is an apt description of the fish in many waters. But smallmouths are also known as trout, brownie, or bronze bass, and occasionally as striper or striped bass for the vertical bars on their flanks.

Spotted bass are also called Kentuckies, Kentucky bass, Kentucky spotted bass, or (rarely) redeyes.

Distinguishing which bass is which (since they occasionally live together) is a popular pastime wherever anglers gather, and it isn't always too accurately done. The most obvious physical characteristics are sometimes similar enough to allow a margin for error. For instance, all three species have a wide variation in color, from silvery through

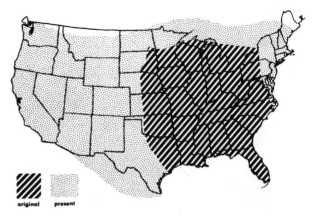

Largemouth bass range.

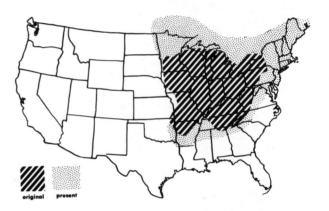

In addition to areas shown on this map, the smallmouth bass has been introduced into selected waters in all states west of the Mississippi River.

Spotted bass range.

Angler Dick Kotis with a bragging-size nine-pound bass.

green to bronze or solid black, depending, it is conceded, on the color and chemical content of the waters they inhabit. Perhaps there is also a slight variation in color from season to season in individual fish—as between spawning season and fall, or when the murky waters of early spring become alcohol-clear in autumn.

Still, largemouths generally tend to shades of green or green-black, while smallmouths are almost always tinged in shades of tarnished brass or bronze. A brown coloration is not unusual. Largemouths may have a horizontal dark stripe along the side; smallmouths never do. Smallmouths may (but do not always) have several vertical dark stripes or blotches; largemouths never have them. Spotted bass usually have a distinct dark spot on the edge of the gill cover, but sometimes largemouths also have such a mark—all of which makes it evident that to depend on markings and color alone is unwise.

Actually, the basses are easy to identify positively by doing a little counting. On all species there is a fine, lateral line that curves all the way from the gill cover at about eye level to the tail. If there are eleven rows of scales between that line and the front of the dorsal fin, it is a smallmouth. If there are seven rows, it is a largemouth. If there are nine rows, it is a spotted bass. Following this scale-row count, you simply cannot miss.

Since spotted bass are the hardest to identify, and since they have actually been called (erroneously) a cross between a largemouth and a smallmouth, try an extra check if the scale-row count measures nine. Run your finger over the tongue, and if you feel a small patch of teeth there, it is a spotted for sure. No other bass have the teeth.

There is still another quick method for making an identification, but it is not so positive as the scale-row count. Project a straight line vertically through the eye of the bass. If the jaw of the fish extends beyond the eye, or your line, you have a largemouth. If not, you have a smallmouth or a spotted.

Size of Bass

Largemouths invariably average much heavier than smallmouths. An exception occurs in waters where both species exist and where the water "type" is best suited to smallmouths. Then the smallmouths will grow larger faster. The world's record largemouth remains a twenty-two-and-a-quarter-pounder taken by George W. Perry in Montgomery Pond near Valdosta, Georgia, in 1932. Perry's catch has been debunked as a hoax, and apparently no really clear pictures of it ever existed. Also, Montgomery Pond no longer exists. But when compiling the original edition of *The Bass Fisherman's Bible*, the writer talked to Perry and was convinced that the catch was genuine. Anything is possible in fishing, but this is one world's record that is likely to last a long time.

The largest fish taken every year in Florida, where largemouths average biggest of all, usually run about fifteen or sixteen pounds, and even these are mighty rare. The best chance for a new largemouth record might result from stocking them in a new, fertile water somewhere, perhaps in Latin America, where there is a year-round growing season. Bass of more than fifteen pounds were taken in Cuba before it was placed off-limits to American sportsmen by the U.S. government. Lago Yojoa in Honduras has produced some jumbos. Some of the reservoirs of southern California now seem to have the best chance for producing a new record with a strain of bass originally imported and introduced from Florida. In 1980 a largemouth weighing twenty-one pounds, three ounces was taken in Lake Casitas by Raymond D. Easley. It is the second-largest bass of which there is an accurate record.

The smallmouth world record, an eleven-pound fifteen-ounce trophy taken in Dale Hollow Lake, Kentucky, stands a slightly better chance of being broken. It was caught by D. H. Hayes of Leitchfield, Kentucky, in 1951. Philip C. Perry, Jr. caught the record spotted bass in Lewis Smith Lake, Alabama, on March 18, 1978. The fish weighed eight pounds, fifteen ounces.

Nationwide, largemouths taken by anglers will average between one and two pounds. Smallmouths will average a pound. Generally both species run larger the farther south they're found, the main reason being a longer active feeding and growing season. North of the Ohio River, a six-pound largemouth is bragging size. South of there it takes a larger fish, say an eight- or ten-pounder, to raise a serious bass fisherman's eyebrows.

The bass of each individual lake and stream have different rates of growth and development. Although a largemouth might reach a pound or more after only six months under ideal conditions, the national average largemouth needs two years to reach ten inches and from one half to three quarters of a pound. Smallmouths need three years to reach comparable growth.

Together, bass and bass fishing are important economic factors in our lives whether we fish for them or not. The best estimates available reveal that 85 percent (or twenty-five million) of all anglers fish in waters that at least contain bass. Figuring that they spend an average of $750 a year for their sport—and that figure is perhaps conservative—bass fishermen pick up an annual check that runs into billions of dollars—more than is spent on baseball, basketball, and football put together. That expenditure includes travel expenses, gas, lodging, boats, motors, special clothing, and meals, as well as tackle, bait, licenses, guides, and the like.

Black bass are important game fish no matter how you regard them.

Life Histories

Toward the tag end of April, in a belt that would stretch from New York to Nebraska, any careful observer can detect a restlessness among the smallmouth bass in any clear stream in which they live. It might even resemble a migration. But actually it's the beginning of spring spawning—the beginning of life for the species.

As water temperatures climb above 55° Fahrenheit, the male bronzebacks spend more time in shallow water, continually searching for a suitable nest site. Then, as if on signal, these same males begin to scoop out nests, or redds, on gravel, coarse sand, or rocky bottoms just as the mercury passes sixty degrees. It is almost as if spawning is triggered by the thermometer. These male-built nests, incidentally, are saucer-shaped depressions from fourteen to thirty inches in diameter, which are

Smallmouth bass inhabit rocky, gravelly bottoms in cold, pure lakes and streams. (Photo by Karl H. and Stephen Maslowski)

"fanned out" by vigorous movements of the tail fin. This "fanning" causes the deformed or reddened tails that anglers often find on bass in early spring.

When the nest is completed the male selects a "ripe" female and drives her to the nest by nudging her with his snout—or by actually biting her on the flank or gill flap. The female usually refuses to remain on the nest the first time; instead she retreats to deeper water. But male bass are persistent, and after several such attempts from a hundred to several thousand eggs are deposited.

Female bass have been found to carry as many as fifteen thousand eggs, but seven thousand is much nearer the average. However, all of these are not deposited at once, nor do all of the deposited eggs mature at the same time. This is a safety mechanism that permits renesting in case predatory fish or spring freshets destroy the first nest. In any case, after egg laying is finished the female either retires or is driven to deeper water by the male, who takes over caring for the eggs and the young.

Smallmouth eggs hatch within three to five days, and at first the young fish (or "fry") sink into crevices in the rocks. From one to two weeks after the eggs are deposited the fry rise and hover over the nest in a school, under the protection of the male parent, who will attack any other fish—or fisherman's lure—that passes close to them. The fry are nearly black in color at this time. They move about rather slowly until all the nourishment in the egg yolk sac is absorbed and until they are a little more than an inch long. This is usually the most critical period in a bass's life, because by now the male parent has grown hungry enough to eat as many of them as he can catch. The lucky ones escape to feed on tiny water creatures called crustaceans and perhaps to grow to catchable size.

About the same time that things are stirring in smallmouth streams and lakes, there is activity in largemouth waters too. Depending on the latitude, this species will spawn sometime between March (south) and June (north)—although largemouth spawning has actually been observed in Florida and points south during every month of the year. In any case, the restlessness in largemouths begins somewhat later than in smallmouths, and serious spawning occurs somewhere between 63° and 68°.

Largemouths' nests are seldom as elaborate as those of smallmouths; sometimes a male will select a site and nothing more. Largemouths prefer to deposit eggs on rootlets of submerged plants or grass, on aquatic vegetation, on either a mud or soft-sand bottom. An average bass nest will be in water three or four feet deep, but the extremes run from a few inches to ten or twelve feet, which is the case in some clear glacial lakes of Michigan. Eggs hatch within three to six days and are cared for by the male parent—until his appetite gets the better of him. Young largemouths that survive feed on tiny water animals called cyclops and daphnia. As they grow older they add larger and larger insects to the menu.

It is obvious that the entire process of spawning is a precarious business. Weather is a factor because a sudden cold spell can interrupt everything. Rains and floods can take a toll; conceivably they can wipe out an entire year's "hatch" overnight in one lake or in one region. Turbidity—the presence of silt or earth in suspension—can interfere with spawning, too, because it diminishes the intensity of rays of sunlight necessary to hatch eggs by slowly heating the water. In lakes, smallmouths sometimes like to spawn in fairly deep water—perhaps in eight or ten

feet. If the sun cannot penetrate that far, the eggs will not hatch.

From the moment the original egg is deposited, a bass's life is one of eating and being eaten. It is an aquatic rat race to survive. Crayfish and an endless host of formidable water insects and amphibians compete to eat the eggs as soon as they are dropped. After they hatch, larger fish are always seeking the fry. Even when a bass reaches several pounds there is no escape, since the sport fishermen then become its problem. But it's only fair to add that anglers are the least serious threat in the entire life cycle of a bass.

Just as bass are always hunted in the eat-or-be-eaten underwater world, so are they always hunting. They may eat anything they can swallow, and there have been many known cases of bass tackling creatures they *could not* swallow. All this is fine for fishermen who show up at streamside with many strange lures. For the record, though, the following have been found in largemouth bass stomachs: an adult red-winged blackbird, muskrats, common water snakes, ducklings, a bottle cap, mice, Micronite cigarette filters, a sora rail, flip-tops from beer cans, and a shoehorn. But the truth is that once they have passed twelve inches in length, 95 percent of any bass's food consists of crayfish and smaller fishes with a few of the larger insects thrown in. In some waters the entire diet might consist of crayfish; in others it might consist of gizzard shad. Those are the staples, but they will feed on anything alive and moving, depending mostly on what is readily available.

Because bass often live in waters that are weedy or dingy and are not as available to observation by divers, all that is known of their movements after spawning is what can be determined through netting from the surface and through stomach analysis, and from information based on a limited number of radio tracking studies and on circumstantial deduction. That doesn't give a biologist as complete a picture, say, as the one a game biologist has of pheasants or white-tailed deer, which live where anyone can watch them.

In large lakes and reservoirs especially, we have not learned everything there is to know about bass after they desert the shallow water where they spawn. Some topnotch anglers suspect that even medium-sized largemouths school up and concentrate in "packs" (at least for certain periods in the year) far more than anyone knows. It has been definitely established by trawling experiments that

Bass fishing takes an outdoorsman to some of the most beautiful fresh waters left in America.

smallmouths in Lake Erie gather in vast schools and travel aimlessly about. No one has been able to find a predictable pattern to these travels.

On the other hand, there is evidence that some largemouths in particular are sedentary—that they establish "territories" that they defend against trespass by all other fishes. This trait has been most evident among bass in captivity.

Summed up, bass are not often "cruising" fish. They commute from shallow to deep water and they even migrate in streams, but this is not a continual or seething movement, such as that which white bass make in fresh water and which tuna, mackerel, and other species make in the salt. At least half of a bass's life will be spent relatively motionless near the bottom, whether the bottom is only inches deep or a hundred feet straight down.

One other point is most evident to observers of bass. Largemouths especially like "edge"—or, in a sense, cover. Fishermen today refer to this as "structure," and that is a word you will read often throughout the rest of this book. Edge or structure may be a sunken log or a stump, a channel or opening in a weedbed, a point of land or a shoal, an old car body, a barn, a flooded fencerow, a drop-off, an old river channel, or the edge of the lake itself. To repeat, there are exceptions, but the "rule of edge" is a valuable one to remember.

Of the three basses, the least known of all is the spotted. In *Fishes of Ohio*, however, Dr. Trautman does point out that they usually inhabit moderate or large-sized streams having gradients of less than three feet per mile with long, sluggish, rather deep pools. Spotted bass spawn in the shallows when water temperatures reach the low sixties, and they appear to be more tolerant of turbid waters than either smallmouths or largemouths.

Dr. Trautman reports that about the time water temperatures reach 50°, there is a pronounced upstream migration into smaller streams, but that by early summer most adults as well as the young retreat again to larger streams and deeper holes. It isn't unusual for the spotted bass to share some water with other bass, and this is especially common in southern reservoirs.

Water temperature plays the major, critical role in governing the life of any bass, but this is especially true, we think, of the largemouth. A wise angler takes advantage of this knowledge. A cold-blooded bass's temperature is the same as the water's, and until it rises above sixty degrees, the fish is not really active. Cold slows down its metabolism, its digestion, and its nervous system. When winter comes, smallmouths apparently hibernate, clustering together under logs, debris, or in crevices until the coldest months pass.

Largemouths become inactive, but do not hibernate. They concentrate in deep water and continue to feed, although not vigorously. They will catch an available minnow, also rendered inactive by cold, and then take days, if not weeks, to digest it. To catch winter bass is a matter of finding the concentrations and fishing slowly on the bottom for them.

A largemouth's life expectancy is also affected by water temperature. The higher the average (year-round) temperature of a lake, the shorter the average life. A northern largemouth from Wisconsin, for example, might reach fourteen to sixteen years, while a Louisiana bass would only average (if never caught) half that age. A largemouth of Ohio or Illinois—in between—could reach ten or eleven years if never hooked.

Many fishermen regard bass purely as sport fish and religiously adhere to catch-and-release practices.

Anglers prepare for the start of a bass tournament; a common scene on bass waters across the country.

But how do you tell the age of a bass? Fish scales can be "read" in almost the same way as the annual rings on a tree stump. Each ring around a bass scale designates one year. Since scales are never shed, each one remains a history of growth; the wider the space between rings, the faster the growth.

Back when there were fewer fishermen, many biologists believed that closed seasons, creel, and minimum-length limits were unnecessary on any bass waters because it is virtually impossible to fish them out. This thinking was based on the fact that the largemouth is the most intelligent of game fishes. Bass are extremely curious, and this results in a good many getting hooked early in life. They soon discover that lures, especially those they see most often, can get them into trouble, and some bass learn not to strike.

While it may be impossible to catch every bass, it has clearly been demonstrated over the past two decades that the pressure of heavy fishing can devastate bass populations if no regulations are imposed. The popularity of the sport is booming, and today's anglers are armed with more knowledge than ever and the most sophisticated fishing gear ever used. In order to insure quality bass fishing in the years ahead, many states are adopting more stringent daily limits and various length limits.

A number of overfished reservoirs in Missouri, Texas, Ohio, Georgia, and other states have been rejuvenated thanks to minimum-length limits generally ranging from twelve to about sixteen inches. Other lakes have benefited from slot limits. A twelve- to fifteen-inch slot limit, for example, allows anglers to harvest bass shorter than twelve inches and longer than fifteen inches. Bass that fall between twelve and fifteen inches must be released. Removing some of the smaller and larger bass decreases the competition for food, which helps the remaining bass grow at an accelerated rate. The bass in the protected slot have an opportunity to spawn and to become larger, more desirable fish before succumbing to anglers.

Many fishermen have come to regard the bass purely as a sport fish and religiously adhere to catch-and-release practices. When they want fish for the table, they'll go for crappies, bluegills, bullheads, catfish, or some other species. This attitude has been widely accepted due to the efforts of bass fishing organizations, such as the Bass Anglers Sportsman Society (BASS). Hundreds of thousands of anglers now belong to BASS and to other bass fishing organizations, most of which sponsor bass tournaments and organize small, affiliated local bass clubs throughout the country. Bass tournaments are conducted on amateur and professional levels, and it's not unusual these days for a major tournament to pay the winner $100,000. Bass caught during the tournaments are kept alive in aerated live-wells, and are released after being weighed at the end of the tournament day. Anglers who bring in dead bass are penalized.

Bass tournaments may not appeal to you, but there's no question that bass organizations and tournament fishing have brought about the surging interest in bass fishing. These organizations have also greatly expanded our knowledge of bass and how to catch them by drawing together anglers from all parts of the country who have shared ideas and tactics. No doubt, the fastest way to learn successful bass fishing methods is to join a local bass club where you can benefit from the advice and experience of its members. In recent years, anglers have taken a more scientific approach to fishing, as is evidenced by the success of magazines such as *Fishing Facts* and *The In-Fisherman* which read more like fishing manuals than typical outdoor magazines. You can also attend bass fishing classes, such as those conducted by the noted American Fishing Institute of Indiana State University. (See Appendix.)

Even though we've learned a great deal about bass and bass fishing, neither is entirely predictable. The very best professional anglers in the country often have days when they catch little or nothing. Even so, the fisherman who knows the most about bass and what makes them tick has a better chance of ending the day with a heavy catch.

Chapter 2

*L*ocating Bass

Only a small percentage of a body of water holds most of the bass at any given time. To complicate matters, bass change locations in response to their spawning urges, the seasons, the movements of their forage, the weather, the time of day, and other factors. The key to success lies in avoiding areas that have few bass and concentrating your efforts where they are most abundant. Fishing at random is inconsistent at best and diminishes your chances of catching bass.

Although a bass has the same basic nature wherever it swims, it must respond to its environment. A bass living in a shallow, weed-choked Florida lake may spend most of its life in water less than five feet deep. A bass living in a crystal-clear canyon reservoir out West may spend most of its life in water deeper than ten feet and will often be found at depths of more than thirty feet. The better you become at assessing the water, the better decisions you will make regarding where to cast and which tactics to employ. Many expert anglers derive as much satisfaction from figuring out the bass as they do from actually catching them.

You must first determine whether the body of water you will be fishing is a reservoir, natural lake, pond, mining pit, or river. Each environment poses a different puzzle, and you'll find that even similar types of waters have dissimilar features. The more you learn about a body of water, the more you will understand the alternatives that are available to the bass. On any given day, bass can be taken from many different areas.

Reservoirs

Bass movements in reservoirs are more dramatic than in other waters, because reservoirs offer bass more options in terms of cover and structure. Reservoirs, formed by building an earthen or concrete dam across a stream or river, range in size from small lakes to sprawling inland seas covering thousands of acres of land. Fish and wildlife agencies usually plant bass into new reservoirs; inundated streams, rivers, and even smaller reservoirs often provide additional stocks of native bass.

Thanks to an abundance of nutrients, bass flourish in newly flooded impoundments and go through a population boom that peaks somewhere between the fourth and eighth year. If you know of an impoundment that is going through its boom stage, make plans to fish there soon. After the peak period, bass populations diminish and tend to level off, but many older reservoirs continue to maintain excellent bass fisheries.

Reservoirs are found all across the country, and

they are as diverse as the terrain on which they were built. You can learn a great deal about the shape and makeup of the reservoir bottom by simply taking note of shoreline features and the surrounding countryside.

If the land is flat, the reservoir will most likely have a bottom that slopes gradually away from the bank. Wide, shallow areas will be common, and the creek channels cutting through these flats will provide the major drop-offs and the only access to deeper water in many areas of the lake. Some of the flats may be flooded fields with little cover, except for the trees and brush along the creek channel banks. Other flats may be flooded forests, a common sight on many excellent bass reservoirs. There will be few, if any, steep banks, and the bottom will probably be sand or mud. The water color may range from murky to clear, with weed growth prominent in clearer water, especially in older reservoirs.

A bass living in a shallow, weed-choked Florida lake may spend most of its time in water less than five feet deep.

A reservoir constructed in high hill country tends to be narrow in regard to its overall length and has many points, steep banks, and deep coves. The water is clear, and the bottom is hard and composed of rock, gravel, sand, and clay. Creek and river channels will often cut close to the shoreline, forming sheer rock bluffs and steep gravel banks. There is likely to be flooded timber, but vegetation is not as common in these reservoirs as in shallower ones.

Reservoirs built in the canyons of the West have towering bluff banks, bottoms that plummet to depths of hundreds of feet, and ultra-clear water. Bass live deeper in these environments and are sometimes taken from depths of fifty to sixty feet. Fish may also be found in the shallow upper reaches of canyon reservoirs during the spawning period.

Most reservoirs fall somewhere between those built on flat land and those built in high hill country. Many larger reservoirs change dramatically from one end to the other. The deeper end of an impoundment where the dam is located may have steep banks, clear water, and a hard bottom, while the upper end may have shallow flats, murky water, and a softer bottom. The mid-lake section will have more structural variation, including some of the features found at the upper and lower ends of the reservoir. Because the environments differ, the bass in each area will be following different patterns. You'll have more success in these types of reservoirs if you approach each area as though it were a separate impoundment.

A map that draws the bottom of the reservoir in contour lines reveals more potential bass hangouts than you could find in years of fishing without one. The map will show drop-offs, points, humps, and creek and river channels. Submerged channels are especially important because bass follow them when they travel, much as you travel roads and highways. The map will also show man-made structures that are capable of holding bass, including submerged roadbeds, bridges, culverts, foundations, and ponds. The better maps also point out areas that have flooded timber, stump beds, and other cover. (Lake maps are covered more thoroughly in the next chapter.)

The largemouth is the only bass in many reservoirs, and is usually the most abundant bass in reservoirs that also have smallmouths or spotted bass ("spots") or both species. A few deep hard-bottomed reservoirs that have clear, cool water have greater numbers of smallmouths or spots.

Bass living in a crystal-clear Western canyon reservoir can often be found more than thirty feet deep.

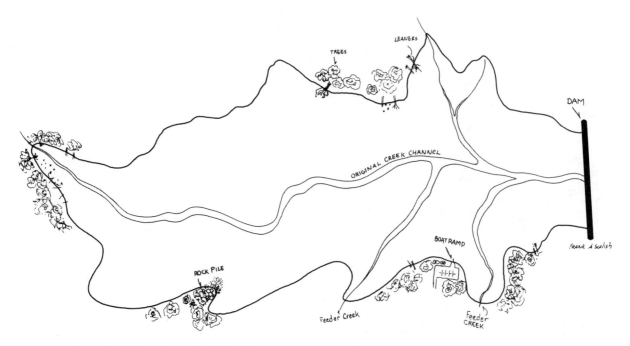

Reservoirs built on flat land will be wide in relation to their length and will have few steep banks and many areas with shallow, flat bottoms.

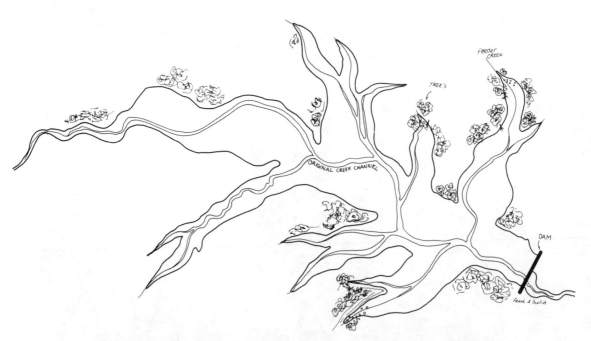

Reservoirs built in hilly country will have many creek arms and often a wide variety of bottom forms, such as steep banks, deep coves and, possibly, shallow flats in the upper reaches of the reservoir near the major tributary.

Reservoirs built in the canyons of the West have towering bluff banks and bottoms that plummet into deep, ultra-clear water.

Aging

As a reservoir ages, bank erosion and siltation will gradually change the shape of the bottom, particularly in the upper reaches where incoming creeks and rivers deposit silt. Creek channels may fill in and become less defined, the bottom may be covered with a layer of soft bottom sediment, and stumps and standing timber will gradually decay, leaving less cover for the bass. The age of the lake should be considered when studying maps, because the bottom features are more likely to have changed in older reservoirs. On lakes that have little bottom cover, bass are drawn to docks and to objects that have been planted by industrious anglers, such as brush piles and Christmas trees.

In some reservoirs, milfoil or hydrilla have become prominent forms of aquatic growth. These weeds grow thick in the summer and form a dense carpet on the surface. At this stage, the vegetation makes it difficult to fish, and many anglers curse its presence. The truth is, the weeds have been greatly beneficial in many instances because they provide the bass with ample cover and a place where they can forage on baitfish. Sam Rayburn

As a reservoir ages, its physical characteristics gradually change. The milfoil weeds on the surface behind the angler will not grow up until this particular reservoir ages several more years.

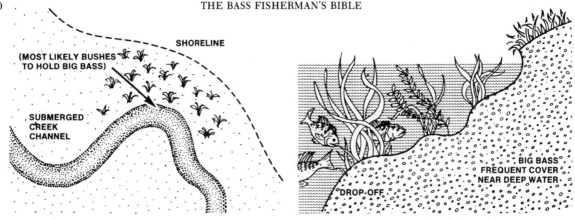

Good fishing can often be found where shallow weedy water drops off into deeper water.

Lake in Texas and Guntersville Lake in Alabama, for example, are two reservoirs where bass have prospered thanks to the growth of weeds.

Weeds

Many types of aquatic vegetation exist on reservoirs, natural lakes, and other bass waters all across the country. Weeds provide bass with shade, oxygen, and food, and they often yield excellent fishing wherever they are found. Weeds need sunlight in order to flourish, so the clearer the water, the deeper the weeds may grow.

Weeds fall into one of three general categories: submergent, emergent, or floating. Submergent weeds grow up from the bottom, but stop short of the water's surface. The tops of the weeds could be a few inches or several feet below the surface. Emergent vegetation also grows from the bottom, but it reaches all the way to the surface and may form a dense carpet. Floating vegetation is not connected to the bottom and is blown about by the wind, either in small clumps, or large clusters.

Natural Lakes

Weeds are the predominant cover on most natural lakes, especially for largemouth bass. The age of the lake has a direct bearing on the type and amount of weed growth present and how the bass relate to the weeds. Young lakes have clear, infertile water, hard bottoms, steep banks, and very little weed growth. Although they may support

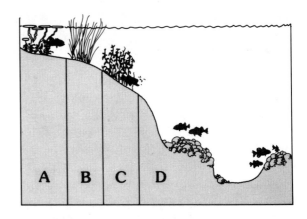

Weeds are the predominant bass cover on most natural lakes, especially for largemouths. A and B show two types of emergent vegetation. C shows a submerged weed bed on the edge of a drop-off, an excellent location to fish. The rock piles in area D will hold smallmouths, if they are present in the lake, and possibly largemouths as well.

other gamefish, such as lake trout, they are poor habitats for bass.

Middle-aged lakes vary greatly in their makeup but generally have fairly clear, fertile water, a mixture of hard and soft bottoms, and a variety of weed growth in the shallows and in deeper water. The bottom may slope gradually in some areas and drop sharply in others. Middle-aged lakes can provide excellent fishing for largemouth and smallmouth bass, as well as walleye, pike, muskellunge, and other gamefish. The better largemouth lakes have ample protected areas for spawning, such as shallow bays and canals.

Bass Under Weeds

I learned a great deal about fishing weed beds in middle-aged natural lakes while visiting 900-acre Paw Paw Lake in southwest Michigan with my good friend Bob Troxel of Athens, Ohio. Our host was Bill Edwards, who then owned a popular tackle shop in South Bend, Indiana. We launched two bass boats shortly after daybreak, and Bob and I were soon skimming over the water, following in Bill's wake. The sun was already burning the mist from the water and would eventually usher in a sultry August afternoon.

Our boats sped past banks lined with houses, cottages, boat docks, and isolated fields of lily pads. Some of the shorelines were also rimmed with thick weed beds that grew up from the bottom and matted on the surface. Other prevalent varieties of submergent vegetation were hidden from sight. According to Edwards, the submergent weeds were yielding bass with the most consistency during the late summer period. Edwards eased back on the throttle and let his boat settle into the water as he approached a lone boat dock on a bare bank.

"An underwater weed patch grows in front of this dock," said Edwards. "Watch your depthfinder and hold your boat in about seventeen feet of water. Cast plastic worms toward the bank and let them sink all the way to the bottom. You'll feel the weeds with your worms."

We did as he instructed and could easily feel the invisible weed growth as we worked our worms through it. We had been casting for less than five minutes when Bob felt a discernable "tick" on the end of his line.

"There he is," he whispered.

Bob quickly dropped his rod tip, cranked in the slack line, and set the hook hard. The rod bowed deeply and the line immediately began climbing toward the surface. An explosion of green, black, and white erupted from the water as a three-pound largemouth tried to free itself of the hook. I netted the bass for Bob a few minutes later, and it proved to be the first of many we would catch over the next few days while fishing submergent weed beds.

—Mark Hicks

While some largemouths use weeds in shallow water throughout the year, most relate to more expansive weed beds in deeper water, except during the spawning period. If the bass is the dominant predator, it will swim freely along the outside edges of weed beds and over the tops of submerged weeds. An abundance of pike and muskies, however, will force the bass close to weedbed edges and into the weeds.

Smallmouth bass in middle-aged lakes search out shallow areas that have rock and gravel bottoms for spawning. Smallmouths tend to be homebodies and after spawning will move to nearby weed beds and rocky structures in deeper water.

Older lakes are very fertile; they usually have extensive, shallow weed flats and can support significant largemouth bass populations. Because the water is somewhat stained, weeds don't grow in the deeper water of older lakes as they do in that of middle-aged lakes. The bass relate to the shallow weeds throughout the year and are likely to be the dominant predators. But very old lakes are on the verge of becoming swamps and may not support any bass. Only carp and other rough fish are likely to be present.

Ponds and Pits

Many farm ponds and mining pits, found extensively throughout much of the country, provide excellent bass fishing. Every year they give up trophy bass, such as Ohio's thirteen-pound, two-ounce largemouth, a state record. Many ponds are less than an acre in size and have fertile, stained water. Mining pits, formed by surface mining for coal, gravel, phosphates, and other minerals, are deeper than farm ponds and have steeper banks and clearer water. Compared to lakes and larger reservoirs, farm ponds and mining pits are relatively easy systems to fish, because the bass have limited options. The bass relate to overhanging

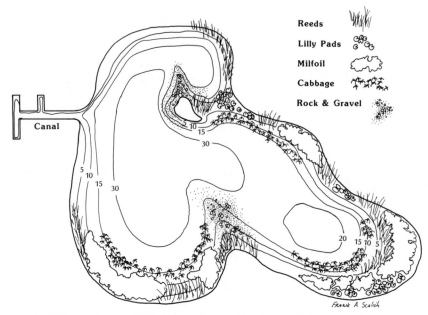

A typical middle-aged natural lake has a mixture of hard and soft bottoms and a variety of weed growth in the shallows and in deeper water.

bushes, bulrushes, and other cover near the bank; and to weeds (often in the form of algae) or to any cover that is planted or left on the bottom during impoundment.

Rivers

Of the approximately 700,000 miles of public fishing streams in the United States, about half can support bass. Smallmouth bass thrive in cool, flowing rivers that are interspersed with long pools and shallow riffles. Largemouths inhabit warmer rivers, and, although they seek slower current areas than do smallmouths, they will sustain themselves near heavy current if need be. The best largemouth bass rivers have connecting backwater ponds and sloughs that can be fished much like small lakes. Spotted bass are also at home in rivers, especially in those that have deep pools and a moderate current.

Many rivers support more than one species of black bass. Anglers on the Ohio River, for example, catch mainly largemouth bass, but also take spots and smallmouths. Largemouths thrive in the backwaters and on the main river, but smallmouths and spotted bass are usually found only on the main river.

The obvious difference between a river system and other bass waters—and the factor that gives most anglers trouble—is current. Although the current is more evident in the main channel of a river system, it influences the backwaters as well. The strength of the current determines where the bass will hold. Because rivers are sensitive to rain and the workings of dams, the water level and the velocity of the current may change from day to day, and even from hour to hour. Small fluctuations may cause the bass to move into slightly shallower or deeper water near a particular physical feature, such as a point that cuts into the main river. A large increase or decrease in current velocity could make the bass leave the point altogether.

Cover and structure on the main river do hold bass, but current breaks should receive more attention. Current breaks, the edges created where fast water meets slower water, are created by structures and objects in the river. A boulder jutting out of the water forms an obvious current break. The primary spot for a bass is behind the boulder, but there could also be a pocket of slack water in front of the boulder. Submerged boulders form current breaks too. You'll find the boulders upstream from the boils that they create on the water's surface. Snags, especially large trees, also form current breaks.

Rusty Kisor of Millfield, Ohio, plays a spirited farm pond bass. Farm ponds are found extensively throughout much of the country and they can produce excellent bass fishing, including trophy fish.

Many mining pits are good bass waters.

Points, bars, and riffles are major structures that interrupt the flow and provide current breaks where bass can rest and can ambush prey. The mouth of a tributary, for example, often has a bar on the downstream side that breaks the current and yields excellent fishing. Another productive area is a bar on the inside curve of a river bend. The fish will hold in the eddy just downstream. When fishing a pool, concentrate your casts at the head of the pool just below a riffle, and also in the slick water at the tail of a pool.

You can also find productive current breaks near bridges, pilings, and other man-made structures. When fishing a navigable river system that has wing dams, never overlook these narrow, riprap fingers that protrude into the river from the bank. Wing dams are constructed to help prevent siltation in the main river channel. Because they create dramatic current breaks, they attract all species of bass that live in the river. Bass usually position themselves near the tip of the dam or cling to the face of the dam in a hole that has been gouged out by the current.

The ability to read a river and determine where fish are holding will not come overnight, but you must learn this skill if you hope to enjoy consistent success. It is equally important to present your offerings in a natural manner. River bass face into a current and expect food to wash down to them. You'll get many more strikes if you cast upstream and retrieve your lures with the current. This presentation will also give you more control and allow sinking lures to stay near the bottom where most river bass are caught.

Seasonal Locations

If you want to catch bass consistently throughout the year, you must change strategies as the bass change their locations, moods, and priorities. Bass tend to follow seasonal patterns, and once you've learned these patterns you can determine the most likely places to find them. Along with lake maps and depthfinders, which will be discussed in the next chapter, another indispensable tool is the temperature gauge. A surface temperature gauge will do for most applications, and there are a number of digital gauges available that provide constant readouts. A less expensive hand-held thermometer will also suffice. Keep in mind that the water temperature is only a general indicator of what the bass are up to.

Large river systems, particularly those that have locks and dams, can be fished easily with modern bass boats.

The surface temperature gauge is an indispensable tool for locating bass, especially in the spring.

Spring: Prespawn

In the spring, use a temperature gauge both to help locate the bass and to determine which lures will be most productive. Since bass are coldblooded, their metabolism slows or increases in direct relation to the water temperature. When the water temperature is between 45° and 54° in the early spring, bass begin their initial movements away from the deep water where they have spent the winter. Smallmouth and spotted bass tolerate cold water better than largemouth bass do, and become active earlier.

Crayfish and other creatures that bass feed upon are beginning to emerge after a long winter of dormancy, and the big, egg-laden female bass are the first to begin actively foraging. The shift is gradual, and the bass are sluggish in the chilly water, but early spring may be the best time of the year to catch trophy bass. They are most active after three days or so of warm sunny weather, because the water temperature is on the rise. Cold weather and a falling water temperature curb their appetites.

You'll find bass in or near deep water during this period. In natural lakes, the largemouths are likely to be holding on the first major drop-off near the mouths of shallow spawning bays. The smallmouths stay near bays, islands, and other areas that have suitable hard bottoms for spawning. In reservoirs, look for bass on bluff banks, submerged points, creek channel banks, and in creek bends away from the shoreline. A few bass may move to shallow water, especially on warm, sunny afternoons, but they won't go far from deep water. Many bass will be in depths from about eight to twenty-five feet, but they can sometimes be taken much shallower. Drop-offs that have cover will attract more bass. Deep weed beds and rock piles are primary locations in natural lakes, while flooded stumps, brush, trees, and boulders will attract bass in impoundments.

Because their metabolism is slow at this time, the bass cannot chase fast-moving lures. A hook-guard jig with a pork or plastic trailer worked slowly over the bottom is the number one producer during the spring. Spinnerbaits and crankbaits will also take bass, provided that you retrieve them slowly. When you catch one bass, concentrate on the general area where you found it because bass tend to gather in loose groups at this time.

When the water temperature in the shallows climbs over 55° and stabilizes above that temperature, bass move up from deeper water, which may be 5° to 10° colder. In natural lakes look for bass in shallow bays. In impoundments search for them in the backs of coves and in wide feeder creeks that have expansive shallow flats. Concentrate on bays and feeder creeks on northern shorelines, since they receive more sunlight and are protected from

Bob Troxel of Athens, Ohio, took the smallmouth (left) and the largemouth from the Hudson River in New York. Many lakes and rivers support more than one species of bass.

Bass often hold in current breaks such as those formed by the boulders in this stream.

cold north winds. They are the first to grow warm and the first to be infiltrated with bass. Murky water warms faster than clear water and is likely to attract more largemouth bass, which are more tolerant of stained water. Areas with abundant cover generally hold more bass than areas with little cover.

The bass feed heavily when they first move into shallow water, and eventually turn their attention to choosing spawning locations. They are relatively easy to catch during this period, and wise anglers release them so they may spawn and insure good fishing in the future. At this stage, a surface temperature gauge can really pay off. Move from one likely spawning bay or creek to another and check the surface temperatures. Chances are that the warmest area you find that day will yield the best bass action, provided the bass have adequate cover.

The warmer water makes bass more mobile and aggressive. A jig is still effective, but Texas-rigged plastic worms, spinnerbaits, crankbaits, and top-water minnows also begin taking their toll. The bass, especially the one- to two-pound males, now roam about on shallow flats, using any available cover such as newly emerging weeds, boat docks, windfalls, stumps, stickups, and boulders. The larger females make occasional feeding sprees into the shallows, but for the most part relate to deeper water nearby. If you're after trophy fish, concentrate on shallow cover that is close to deeper water. The bass are more active during warming trends and may feed throughout the day. A calm, cloudy day after a warming trend can also serve the angler well. A severe cold front, however, can shut things down overnight.

One effective tactic at this time is to tie on a spinnerbait or shallow running crankbait and to cover the shallows quickly with many short casts to likely cover. Longer casts will be necessary if the water is clear. You'll usually find the bass holding tight to cover on sunny days, whereas they may be cruising about on overcast days. Vary the speed of your retrieves until you find what the bass want. When the water temperature is in the upper fifties, use slower retrieves. As the water temperature climbs into the sixties, faster retrieves may be more effective. Try steady retrieves, stop-and-go retrieves, and be sure to bump your lures into the cover.

The bass eventually scatter and become more territorial as they select spawning sites. Spinnerbaits and crankbaits are still useful, but plastic

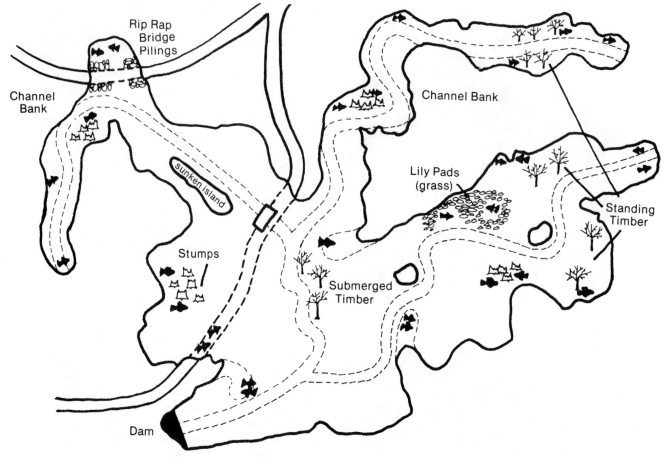

This reservoir map shows the possible locations of bass in the spring. (Courtesy American Fishing Institute of Indiana State University)

worms and floating minnows should move to the top of your list. Although bass do not feed while spawning, they will strike lures that trespass onto their beds. It is legal to fish for bedding bass in many states, but some anglers prefer to leave them alone so they may spawn unhampered. This doesn't mean that you must stop fishing altogether, because not all the bass spawn at the same time. By locating bays or creeks with cooler water temperatures, you can fish for bass that are still in a prespawn condition. Since the water on the main body of a lake or reservoir usually warms last, it is an excellent place to catch hungry prespawn bass when those in shallow creeks and bays are spawning.

Postspawn

The period following the spawn is one of the most frustrating for a fisherman. At first, some bass re-

main in shallow water to protect the young bass fry, and they readily strike spinnerbaits, plastic worms, jigs, and topwater lures. But after this brief period, many bass leave the shallows and head toward their summer feeding areas. During this time of transition, bass are hard to locate. Your best bet is to keep on the move, since you'll probably have little luck finding a concentration of bass. You may catch bass from the heads of major creeks, from coves, points, deep weed beds, and creek channel banks all in the same day. Probe the water with a wide variety of lures, since many different lures may draw strikes.

Summer

Bass get into regular feeding patterns in the summer. Since the warm water accelerates their metabolism, they are extremely mobile and must consume more food to sustain growth and maintain

Bass pro Joe Thomas knows that you'll find bass near deep water in the early spring and that the jig and pork is an excellent lure at this time.

Shallow areas with abundant cover are most likely to attract more bass in the spring.

their energy output. So why do many anglers have trouble catching bass in the summer? One problem is that the bass are no longer limited to shallow spawning areas, and therefore disperse to other structures and covers throughout the lake or reservoir. In addition, forage minnows and other foods are abundant in the summer. With such plentitude, the bass can afford to be more selective about what they eat and may be more inclined to overlook lures.

Water temperature isn't nearly as important in the summer as in the spring. Largemouth bass prefer water temperatures between 68° and 72°, but they can be perfectly comfortable in water that is nearly 80°. They even move into much warmer water on feeding sprees. Smallmouths and spotted bass seek cooler temperatures than largemouths do, and are often found in deeper water in the summer. Bass often forgo optimum temperatures to be near their food source. In water much warmer than 80°, however, they may undergo stress and become lethargic or even die.

Because bass can survive in a wide range of water temperatures, there are usually many productive summer patterns. If a bass can find food, adequate

water conditions and cover or depth, it may remain in the same general location until conditions change. On many lakes you can catch bass anywhere from the shallows to the depths. The low light hours of dawn and dusk are prime feeding periods for summertime bass, so it is imperative that you fish at these times. On especially clear lakes, the best fishing may occur after dark. But the bass in murky lakes may be more active in the shallows during midday hours.

If you prefer shallow fishing, look for summertime largemouths in thick green weeds where bass are likely to have plenty of food, shade, and cool water. A big bass may burrow under the vegetation and reside in the area all summer. On many reservoirs, even in the South, you can catch shallow bass by fishing the headwaters of major feeder creeks. The larger creeks often bring in cooler water that is high in oxygen and nutrients, so any bass living there are comfortable and have plenty to feed on. The headwaters are usually murky which makes for better shallow fishing, since you can approach bass more easily without frightening them away. Extremely muddy water, however, will make for tough fishing.

You'll take more bass on the main body of a lake or reservoir in the summer than in any other period. Anglers who love to probe deeper structures come into their own at this time. However, keep in mind that not all bass on the main lake are taken this way in the summer. Early and late in the day, groups of bass may come up from deeper water to feed in creek mouths and on shallow points, weed edges, and humps. You may get fast action for brief periods with topwater plugs, buzzbaits, spinnerbaits, or crankbaits.

When the sun climbs above the horizon and the shallow feeding activity shuts down, fish deeper water. The key to structure fishing is to probe edges that drop into deeper water. Fish the outside edge of a deep weed bed, the drop-off on the end or side of a submerged point, the edge of a creek channel bend, and so on. Instead of fishing the whole structure, concentrate on these edges. If you can find an object or break along an edge, you've hit the most likely spot to catch a bass. A stump, a cluster of boulders, a patch of weeds or clean gravel—all can serve as a break. Whatever the break, it is a high-percentage spot to catch a bass and possibly several of them. One of the advantages of structure fishing is that you may hit a school of bass and catch a limit in minutes.

When bass are shallow and active in the spring, Bob Troxel knows that the spinnerbait is an excellent lure for finding them fast.

The Texas-rigged plastic worm is the undisputed king of summertime structure lures for large-mouths. It is an extremely snag-resistant lure and you can fish it as deep as you like by changing the weight of the slip sinker. Spotted bass also go for plastic worms, especially the smaller versions, but smallmouths are more susceptible to jigs, even in the summer. Deep-diving crankbaits also produce many summertime bass. Because the bass's metabolism is high, medium to fast retrieves are often best. Use smaller crankbaits early in the summer to match the size of forage minnows, which are still small. Go with bigger crankbaits later in the summer, since forage minnows will have grown by then and the bass will look for larger baitfish.

Fall

In the early fall, bass go on longer feeding sprees in response to falling water temperatures and the subsiding intensity of the sun. The diminishing

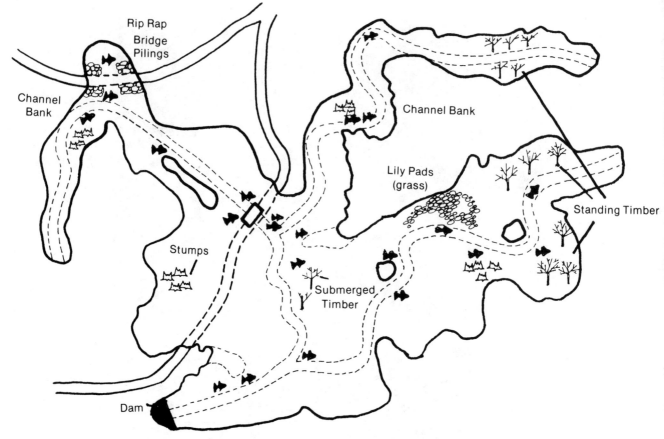

This reservoir map shows the possible locations of bass in the summer. (Courtesy American Fishing Institute of Indiana State University)

food supply also forces them to stay on the prowl. Larger lures are in order, because the remaining baitfish have grown large over the summer. Buzzbaits and spinnerbaits in ⅜- to ½-ounce sizes, and larger crankbaits and topwater plugs, make good choices now. Bass are very mobile during the early fall, so fish these lures at moderate to fast speeds and keep moving until you find the bass. The plastic worm is still deadly, but as the water cools, the bass prefer a hook-guard jig. This is a prime time to hit schools of feeding fish, especially in the mouths of feeder creeks, and on main lake points and islands.

When the surface water cools to about 60 degrees, it becomes heavier and sinks, allowing warmer water beneath it to rise. This phenomenon, called the turnover, eliminates the thermocline and reoxygenates the water. The process may last several days and fishing is poor until it is completed.

When the surface water temperature dips to about 55°, the turnover ends and one of the best big bass periods of the year begins.

The bass seem to sense that this is their last chance to fatten up before winter, and they remain in a positive feeding mood, even though their metabolism is slowing. They gradually begin moving back toward their deep winter homes, and you may find them on the same bluff banks, creek channel banks, points, and deep weed beds where you caught them early in the spring. The fishing methods are basically the same, so rely heavily on a hook-guard jig and don't hesitate to try crankbaits and spinnerbaits with slow to moderate retrieves, especially after warming trends. The colder the water becomes, the deeper and more slowly you will have to fish. You may have to endure cold hands and feet, but the reward may be the biggest bass of your life.

Summer bass can often be found in shallow weeds.

Winter

In winter bass stay deep and become lethargic in water temperatures that dip below 45°. But they can be caught, especially on southern reservoirs that don't freeze over. The jig will still take them, as will deep structure lures such as jigging spoons, tailspinners, and vibrating blades. Bass may winter by deep drop-offs, creek channels, the ends of deep points, bluff banks, and submerged timber. Dropping your lures straight down and fishing vertically is especially effective in cold water, because it allows you to keep the lure working right in front of the fish which are usually slow to respond. Winter bass fishing isn't for everyone, but those who have mastered it sometimes put together surprisingly good catches.

Changing Conditions

Whatever the season, you must be aware of daily changes in weather and water conditions that will influence the movements of bass and how you must fish for them. The intensity of the light is one of

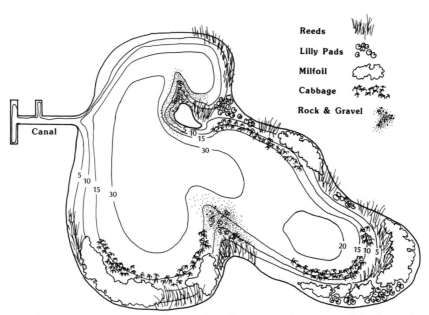

In the spring, largemouths in natural lakes relate to spawning areas such as the canal and the shallow cove on the far eastern shoreline. In summer, some of the bass relate to the shallow milfoil weeds, but most of them relate to deeper weed beds, such as the cabbage. In late fall, almost all of the bass will be found on the deepest green weeds near deep water. Smallmouth bass relate to the rocky point and island, moving shallow in the spring and fall, and deeper in the summer and winter.

the most critical and most frequent changes. When the water is warm enough for the bass to be active, they generally chase lures under low light conditions, such as early and late in the day and under heavily overcast skies. At these times you will often find them in shallower water than you do when the sun is shining. Topwater lures and spinnerbaits are excellent choices under low light conditions.

At the other extreme is the bright, cloudless, bluebird sky that occurs after the passing of a cold front and may be accompanied by a drop in the surface water temperature. Although pretty, such days allow the greatest light penetration and force bass to go deeper or to move tighter to cover. The bass are not as willing to chase lures under these conditions, so you must slow down and put your offerings right in front of their noses. Jigs and plastic worms tend to produce better results under clear skies.

Under normal sunny or partly sunny skies, bass are more active than on ultra-clear days but not as

The Texas-rigged plastic worm is the undisputed king of summertime structure fishing for largemouths.

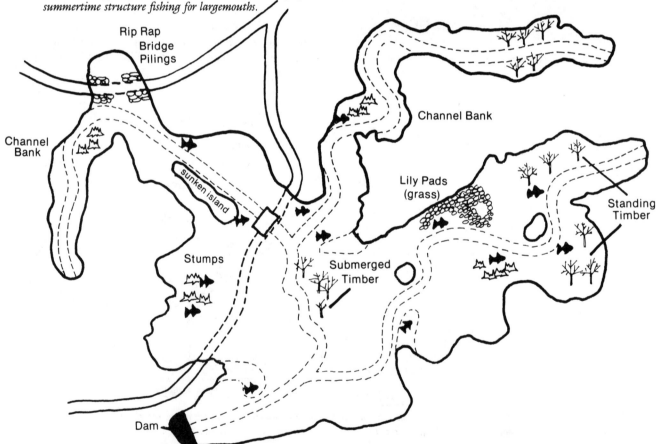

This reservoir map shows possible locations of bass in the fall. (Courtesy American Fishing Institute of Indiana State University)

active as on overcast days. They hold in the shade of cover, and anglers who consistently retrieve their lures through the shadows will catch the most bass. Bass in deep water are not as adversely affected by the passing of a cold front as bass in shallow water and tend to provide more consistent fishing. But remember that during the cold-water periods of early spring and late fall, warm sunshine may actually draw bass into the shallows and make them more active.

The wind, or lack of it, also influences bass. In dead calm water, bass may spook very easily, especially in clear water and on sunny days. You must make long casts so the fish will not see you. Even when you do manage to attract their attention, they may not strike in calm water because they can easily see that your lure is a fake. More successful fishing usually occurs when a breeze puts a good chop on the water's surface. A surface chop decreases light penetration, hides you from the bass, and makes your lures look more natural. A strong wind gen-

Crankbaits are deadly on bass in the fall, when they feed for winter.

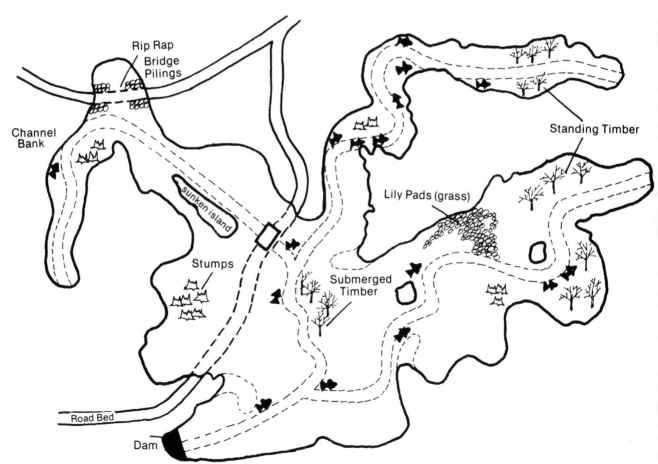

This reservoir map shows possible locations of bass in the winter. (Courtesy American Fishing Institute of Indiana State University)

erates bigger waves which further reduce light penetration. Fishing can be good under windy conditions, provided you maintain proper boat control and lure presentation.

The wind frequently concentrates bass into small areas and encourages them to go on feeding sprees. This commonly happens when the wind pushes schools of shad or other baitfish against windward banks, making them easy prey for bass. The bass move up to feed on the hapless forage, and wise anglers can enjoy good fishing here with lures that emulate the baitfish. The wind also creates water currents that influence where the bass hold in relation to cover and structure. The bass must face into the wind and the current to maintain their position, and will station themselves at the upwind side of objects when feeding. A bass in a cluster of lily pads, for example, would likely move to the windy side of the pads. If the wind is very strong, the bass may hold in eddies formed by riprap points, bridge pilings, and other objects.

A light rain may have little effect on the bass, but a heavy rain can have a major influence, particularly in reservoirs where feeder creeks carry in muddy water. An influx of very cold muddy water, 50° or less, will make bass fishing nearly impossible. You'll have better luck if you stay out on the main lake near the dam, where the water is likely to be clearer and warmer. Sometimes warm muddy water can improve the fishing, especially when it increases the water level and merely stains the water, rather than turning it to mud. When the water is rising, bass often move up to shallow cover and become active feeders.

Falling water, on the other hand, generally spells tough fishing because the bass vacate the shallows, head for deeper water, and become less willing to strike. Falling water is common on many reservoirs. Sometimes the water falls so slowly that you may not even realize why the fish have stopped biting. The basic rule is to fish deeper when the water is falling and shallower when it is rising.

Pattern Fishing

Many significant advances in fishing knowledge and technique have come from tournament bass angling. One of the most important innovations is a strategy known as "pattern fishing." In pattern fish-

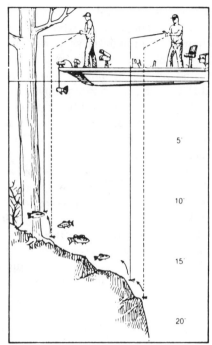

Fishing vertically is an excellent method for catching deep, sluggish winter bass. (Courtesy American Fishing Institute of Indiana State University)

ing, the angler establishes a set of conditions that are producing bass in one location and then searches for similar conditions in other locations. Wherever you find areas that closely match the initial pattern, you stand an excellent chance of catching more bass. Pattern fishing puts the odds in your favor by keeping your baits and lures constantly in productive water. Instead of fishing in a haphazard manner, you concentrate on spots that are most likely to hold bass and on techniques that are most likely to yield strikes.

There are usually several productive patterns for bass on any body of water at any given time. Some bass may be shallow, others deep. Some may be relating to rocky structures, others to weeds, wood, or some type of current. The list of variables can be mind-boggling. Fortunately, you don't have to unlock every pattern. One good pattern, or perhaps two, should get you plenty of action.

How do you go about finding patterns? By experimenting with a variety of lures in varied locations until something produces good results. To start, determine the type of water you will be fish-

Chip Ratajik took advantage of rainy weather and found this trophy bass in shallow water.

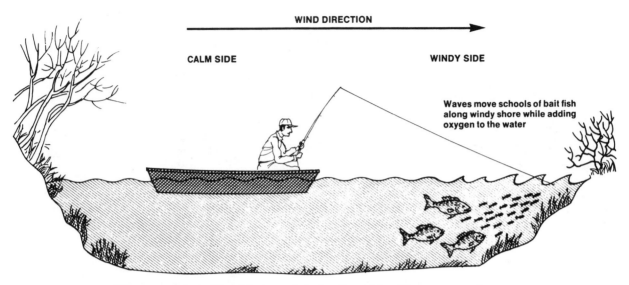

Waves move schools of baitfish along windy shorelines while adding oxygen to the water.

Fishing the backs of protected canals may be an effective "pattern" in the spring.

Bass often move shallow under low light conditions, and move deeper and tighter to cover when the light is bright.

ing, as discussed earlier in this chapter. Then determine probable bass locations according to the season and existing weather and water conditions. Finally, fish these areas with high-percentage lures and techniques, such as those covered in Chapter 4. Something will eventually turn up. Perhaps you'll catch a few bass on a spinnerbait in the back of a cove. If so, the chances are good that the spinnerbait will catch bass in the backs of other coves, too. If this proves to be the case, you will have discovered a pattern that could keep you busy with bass all day, possibly for several days.

Chapter 3

Underwater Eyes

In order to better understand where to find bass in a lake or reservoir, you need to establish a mental picture of the total environment—the environment that you can see from above the water, *and* that which lies hidden beneath the surface. You needn't be a scuba diver to accomplish this task. You can quickly learn a great deal about the lake bottom without ever getting wet, through a process called visualizing.

Visualizing is the ability to draw a mental image of the lake bottom. All good structure fishermen visualize. With remarkable clarity, they can picture a creek bend complete with its stump row, a submerged weed line, an underwater island, and whatever else there might be. The better you can visualize the bottom, the more accomplished you will become at finding and catching bass.

Lake maps and depthfinders are the primary tools for this process. You will also find that a compass and several marker buoys can be very helpful. Use buoys that will unwind when tossed into the water and will maintain their position even in wind and waves.

Map Reading

You wouldn't dream of driving cross-country without highway maps. Nor should you go bass fishing without lake maps, especially when venturing onto a strange body of water. Lake maps help you find your way around—and they help you find bass. With detailed maps, you can often determine productive fishing areas before ever getting onto the water. The key is to study lake maps while bearing in mind the season and the habits of the bass, as covered in the previous chapter. In the spring, for example, you can use maps to locate shallow, protected spawning bays and coves. Maps also reveal underwater structures that most anglers never fish.

If you've been fishing without lake maps, you've been pretty much limited to fishing cover and structure that you can see with your eyes. Although visible areas are often excellent, they are obvious to other anglers and receive the most fishing pressure. Those who have the ability to find underwater structure away from the bank can enjoy relatively untapped fishing. Lake maps will help you find such spots.

Some maps are more detailed than others, but you can manage nicely with any map that has accurate contour lines. Contour lines draw the shape of the bottom by revealing a specific depth throughout the lake. For the most detail, purchase maps that have contour lines no more than ten feet apart. A map with contour lines at five-foot intervals would be even better.

Mapping the Catch

I learned the importance of map-reading years ago while fishing small reservoirs near my home in southeast Ohio. Early one spring, Chip Ratajik and I were having exceptionally good luck with big prespawn bass on a particular reservoir. After catching a number of bass over five pounds from the same banks on several consecutive outings, we studied a contour lake map to try and determine what was holding the fish.

Our map reading session revealed that creek channel bends cut close to the banks at all of the most productive spots. The water temperature was still in the upper 40s to low 50s, and the bass had yet to move out of the depths and disperse into the shallows. The creek channel bends provided a place where the bass could move quickly from deep to shallow water, and feed without expending much energy.

If we could catch bass from creek channel banks on one reservoir, we reasoned, why wouldn't similar places yield bass on other reservoirs? We studied the map of a nearby reservoir, searching for areas where the creek channel swung in close to the bank and back out again. The map showed us a number of spots that had potential, but one creek channel bend

looked very similar to those that had produced on the first lake. We decided to check it out the following weekend.

Chip killed the outboard as we approached the bank by the creek channel bend. The spot didn't look any different from the rest of the shoreline, and I had to double-check the map to be certain our bearings were correct. Chip studied his depthfinder as he eased into casting position with the bow-mounted electric motor. He placed the boat directly over the thirty-foot-deep creek channel. I tossed a jig with a pork rind trailer up on the shallower lip of the creek channel bend, and the lure was promptly inhaled by a largemouth weighing almost five pounds. It was the first of three big bass and a number of smaller fish that we took from the creek channel bend that day.

Thanks to the lake map, we had been able to find the bass before we even got onto the water, and the spot probably would have gone undiscovered without a map. Since then, I've done this sort of thing many times, and you will too—provided you learn how to read lake maps.

—Mark Hicks

Keep in mind that lake maps cannot provide all the information you need to know about a given structure. A firsthand inspection with a depthfinder and fishing lures is necessary before you can visualize the bottom accurately. Reservoir maps tend to be more detailed, because they are usually made before impoundment while the eventual lake bottom is visible to the naked eye. Maps of natural lakes are less detailed and often overlook major structural elements, such as reefs. Nevertheless, contour maps provide a good feel for the lake and get you started in the right direction.

Contour maps are usually available at bait and tackle shops near popular lakes and impoundments. Many feature color coding for easier interpretation, and they may point out navigation markers, roads, and trails around the lake, as well as the locations of marinas, resorts, restaurants, and campgrounds. Reservoir maps may also show submerged buildings, roads, railroad tracks, bridges,

stumps, trees, ponds, and other structures. If you plan to visit a lake for a vacation, call or write the local chamber of commerce or a local bait and tackle shop and see if they can provide you with maps before you go. The state's department of natural resources may be another source for maps.

In many cases, the best maps are those published by the U.S. Army Corps of Engineers or the Department of the Interior, Geological Survey. These topographic maps, as they are called, may not show the depth contours of some natural lakes, so check before buying them. If the lake you're interested in is within the jurisdiction of the U.S. Army Corps of Engineers, they may have a map. To find out, contact the Northcentral Division, U.S. Army Corps of Engineers, 536 South Clark St., Chicago IL 60605.

U.S. Geological Survey maps are usually the most detailed. To find out if they have maps that show depth contours of the lakes you're interested

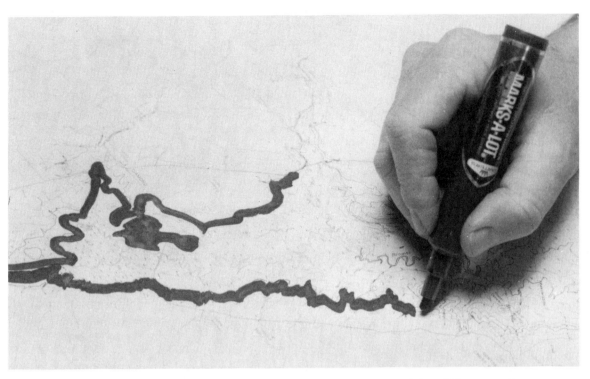

If you get a contour map that was made before a reservoir was impounded, you'll have to outline the shoreline (the normal pool elevation) with a felt pen.

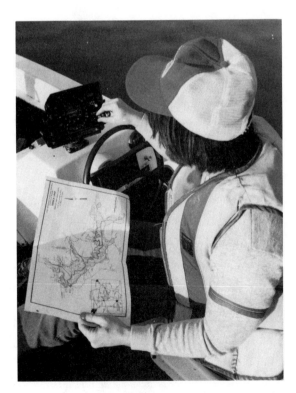

Lake maps and depthfinders are the primary tools for "seeing" what is under the surface of the water.

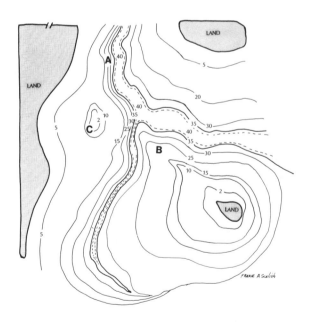

This illustration shows how a contour map might depict a section of the reservoir where two creek channels meet. The lines close together at point A reveal a sharp drop-off. The lines pointing away from the island at point B show an underwater point. The circular contour lines at point C show a submerged hump or island.

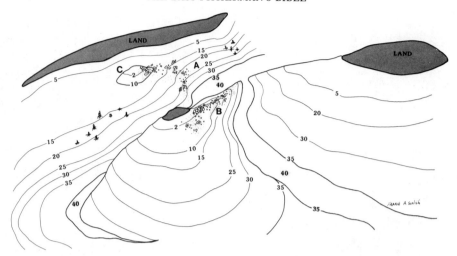

This illustration gives an idea of what the shape of the bottom—drawn by the accompanying contour map—might look like.

in, contact the National Cartographic Information Center, U.S. Geological Survey, 507 National Center, Reston VA 22092. Telephone: (703) 860-6045.

When dealing with reservoirs, dated maps that were printed before the lake was impounded are often the best. If you get a map that was made before impoundment, outline the shoreline with a felt pen. You must first determine the normal pool elevation of the lake, which is usually listed in the margin of the map in "feet above sea level." You may also get this information from the U.S. Army Corps of Engineers. Simply find the contour that coincides with the lake's normal pool elevation, and follow the contour with a marking pen.

Along with contour lines, the map will have other marks and symbols showing foundations, roads, and many other bottom features that may hold bass. A publication entitled *Standard Symbols*, available from the Geological Survey, will make it easier to identify such features on the map.

Your ability to read contour lines, more than anything else, will determine how well you interpret the shape of the bottom and locate underwater hot spots. A submerged point, one of the most prominent structures, appears as a series of contour lines pointing away from the shoreline like a finger. A drop-off exists anywhere the contour lines come close together. A reef, hump, or submerged island appears as a contour line in an irregular circle surrounded by deeper circles. The more you learn about map reading, the better you will become at finding these and other structures.

Again, when looking for structural elements, keep in mind the season of the year and the habits

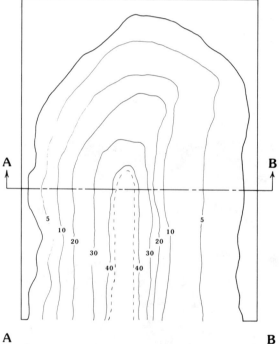

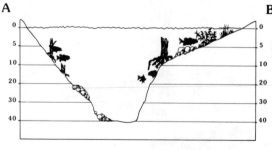

This illustration shows how a contour map depicts the bottom (top), and how the bottom might actually look in the cross-section (bottom).

Crisscross structures while studying your depthfinder to learn more about their general shape, to locate unusual features, and to look for bass and baitfish.

of the bass. Once you have picked out several spots on your map that appear to have potential, it's time to find them on the water. Say that you want to check out a submerged point that reaches far out from the bank before dropping into deeper water. Your map will guide you to the general vicinity of the point. Then you must use your depthfinder to determine the exact location and shape of the point.

You may want to begin by crisscrossing the point a few times to get a general feel for it. Then follow the outline of the point at a specific depth, such as twelve feet deep. Drop marker buoys at intervals as you follow the twelve-foot contour. When you're finished, the markers will outline the point, making it much easier to visualize its shape. If your map or depthfinder shows that one side of the point is bordered by a sharp drop-off, the bass are most likely to be found on this edge. Remember, bass are edge oriented, whether they are using shallow

cover or a deep structure. Should your depthfinder reveal an especially promising feature, such as a stump or rock pile, mark it with a buoy.

After marking a structure with buoys, fish it with a bottom-bumping lure, such as a jig or Texas-rigged plastic worm, so you can feel the bottom through your rod tip. This is an important part of the visualizing process. It will help you determine whether the bottom consists of mud, gravel, rock, or some other substance, and will let you know if the structure has weeds, boulders, stumps, or other features that attract bass. Very often a single stump or a small patch of weeds may hold an entire school of fish. Note the spot's location even if it fails to produce, because it may hold bass at another time.

Before retrieving your markers, locate landmarks so you can quickly find the place at a later time. First find an obvious object on the shoreline, such as a house. Then line up another object directly

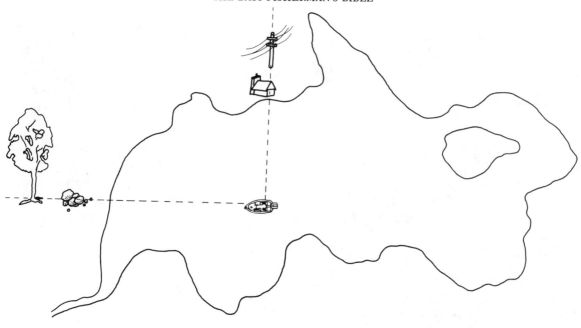

You can easily return to underwater structures by taking landmarks as illustrated here.

Marking an underwater structure with buoys helps you visualize its shape and keep your lures in the most productive areas.

behind the house, perhaps a telephone pole. Find another shoreline object at right angles to the house and line it up with another that is directly behind it. Jot these landmarks down in a notebook. When you return, position your boat so that the landmarks line up and you will be directly over the structure.

Another method is to find a shoreline object and to take a compass bearing on it. Then find another shoreline object at right angles to the first and take another compass bearing. To find the spot later, head toward one of the objects while following the compass bearing until you cross the second bearing.

Visualizing may not come easily at first, but with practice it will become second nature. With a lake map and a depthfinder, you can learn more about the bottom of a lake in a few days than you could in years of fishing the lake without these tools.

Depthfinders

When Carl Lowrance introduced the first depthfinders in 1959, they were not immediately accepted by the general angling public. Fishing traditions were hard to break, and most bass anglers

A compass helps you find and relocate underwater structures.

The flasher on the left can be mounted anywhere there is a flat surface. The one on the right is made to be mounted in the console so it is out of the way. (Courtesy Techsonic Industries)

remained content to plug visible cover near the shoreline as they had always done. As more anglers discovered that depthfinders let them "see" what was under the surface, interest in these devices accelerated. Since then, depthfinders have dramatically changed the scope of bass fishing, allowing anglers to get away from the bank and find bass in deeper water. Today, you'd be pressed to find a serious bass angler who doesn't own at least one depthfinder, and many have two or three.

Advancing technology has improved depthfinders and has allowed for the development of various types of displays: first the flasher, then the paper graph, and now the video and the liquid crystal display.

The depthfinder also reveals cover and structure, such as weed beds, stumps, and rock piles. It distinguishes between hard and soft bottoms and even shows fish. Some anglers call these devices "fish finders," but they don't find the bass, *you* do.

Flashers, graphs, liquid crystals, and videos all work on the principle of sonar. They only differ in how they display the information they receive. Sonar devices create electrical impulses that are fed to a transducer in the water. The transducer changes the electrical impulses to sound pulses that bounce off the bottom or off fish—whatever objects are under the boat. The transducer then converts the reflected signals back into electrical impulses, which create the images you see.

Many inexperienced anglers believe that you simply ride around until the sonar displays the bass, and then you proceed to catch them. In reality, you won't actually see bass on the sonar in most cases. Sonar mainly helps you learn the bottom of the lake and find structure and baitfish. Sometimes you'll see the bass, but don't count on it. Bass often stay so tight to cover that they are difficult to pick out on the display. In water less than 15 feet deep, they may shy away from the path of your boat and escape the range of your sonar altogether. Using sonar and accurately interpreting the information it provides requires skill, knowledge, and experience. The more you know about the habits of bass, the more you will benefit from sonar's use.

Flashers

The flasher was the first type of fishing sonar. Thanks to current technology, the better units are highly refined. Flashers are the least expensive sonars, yet they are capable of displaying more detail than most other types. Many of the top professional bass anglers started out with flashers and prefer them to all other sonars.

Despite its advantages, the flasher's sales are declining. Flashers are the most difficult sonars to interpret. The bottom, fish, cover, and anything else under the boat are all displayed on a dial as red flashes. You must learn how to read the flashes and draw a mental picture. Other sonars display two-dimensional pictures that simplify this mental process. Some fishermen believe that flashers will soon be obsolete because of the increasing popularity of other sonars, particularly the liquid crystal models. But flashers are going to be around for awhile, and they are excellent fishing tools, provided you're willing to learn how to use them.

This flasher depthfinder has a thirty-foot scale, a good choice for bass anglers who rarely fish deep water. (Courtesy Lowrance Electronics)

The top-of-the-line paper graphs deliver sharper and more detailed images than any other picture sonar. (Courtesy Eagle Electronics)

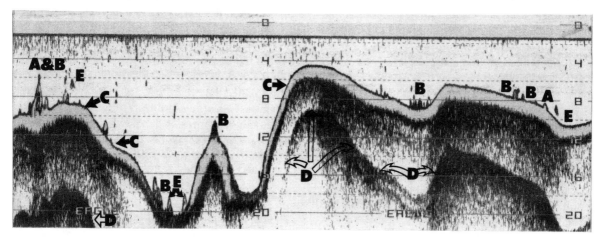

This reading from a paper graph clearly shows rocks (A), stumps (B), the bottom (C), second echo (D), and fish (E). (Courtesy Lowrance Electronics)

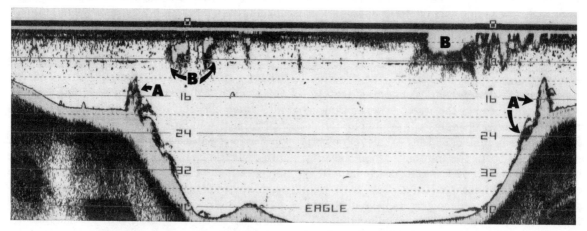

This paper graph reading shows brush on a river channel with fish (A), and baitfish (B). (Courtesy Lowrance Electronics)

A flasher with a 0-to-60-foot scale is an excellent choice for most bass waters. If you spend most of your time fishing very shallow lakes, you may be better off with a 0-to-30 foot scale. You'd be wise to select a flasher that has dual or triple ranges, such as 0-to-60 and 0-to-120. All flashers have the ability to wrap around past the point of 0 when measuring water that's deeper than the range of the scale. For example, if you were over 40 feet of water with a flasher that had a 0-to-30 foot scale, the bottom would show up at 10 feet.

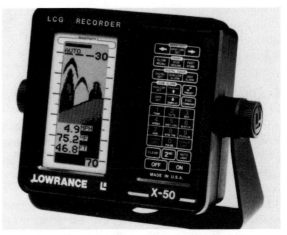

Liquid crystal sonar recreates what's under the boat with tiny blocks called pixels. The smaller the pixels, the finer the definition. (Courtesy Lowrance Electronics)

Graphs

At this writing, the top-of-the-line paper graphs deliver sharper and more detailed images than do any other picture-type sonar. Many anglers fail to realize this, because paper graphs have been around for some time, whereas videos and liquid crystals are the latest technological achievements. A topflight paper graph has 10 times the resolution of the very best liquid crystal, and the images drawn on paper have more contrast and are easier to see. Liquid crystals and videos are continually being refined, however, and may soon have resolution that approaches that of the paper graph.

A graph draws a picture with a series of fine lines as a roll of paper is pulled across the screen. The shape of the bottom is obvious, and it's easy to recognize stumps, standing timber, brush, and weeds. Fish are drawn as arches. Larger arches indicate larger fish, but you can't tell the species of fish from these images. No sonar can do that. If you are familiar with the habits of bass, on the other hand, the location of the arches will give you a good idea whether the indicated fish are bass.

Graphs are available with multiple depth ranges, zoom functions, and many other capabilities. The best graphs cost no more than the best liquid crystal units. You must change the paper periodically, but this is a simple chore that takes only a few minutes. One roll of paper should get you through several fishing trips if you use a graph in conjunction with a flasher. If you do this, use the flasher for running and locating structure, then switch over to the graph when you want to really look over a specific area.

Liquid Crystals

Liquid crystals recreate what's under the boat with tiny blocks called pixels. These units are the cur-

rent craze in sonar, but only the very best models have enough resolution to make them serious fishing tools. The smaller the pixels, the better the resolution. The best units now available have about two hundred pixels from the top to the bottom of the screen. These units do a good job of revealing the shape of the bottom and the presence of stumps, weeds, and other cover. They can also arch fish. However, units that have larger pixels cannot arch fish and they show little detail.

On the other hand, small pixels create an image that lacks contrast, and some units are difficult to see under certain light conditions.

One reason for the popularity of liquid crystals is that they can be used in an automatic mode. They are easier for beginners to use and do a fair job on automatic, but you should learn how to use them in the manual mode in order to get the most out of them. Most liquid crystals have multiple depth ranges, and many have zooms, fish alarms, and a variety of other functions.

Videos

Videos are getting a lot of attention from fishermen these days, and the better units have good resolution. Some models display in monochrome, whereas others have multiple colors that help distinguish between fish and objects from the bottom. Most have multiple ranges, zoom and many other functions. Like liquid crystals, videos are easy to use.

One problem with videos is that they are difficult to see in bright light. They are also expensive. A quality video costs more than a quality graph, yet the graph provides more detail.

Tuning Sonar for Optimum Performance

Even though some sonars can be operated in automatic modes, most of them must be tuned manually to get the most detail. The key control is sensitivity. Many anglers set the sensitivity so low that they get only a bottom reading. In order for your sonar to pick up fish, along with weeds and other cover, you must increase the sensitivity until you get a double reading called an echo. For example, if you are over fifteen feet of water with a flasher, you increase the sensitivity until the bottom flashes at fifteen feet and the echo flashes at thirty feet. With picture-type sonars, the echo is displayed beneath the bottom. You have to change the sensitivity throughout the day, because it must be turned up in deeper water and turned down in shallower water.

In addition to providing more detail, the echo can tell you a great deal about the makeup of the bottom. When you're over a soft bottom, the echo will be weak or may even disappear. That's because a soft bottom absorbs the transducer's signals. The echo will be bright and distinct over rock or gravel, because a hard bottom reflects strong signals.

The suppression control reduces interference and is generally used when running the boat at high speeds. Leave the suppression off when idling or fishing. It reduces the quality of the display, making it more difficult to distinguish fish and other objects. If the unit has been installed properly, you should have few problems with interference at slow speeds.

Installation

Those who fish from car-toppers or rental boats need not deny themselves the benefits of sonar. There are many portable units available that run on lantern batteries. The transducer is fastened to the transom with a rod-like holder or with a suction cup device.

When installing a stationary unit, place it where you can read it easily when running the primary motor and while fishing. If you run your boat from one position and cast from another, you may need two sonars. In many cases, a swivel-base mount

Video depthfinders come with screens that display in monochrome or in multiple colors. (Courtesy Techsonic Industries)

This illustration demonstrates how a rock pile that is holding smallmouth bass and walleye might be displayed on a flasher depthfinder. (Courtesy Lowrance Electronics)

will allow you to read your sonar from different locations in the boat.

Most bass boaters mount one or two sonars on the console, perhaps a flasher and a graph, and another in the bow of the boat for use when fishing. The transducer for the sonar on the front deck is generally fastened to the bottom of the electric

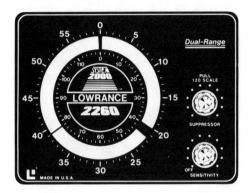

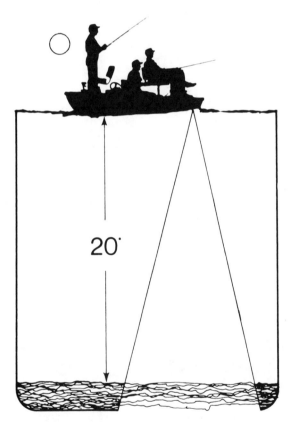

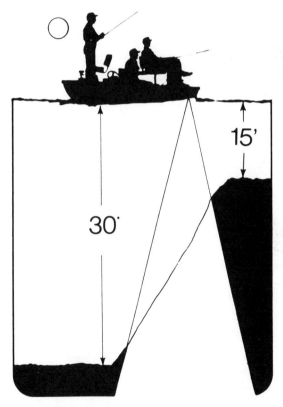

The sensitivity on your sonar should be turned up until you get a second reading below the bottom called an echo, here shown at 39 feet on the flasher's dial. Only use the suppression when boating at high speeds. (Courtesy Lowrance Electronics)

A smooth sloping bottom is displayed on the flasher as a wide, nearly solid signal. (Courtesy Lowrance Electronics)

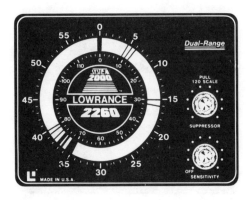

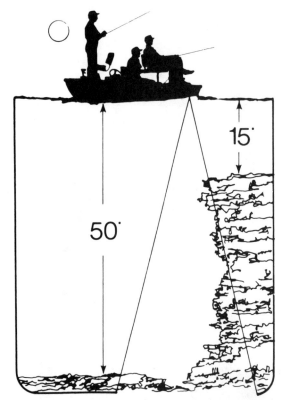

A steep rocky ledge is displayed as a wide broken band. (Courtesy Lowrance Electronics)

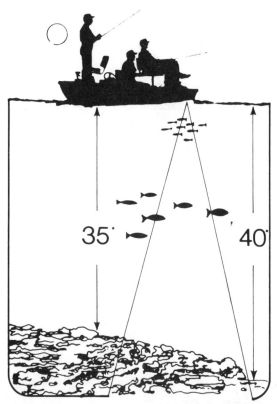

The width of the signal on a flasher indicates the size of the fish. Thin lines could be small fish or baitfish. Wider, brighter signals indicate larger fish. (Courtesy Lowrance Electronics)

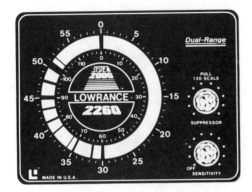

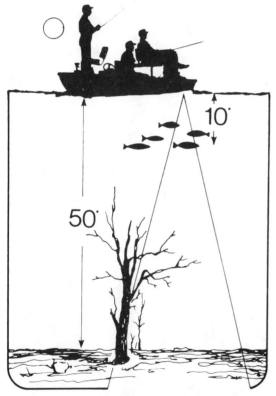

A broken signal could reveal a tree and gamefish. The more you know about a given lake and how to use your sonar, the better you will become at interpreting the signals. (Courtesy Lowrance Electronics)

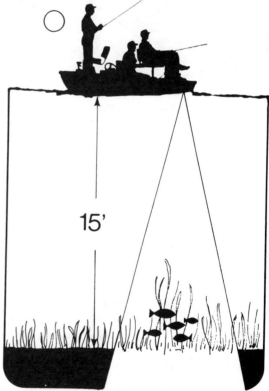

Weeds return pale, thin signals that tie in with the bottom signal. (Courtesy Lowrance Electronics)

This liquid crystal depthfinder is fastened to a swivel mount. The angler can rotate the unit so it can be seen from anywhere in the boat. Note the in-dash flasher that is used for high-speed running. (Courtesy Techsonic Industries)

Portable depthfinders are available for use with car-toppers, canoes, rental boats, rafts, and similar watercraft. (Courtesy Ray Jefferson)

maneuvering motor. In this way the sonar shows the angler what is directly beneath him, not what is beneath his transom fifteen to twenty feet behind. Some transducers can be attached to electric motor housings with radiator hose clamps. Other kinds of attachment devices are also available.

Most problems with sonars result from improper transducer installation. A transducer can send and receive signals through water, but not through air. As long as the head of the transducer remains under water, it should perform well. Transducers are often fastened to a mounting bracket that is held to the transom with screws, or to a flip-up bracket. These mountings give good performance at slow to moderate speeds. At fast speeds, however, your hull may create air bubbles under the transducer that will cause interference. With some boats, you can eliminate this problem by mounting the transducer flush with the bottom of the hull in an area that creates the least turbulence.

This angler has found that a portable liquid crystal sonar is the ideal match for his small boat. (Courtesy Lowrance Electronics)

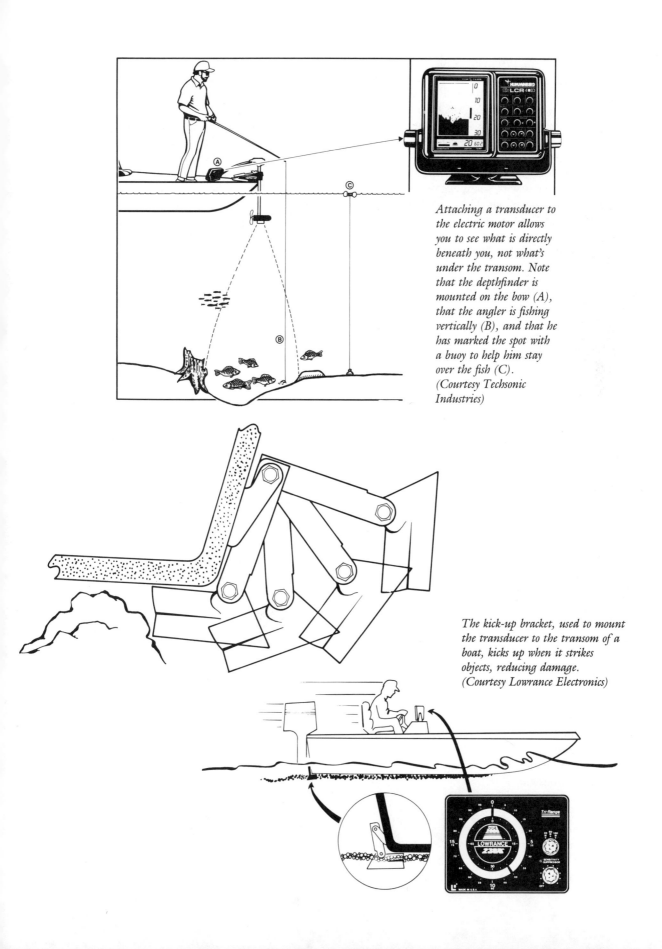

Attaching a transducer to the electric motor allows you to see what is directly beneath you, not what's under the transom. Note that the depthfinder is mounted on the bow (A), that the angler is fishing vertically (B), and that he has marked the spot with a buoy to help him stay over the fish (C). (Courtesy Techsonic Industries)

The kick-up bracket, used to mount the transducer to the transom of a boat, kicks up when it strikes objects, reducing damage. (Courtesy Lowrance Electronics)

You'll have fewer problems with water turbulence and possible damage to the transducer if you mount it to shoot through the hull. A transducer will send signals through fiberglass. It will not shoot through aluminum, wood or foam flotation, so be sure there are no layers of these materials between your transducer and the water.

For through-the-hull installation, thoroughly clean the bilge area with soapy water. Then sand the bottom where you've decided to mount the transducer, and form a small circular dam with caulk. Mix a two-part epoxy (a slow-drying type will allow air bubbles to escape before hardening).

Smear epoxy on the face of the transducer and on the area you've prepared for the transducer. Put the transducer in the center of the caulk dam and place a weight on it until it dries.

There is more to the art of using sonar than can be covered in this brief chapter. Whatever type of sonar you get, be sure to study the owner's manual thoroughly. For in-depth information on using sonar, consider obtaining a copy of "The Comprehensive Guide to Fish Locators" by Babe Winkelman, Babe Winkelman Productions, Inc., P.O. Box 407, Brainerd, MN 56401.

Chapter 4

The Right Lure for the Job

There's something mystical about bass lures. Deep within every angler springs the eternal hope that his next lure will slay bass like nothing before. We snap up the latest creations that hit the market, or whatever the pros have used in winning recent tournaments, or perhaps something a fishing buddy has whispered to us. Fiddling with new lures is part of the fun of bass fishing, but it's easy to let things get out of hand.

The most consistent bass anglers realize that there are no magic lures. They regard their lures as tools and they strive to fill their tackle boxes with an assortment that will allow them to handle any fishing chore they encounter. Instead of buying lures according to whim, you should break them down into categories. The basic lure categories are plastic worms, jigs, spinnerbaits, crankbaits, and topwater and specialty lures. Your goal should be to fill each of these categories with a selection that will allow you to fish from top to bottom, regardless of the lake you are fishing or the cover or structure that confronts you. When selecting a lure, you should consider—in the order of importance—its depth, speed, action, and color.

The first step toward improving your success with any lure is to sharpen the hooks and keep them sharp. A truly sharp hook should dig into the back of your thumbnail at the lightest touch, but very few hooks are sharp enough to fish with straight from their packages. Taking time to do this simple chore will increase your catch by 25 percent or more. Large hooks, such as worm hooks, may be sharpened first with a flat file and then finished with a small stone. Hone small hooks with a stone only. Some of the available hook-sharpening devices also work quite well.

Plastic Worms

The plastic worm reigns as the number one bass lure, and its virtues have been widely extolled for over two decades. Successful bass anglers everywhere, including most top tournament professionals, rely heavily on this lure. The worm is deadly whether at a water depth of one foot or over thirty, and can even be fished on the surface. It will produce bass from the thickest cover imaginable or from clean bottoms, and under all but the coldest of water conditions.

It is difficult to explain why plastic worms are so effective. They do not really resemble anything in nature except night crawlers, which are not aquatic and are nowhere an important part of a bass's diet. Plastic worms do look somewhat like leeches or lampreys, on which bass will feed, but these are

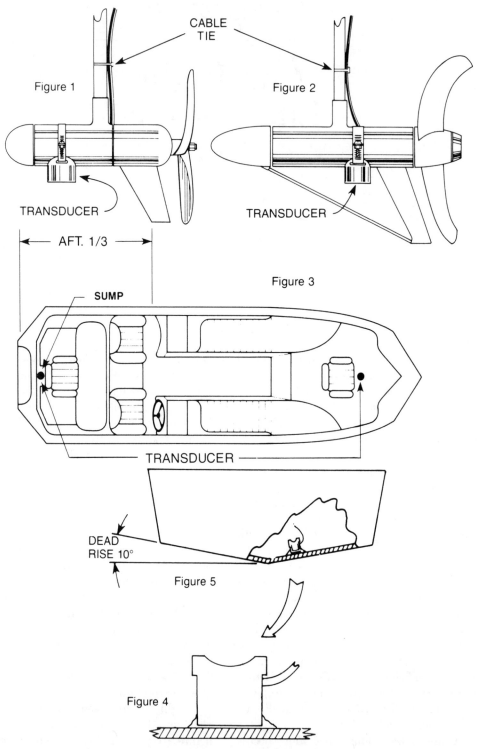

CABLE TIE

Figure 1

Figure 2

TRANSDUCER

TRANSDUCER

AFT. 1/3

Figure 3

SUMP

TRANSDUCER

DEAD RISE 10°

Figure 5

Figure 4

(Figure 1 and Figure 2) It is wise for anglers who fish from bow-fishing platforms to clamp a transducer to the trolling motor housing. Transducers also shoot through the hulls of fiberglass boats, which prevents damage to the transducer and provides better readings at high speeds (Figures 3, 4, and 5). (Courtesy Lowrance Electronics)

The plastic worm reigns as the number one bass lure of all time.

not abundant in typical largemouth bass waters. The worm's appeal probably derives from its soft texture and lively action, which make it appear and feel more lifelike than any other lure.

Recent studies have revealed that the plastic worm is the only lure that bass do not become conditioned to after repeated exposure. This is extremely important to remember on heavily fished waters where bass see all popular lures on an almost daily basis. The bass may eventually shy away from other lures, but the plastic worm will continue to entice strikes, day after day and year after year.

These days, the many styles and colors of plastic worms make for a mind-boggling choice. Do yourself a favor and limit your initial selection to a few straight and swimming tail designs in four, six, and seven-inch sizes. Smaller sizes generally work better in clear water, whereas larger sizes should be your first choice in murky water. If you fish Florida waters that are noted for big bass, you may also want to have worms measuring eight inches or longer. Keep worm colors to a minimum when you

start out. Black, dark purple, and motoroil are proven producers in stained water. Blue, green and red are good bets in clear water.

The Texas Rigged Plastic Worm

Of the many ways to fish plastic worms for bass, the Texas rig is the most widely used. The point of the hook is embedded into the body of the plastic worm, making it virtually snag-free. You can cast this lure into weeds, brush, and fallen trees, and the worm will usually slither through and over the obstacles without hanging up. Because a Texas-rigged plastic worm will penetrate heavy cover where bass love to lurk, it can be used to extract bass that most other lures can't reach.

The Texas rig requires worm hooks that have been specifically designed for this setup. Many of these stout hooks have unique bends in them that facilitate Texas-rigging and improve hook setting. Most also have one or more tiny barbs on the shaft just below the line tie to prevent the worm from sliding down. Some popular worm hooks include the Tru-Turn, Eagle Claw's 95JB, Mister Twister's Keeper, and Mustad's Superior Point Sproat Worm Hook. For most four-to-seven-inch worms, 1/0 to 3/0 hook sizes will do. The thicker the worm, the larger the hook. You may need larger hooks than normal when you have to force bass from heavy cover with stout tackle.

The final component of the Texas rig is the slip sinker. This bullet-shaped weight has a hole through its center for the line. You'll need a variety of sizes from 1/16 to one ounce. As a rule of thumb, use the lightest slip sinker that effectively does the job. The wind, the depth of the water, and the thickness of the cover will determine the proper weight. Light slip sinkers are sometimes needed when fishing for temperamental bass in clear water, but you should stay with heavier weights, say 1/4 of an ounce, until you become more skilled at fishing with the Texas rig. You may need to use a heavier sinker on windy days, or when fishing deep, or when you need to penetrate heavy cover. Lighter sinkers make it more difficult to control the worm and detect strikes.

To rig a worm Texas-style, first thread your line through the hole on the pointed end of the slip sinker and tie it to your hook. Then push the point of the hook into the top of the worm from about 1/4 to 3/4 of an inch, depending on the style of hook you are using. Push the point out the side of the

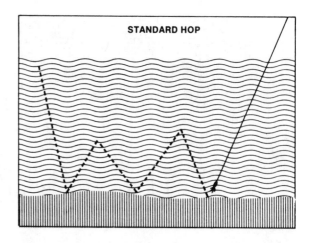

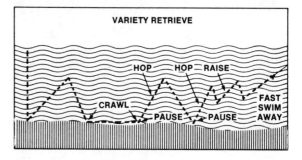

Mark Hicks with a largemouth bass he caught on a Texas-rigged plastic worm.

worm and pull the hook through until the eye is buried in the worm's head. Then turn the point of the hook 180 degrees and push it into the body of the worm so that the worm hangs straight.

Many anglers let the sinker slide freely on the line when fishing with the Texas rig. They claim that this gives the worm better action, prevents the bass from feeling any unnatural weight, and allows the hook to penetrate more easily. Some anglers peg the slip sinker by jamming a toothpick into the hole with the line and snipping off the excess wood. This prevents the sinker from sliding and holds it to the head of the worm. Proponents of this method claim that you can feel strikes better and that the sinker will not foul up in weeds and other cover as it sometimes does when allowed to slide on the line. Try both methods. You may find that you prefer to peg the sinker when fishing dense cover and to let the sinker slide when fishing more open conditions.

A slow bottom-hopping retrieve is effective in most instances. When bass strike a plastic worm it is almost always while it is falling, so be especially alert as the worm sinks after the cast. Once the worm touches the bottom, lift it with your rod tip only six to twelve inches and let it fall back to the bottom on a semi-tight line. Tune all your senses to the lure as it sinks. Be patient and be sure your worm touches the bottom again after each lift. You'll have an easier time detecting strikes if you hold the rod at a 90-degree angle to the worm. This keeps your rod in the ten-to-twelve o'clock position during most of the retrieve. You may want to give the worm two or three hops before taking up slack line with the reel. Do not move the worm by cranking the reel.

It pays to experiment with how high and fast you work the lift-drop retrieve, because the bass will show a preference. On some days you may have to soak the worm on the bottom for several seconds between hops. On other days you may have to give the worm several short consecutive hops before pausing. When the worm is in cover, such as a submerged brush pile, you can often encourage strikes from reluctant bass by methodically lifting

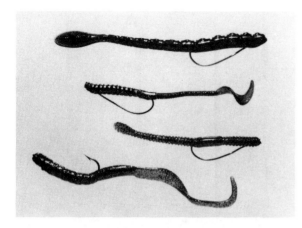

A few of the many styles of plastic worms available. Note that the bottom worm has been rigged on the hook with a kink so it will spin when retrieved.

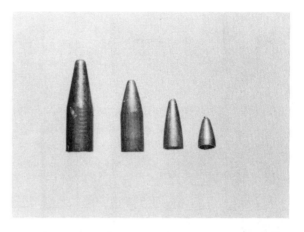

You'll need slip sinkers in a variety of sizes to fish for bass under different circumstances.

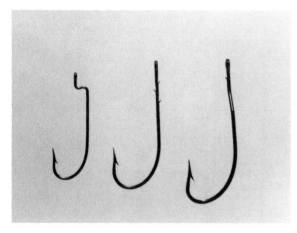

"Worm hooks" designed for the Texas-rigged worm come in a variety of styles.

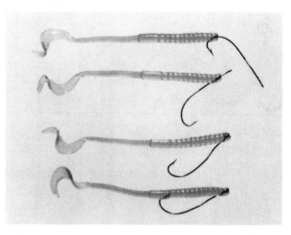

These four steps, from top to bottom, show how to insert a hook for the Texas rig.

and lowering the worm in one place while the line is draped over a limb. Another productive tactic, called doodling, is to shake the rod tip. This gives the worm an alluring action while staying right in front of the bass.

Distinguishing the feel of a strike from the feel of other things your worm might touch is the most demanding aspect of fishing the Texas rig. The strike will often come as a distinct tap, but you may feel only a slight heaviness. These sensations are similar to those you'll feel when your worm bumps a rock or limb, or when it pulls against a strand of aquatic vegetation. No one can tell you exactly what the strike feels like. Experience is the only teacher.

A sensitive rod that has a high content of graphite or boron will help you feel strikes. The rod should also have a medium-heavy or heavy action, because it takes plenty of backbone to drive the hook through the plastic worm and into the mouth of the bass. (Rods are covered in Chapter 5.) A highly visible clear or blue fluorescent line will also help you determine strikes, since you will often see strikes that you never feel. Whenever you see your line jump slightly and start moving off, you can be certain that a bass has engulfed your worm. Although 14-pound test line is excellent for a wide variety of circumstances, you should drop down to 8- or 10-pound test when fishing deep, clear water

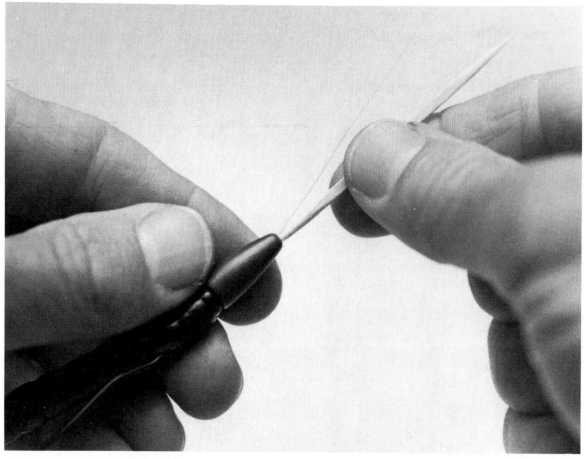

To prevent the slip sinker from sliding, firmly insert a toothpick into the hole with the line. Then snip or break off the excess wood and the slip sinker will stay at the head of the worm.

that has few snags. When fishing extremely dense cover, you may have to go as high as 25- or 30-pound test to prevent breakoffs.

Many anglers have a hard time deciding when and how to set the hook after a bass picks up their worm. Even though bass will frequently swim off with your worms and sometimes swallow them, they are just as likely to eject worms moments after taking them. You'll put the odds in your favor if you set the hook as soon as possible after the strike. When you let a bass run with your worm, you increase the chance of excess slack getting in your line, reducing the effectiveness of your hook set.

The instant you sense a strike, point your rod tip toward the bass and take a few quick turns on the reel, but leave a little slack. Repress the urge to reel in every last bit of slack line, or the bass may feel resistance and drop the worm. Snap the

rod up and back while holding your elbows close to your body to generate maximum leverage. That little bit of slack you left in the line will allow your rod to get moving fast before hitting the bass. Hold your rod tightly, because the sudden stop should be jarring. Do you really have to set the hook that hard when fishing the Texas rig? Absolutely! Halfhearted hook sets result in lost fish.

The Carolina Rig

Another deservedly popular plastic worm rig is widely known as the Carolina rig. Unlike the Texas-rigged plastic worm which is designed to make regular contact with the bottom, the Carolina-rigged plastic worm swims freely above the bottom. First thread a slip sinker with the line, followed by a

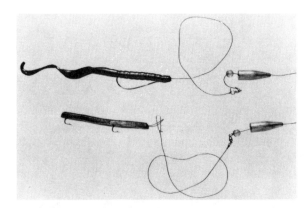

The Carolina rig allows the worm to swim freely behind a heavy slip sinker. Both Texas-rigged worms and open-hooked worms may be used.

plastic bead about ¼ of an inch in diameter to protect the knot from the sinker. Tie the line to a two-way swivel. To the other end of the swivel attach a leader anywhere from twelve to forty-eight inches in length, depending on how high you want the worm to float above the bottom. A short leader will keep the worm close to the bottom, whereas a long leader will let the worm swim higher over the bottom. Longer leaders keep the worm swimming over weeds or some other cover.

Rigging the plastic worm with a worm hook, such as those used with the Texas rig, helps prevent snagging. When the bottom is pretty much free of snags, rigging the worm with the hook point exposed will insure better hookups with bass. For a deadly alternative, rig the worm on the hook so that it has a pronounced kink that will make it gyrate as it swims. Another type of worm that works well with the Carolina rig has two or three small exposed hooks formed into the body of the worm, from the head to the tail. One of the most popular is the "Do Nothing Worm," which Jack Chancellor used to win a Bass Masters Classic on the Arkansas River. The small hooks penetrate easily and the hook in the tail insures the catching of short-striking bass. This type of worm is also available with hook guards to prevent snagging.

Anglers most often use the Carolina rig with slip sinkers weighing from ½ to 1 ounce. The heavy weight allows for long casts, keeps the sinker in constant contact with the bottom, and itself attracts bass. When the sinker is plowing through a soft bottom, it kicks up clouds of silt that arouse a bass's curiosity. Bass are also drawn to the commotion caused when the sinker bounces over broken rock

and into stumps, brush, and other objects. When the bass comes around to check things out, he spots the plastic worm swimming enticingly above the bottom and has a hard time resisting the apparently easy meal.

You'll find the Carolina rig to be especially productive when fishing large areas in water that varies from middle to very deep, such as long wide points, flats, and stump fields. Make long casts over these areas and give the sinker time to reach the bottom. Retrieve by cranking the reel at a pace that is slow enough to keep the sinker working on the bottom. Raise the rod tip only to lift the sinker over obstacles, and continue retrieving with the reel. When a bass inhales the worm, you may feel only a heaviness on the line. If you're using a worm with a large hook, snap the rod up sharply to embed the barb. With worms that have small, exposed hooks, just lift up slightly on the rod and continue reeling.

For shallow-water fishing, modify the Carolina rig by using a lighter slip sinker, say ⅛ to ¼ of an ounce, with a short leader. When fishing for temperamental bass in clear water, you can often encourage strikes by simply placing a split shot on the line a foot or two above the hook. This lets the worm sink with a very slow and natural movement.

Jigs

The jig is the oldest and simplest of all lures, consisting basically of a lead head molded onto a hook that is dressed with rubber, plastic, hair, or feathers. Even though jigs have long been effective on all species of black bass, many anglers overlook them in favor of lures that spin and wobble when retrieved. As with a plastic worm, you must impart action to the jig and develop a feel for strikes. Whether you fish these lures in the shallows, middepths, or deep water, they give you ample opportunities to set the hook. Successful jig fishing requires concentration and dedication, but the rewards are well worth the effort.

Jig and Pork = Big Bass

In the past, you couldn't fish a jig in the heavy cover where bass often lurk, because the exposed hook would snag on almost every cast. The development of the hook-guard jig has allowed anglers

When fishing the Texas rig, you'll feel strikes more easily if you hold the rod high and move the worm with the rod tip.

to probe the thickest bass cover imaginable, from flooded bushes to thick weed beds. The most popular style of hook-guard jig is usually tipped with a pork rind trailer, and the lure combination is commonly known as the "jig and pork." Over the past decade, the jig and pork has proven beyond question that it consistently catches more big bass than any other lure. If you dream of catching trophy bass, you could do no better than to master this lure.

Why does the jig and pork have such universal bass appeal? Most experts believe that it looks and can be made to act more like a crayfish than any other lure, and these crustaceans are a major food source for bass everywhere. Since crayfish are generally dark in color, many excellent jig and pork anglers rely mainly on black or brown or combinations of these colors. Some anglers also like a touch of another color in the jig's head, skirt, or trailer to add flash. Blue, red, orange, and green are widely used flash colors.

The typical hook-guard jig has a wide, stable head that holds the hook upright when resting on the bottom. The hook's eye is at the tip of the head which helps the lure slither through weeds and climb over rocks, limbs, and other obstacles. Molded into the jig's lead head and protruding in front of the hook's point is a hook guard comprised of nylon or monofilament bristles or a plastic "Y." The guard protects the hook from snags, but folds back and exposes the point when you set the hook.

A rubber skirt is the most popular dressing. The lively legs sweep back over the hook, giving the jig bulk and a life-like appearance. The skirts on most jigs reach beyond the bend of the hook. The long legs move slowly in the water and appeal most to sluggish bass in cool water. In warm water, when bass are more active, trim the skirt to be even with the bend of the hook. This modification lets the jig sink faster and gives the legs a more abrupt movement. In very cold water, when bass are least active, a hair dressing, such as bucktail, may be the most productive type. The hair dressing gives the jig bulk, but adds little action.

Anglers have made the Uncle Josh No. 11 Pork Frog the most widely used jig trailer nationwide because it closely imitates a crayfish. The two thin trailing legs resemble pinchers, and the fatty portion gives bass the feel of something real. Smaller and larger pork frogs are available, as well as many other styles of pork rinds. Split-tails, spring lizards, and eels are among the most popular. A larger trailer is often used to give the jig more bulk and to slow its fall. A small trailer reduces the size of the jig and allows it to sink faster. Some anglers modify their pork frogs by trimming the fatty portion for more action and a faster sink rate. Pork remains supple in cold water, but will dry up and become useless if left out of the water too long. On a hot summer day, it can dry up quickly.

Plastic trailers aren't as lively as pork in cold water, but, since they won't dry out, many anglers favor them during the summer. Crayfish imitators make the most popular plastic trailers, and some seem remarkably lifelike. Swimming tail worms and grubs also serve frequently as trailers, and many more styles and colors of trailers are available in plastic than in pork.

While hook-guard jigs come in weights from ⅛ to one ounce, the ¼-to-⅝-ounce sizes are used most often. Lighter jigs fall more slowly and are preferable when casting to shallow cover, when working over the tops of submerged weeds, or whenever bass simply prefer a slower presentation. Smaller jigs also work more effectively when you're going for smallmouth and spotted bass. A heavier jig falls faster, making it better for deep-water fishing, especially under windy conditions. It is also the best choice when you want to penetrate thick cover, such as brush or matted surface weeds, to reach the bass below.

Many jigs come with heavy hooks that will not straighten when used with the "flippin'" method, which employs a long, stout rod and heavy line. See Chapter 5 for more detail on flippin', but suffice it to say here that this technique allows you to work a jig into heavy cover and force bass out before they can tangle the line. The heavy hook is beneficial when flippin', but it is difficult to set with conventional tackle. You'll have fewer problems if you go with jigs that have standard hooks when you're not flippin'.

Few lures can compete with the jig and pork in cold water, say 45° to 55° Fahrenheit. Bass are sluggish under these conditions and they respond much better to the slow, teasing action of a jig than to other lures. For years the jig and pork was considered to be only a cold-water lure, but more anglers are discovering that it will take bass throughout the seasons. It will also produce bass in waters ranging from clear to muddy.

A bottom-hopping retrieve is deadly, especially when you keep the jig and pork working through and bumping into cover. In cold water, a slow lift-drop action works best, but faster retrieves can work well as the water warms. Most anglers retrieve jigs from shallow to deeper water, but you may fare better retrieving from deep to shallow, a tactic that keeps the jig in constant contact with the bottom. A swimming retrieve can work well on occasion, particularly when fishing over submerged weed beds.

Bass usually inhale the jig as it sinks, so you must be alert in order to detect the light strikes that often occur. The process of retrieving and setting the hook is very similar to that described in the section on fishing a Texas-rigged worm. The bass generally holds the jig long enough for you to drop the rod tip and take in slack line before ramming home the hook. A line of about 12-pound test is as light as you should use for most situations, and 14-pound test is the minimum when fishing around cover. When flippin' jigs into thick cover, you'll need heavier line to withstand its abrasive nature—something on the order of 25-pound test.

If you flip a jig right on top of a bass, it will often respond with a reflex strike, engulfing the lure before it reaches bottom. At other times, you may have to lure the bass to your jig or tease it into striking. Allow the line to drape over a piece of the cover, such as a limb, branch, or root. Lift and drop your rod tip so that the lure swims up and down in one place. You may sometimes have to work the jig in one spot for a minute or more before the bass finally decides to strike.

Plastic, Hair, and Feather Jigs

Hair, feathers, or a combination of these materials once formed the standard dressings on bass jigs. While they are still productive, most anglers overlook them in favor of jigs dressed with plastic bodies, because plastic jig bodies exist in an endless variety of styles and colors. They also have more action and a natural texture, and rig inexpensively and easily. Simply take a plain jig, thread the plastic

Deadly on all species of black bass, jigs are proven producers of big fish.

body onto the hook's shank, and you're in business. Some jigs come with barbs on their collars to help hold the plastic in place. A drop of Super Glue where the hook shank enters the jig head will also prevent the plastic from sliding back.

Many plastic bodies imitate baitfish, which is exactly the case with plastic grubs that have straight or swimming tails. A number of plastic dressings are also shaped like shad and have tails that shimmy when pulled through the water. One of the most effective baitfish emulators to come along in recent years was devised by an innovative angler who fishes deep, crystal-clear canyon reservoirs out West. The body, called a Gitzit, is a hollow tube with many fine legs cut into its tail. The jig head is hidden inside the tube, giving the lure a very natural appearance and feel. Anglers currently use the Gitzit in clear-water situations all across the country with excellent results.

A four-inch plastic worm makes an excellent jig dressing, as do the many crayfish designs. The truth is, there are so many styles and variations of plastic jig dressings that it would be futile to try and cover them all. Most of them will catch bass when used under the right conditions.

Plastic jig bodies in translucent colors work best in clear water. The colors of smoke and light green seem to have universal appeal. Other proven colors include smoke with red flake, motoroil with red flake, and clear with silver flake. In stained water, you may have better results with white, chartreuse, fluorescent red, and black.

Some jigs in this category have hook guards or can be made snagless by embedding the hook into the body of a plastic dressing. They are most often used, however, with exposed hooks when fishing over a clean bottom or in any situation in which snagging is less of a problem. Swimming them down rocky bluff banks is one particularly effective application. When fishing for temperamental bass in clear water, these jigs function with special productivity when paired with light lines from 4- to 8-pound test. Jig heads weighing ⅟16 to ⅜ of an ounce are used most often, with the ⅛- and ¼-ounce sizes acting as the workhorses. The jigs should have fine wire hooks that penetrate easily, allowing the use of medium-action spinning outfits.

Jig Head Variations and Retrieves

Most often, anglers work jigs slowly over the bottom with a lift-drop action. This simple retrieve is often deadly, since bass usually relate to some type of bottom structure. Ball and oval head jigs perform well all around. Their even balance makes them good for swimming retrieves, and they tend to swim through the water with a smooth level glide.

Weeds hold bass in many lakes, and if weed growth isn't too thick you can fish it effectively with a jig that has a pointed head, such as the Pow-RR head made by Mister Twister. This jig has the hook eye at the very tip of its pointed nose, so it will rip through many weeds without snagging. The jig also has a wide flat base, enabling it to stand upright on the bottom when at rest. During cold water periods and after cold fronts, try fishing this jig with short hops, occasionally letting it stand on the bottom for several seconds. At those times when bass are too sluggish or finicky to strike a moving jig, they may find it hard to resist the temptation of an apparently tasty morsel sitting on the bottom.

When bass are suspended in open water, they can be extremely difficult to catch; however, swimming a jig in this situation may get results when other lures fail. The slider head jig, designed by Charlie Brewer, is extremely well suited to swimming retrieves. The thin, flat jig head glides through the water because the flat side rides parallel to the bottom. It lets you retrieve slowly while maintaining a specific depth. The slider jig is normally paired with a four-inch plastic worm. You simply cast the lure out, let it sink to the desired depth, and then retrieve steadily while holding the rod tip as still as possible. Charlie Brewer calls this his "Do Nothin' " retrieve. He believes that gamefish see the slider's easy glide as the effortless swimming action of a minnow.

Smallmouth bass taken on a jig in Tennessee.

The jig and pork is the number one producer of trophy largemouth bass.

Mark Hicks with one of many sizable bass he has taken on jig and pork combinations.

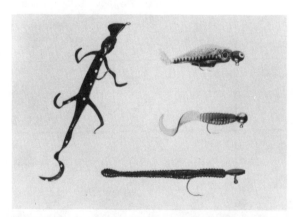

Plastic bodies can be threaded onto the hooks of assorted jig head designs to take advantage of varied fishing conditions.

These are typical hook-guard jigs. Rubber and hair dressings are both productive.

Pork rind trailers come in many shapes and sizes. The Uncle Josh No. 11 Pork Frog (left center) is the most widely used.

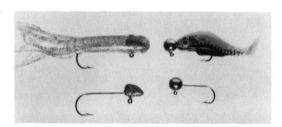

The tube jig (right) and plastic minnow are just two types of plastic bodies that can be used in conjunction with jigs. Note how the jig head slides into the tube.

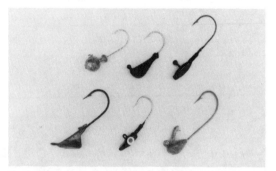

Jig heads come in many shapes and sizes: ball head, banana head, and slider head (top row); and Pow-RR head, flat head, and keeper head.

*Bass pro Joe Thomas hauls a bass out of heavy cover. Most anglers favor jigs when flippin'
into the thick stuff for bass.*

Spinnerbaits

Even though spinnerbaits don't look like anything
a bass would want to eat, they are probably the
most versatile bass catchers you can own. These
flashing lures encourage reflex strikes from bass
throughout the seasons, and work effectively in
both clear and muddy water. They are mostly used
from the surface down to depths of about ten feet,
but can also be used successfully in deeper water.
Thanks to their ability to climb over snags, no other
lure can explore shallow cover faster or more efficiently. Is it any wonder that the spinnerbait may
be the most popular bass lure in the country?

The overhead spinner design has won the respect
of bass anglers everywhere. This lure, built around
a V-shaped wire, has the blade or blades attached
to the top prong, and the lead head and hook
molded onto the bottom prong with the hook riding
up. A line tie is formed in the crotch of the V, and
the wire arrangement serves as an effective hook
guard. The lead head, painted and dressed with a
skirt that is usually made of rubber, gives the lure
more bulk and action. Better spinnerbaits have ball
bearing swivels connecting the trailing blades to
the overhead wires. The bearing is a key component, since it lets the blade spin freely with the
slightest movement of the lure. Cheap swivels can
hinder the blade's movement.

Spinnerbaits are the most versatile lures you can have in your tackle box.

Mark Hicks used a single bladed spinnerbait to take this dandy largemouth.

Spinnerbaits that have long overhead wires are more snag-resistant and should be used when fishing weeds, brush, and other heavy cover. Short overhead wires give spinnerbaits better balance with falling retrieves, but are more prone to snagging. Use short-arm spinnerbaits over bottoms that have fewer snags.

Tandem-bladed spinnerbaits give off more flash, provide more lift during the retrieve, and are generally preferred when fishing less than six feet deep. Single spins give off a stronger thump and sink faster. They are the best choice for falling retrieves, and for use in murky water where the blade's vibration attracts bass more than its flash.

The three blade styles used most often include the Colorado, willow leaf, and Indiana. The broad-beamed Colorado blade spins in a wide arc, creating the most resistance and the strongest throb. The Colorado produces well under all water conditions but especially in murky water and with falling retrieves. The long, slender willow leaf blade rotates faster and in a tighter arc. It gives off more flash and less vibration, and fishes best in clear water where bass can see the flash from greater distances. The Indiana blade falls between the Colorado and the willow leaf and is effective under a wide variety of conditions. Tandem spinnerbaits often mix blade styles.

Nickle, copper, and gold-plated blades are the mainstays, because their metallic flash mimics that given off by baitfish. There are also painted blades available in myriad colors. Many anglers believe that nickle blades work better in clear water, while gold and copper blades work better in murky water and on overcast days. Some anglers, including some of the top professionals, use two blades of different colors when fishing with tandem spinnerbaits to be sure they have something that will appeal to the bass. Spinnerbaits that have snaps attached to their swivels easily allow you to change the trailing blades until you find something that works.

The rubber skirts on many spinnerbaits can also be easily exchanged. Chartreuse, white, and black are the basic colors, and you would do well to start out with them or with skirts that have combinations of the three.

Although spinnerbaits readily take bass without trailers, most anglers do use them. Plastic curl-tails and twin-tails make the most popular trailers. Pork frogs and other pork rinds are also frequently used.

A Pocketful of Color

When you consider the various sizes and colors of spinnerbait heads, blades, skirts, and trailers, you realize that there are an infinite number of combinations. Some anglers are overwhelmed by the endless possibilities. I discovered a novel way to simplify and hasten spinnerbait selection while fishing with Paul Wright of Dallas, Georgia, who is one of the most proficient spinnerbait anglers I've ever met.

We were fishing the upper end of West Point Lake, Georgia, where the water had more color to it than that in the clearer, lower end of the lake near the dam. Wright had been catching bass in shallow water on spinnerbaits. He started out with the lure that had been producing for him, a ½-ounce tandem spinnerbait with a medium-sized silver Colorado trailing blade. We were fishing some of his favorite banks, retrieving our spinnerbaits close to submerged stumps, fallen trees, and other prime wood cover. After fishing two such areas without a strike, Wright decided it was time for a change.

"I think these bass need a spinnerbait that has more flash and color," he said.

I figured that Wright would sort through one of his tackle boxes to find the desired lure. Instead, he opened the snap-swivel on his spinnerbait and removed the trailing Colorado blade. He then dug deep into one of his pants pockets and dredged up a varied assortment of spinnerbait blades, from little Colorado blades to oversized willow leaf blades. Most of them were plated with shiny metal finishes, but a few were painted white, chartreuse, or fluorescent red. He selected a large gold willow leaf blade and returned the rest of the cache to his pocket.

After fixing the willow leaf blade to the swivel, Wright removed the spinnerbait's white skirt, reached into another pocket, and hauled up a handful of colorful skirts. He found a chartreuse and blue skirt to his liking and returned the rest.

"This should work better in this stained water," he said as he pulled the spinnerbait alongside the boat to study its performance.

The lure had an entirely different appearance. The big blade gave off an enormous flash, and the chartreuse and blue skirt was highly visible in the stained water. At the next bank we visited, Wright pitched the big spinnerbait past a cluster of logs that looked similar to much of the cover we had already fished. The spinnerbait had just cleared the outermost log when a three-pound bass clobbered the lure and put a deep bow in Wright's rod. No doubt the bass was partial to the face-lift that Wright had given his spinnerbait. So were the many other bass he caught that afternoon.

Many bass anglers carry assorted blades and skirts in their tackle boxes, but few will stop and search for these items, even when their spinnerbaits need modification. Because Wright keeps his blades and skirts in his pockets, he has no qualms about making changes. He can modify his spinnerbaits quickly and easily, and he often does so many times throughout the day until he finds a combination the bass prefer.

—Mark Hicks

Trailers give the lure more bulk and action, and the feel of something alive. They can also provide the lure with a contrasting color, as in the case of a chartreuse curl-tail behind a white skirt. In some cases, you may want to remove the skirt and use a plastic trailer only. This is commonly done when using falling retrieves, because it lets the spinnerbait sink faster.

When you feel bass hit your spinnerbait but can't seem to hook them, switch to a larger trailer which will often bring on more aggressive strikes. If that fails, try adding a trailer hook. These special hooks have large eyes that slip over the barbs on spinnerbait hooks. Some trailer hooks come with a piece of surgical tubing over the hook eye, or some other device that holds it securely in place. However, trailer hooks do have a drawback. They reduce the ability of a spinnerbait to avoid snags. When fishing extremely thick cover, a trailer hook may be more trouble than it's worth.

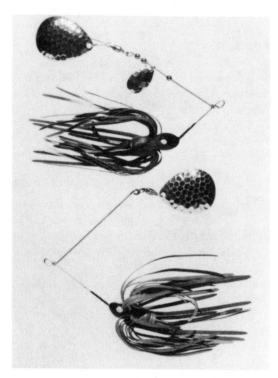

Short-arm spinnerbaits have better balance for falling retrieves, but are more prone to snagging.

These spinnerbaits have long, overhead arms to prevent snagging. The tandem model (top) gives off more flash and provides more lift. The single spin (bottom) gives off a stronger vibration and sinks faster.

The three blade styles used most often are the Indiana, Colorado, and willow leaf.

Spinnerbait sizes range from ⅛ to one ounce, and the weight designation refers only to the lead head. The lure is actually heavier, since it also has the weight of the wire, blades, and other components. Smaller heads are generally matched with smaller blades and vice versa. Light heads with oversized blades tend to lift more during the retrieve. Heavy heads with small blades sink faster, which makes this combination appealing for falling retrieves.

Many factors can influence which size spinnerbait the bass will prefer. If you can determine the baitfish the bass are feeding on, select a spinnerbait that matches them in size and color. When bass are in a negative mood due to the passing of a cold front or to heavy boat traffic, you may find that smaller spinnerbaits are more productive. Larger spinnerbaits usually draw more strikes when bass are aggressive, when the sky is overcast, and when there is a heavy chop on the surface. Big spinnerbaits also consistently catch bigger bass.

Spinnerbaits with oversized willow leaf blades have really caught on in recent years, and these lures have accounted for many heavyweight bass catches. The big lures have so much more flash and vibration than conventional spinnerbaits that they can draw bass out of thick cover and from greater distances. They are especially appealing to trophy-sized fish, because a big bass may prefer not to chase down a meal unless the reward is worth the effort. A trophy bass may ignore a small spinnerbait, but a big-bladed spinnerbait is likely to goad it into action.

The heart of the spinnerbait is a willow leaf blade ranging in size from a number 5 to a number 8, the latter measuring well over three inches in length. The molded heads of these lures must be heavy enough to balance the big blade, and they generally run from ⅜ to ⅞ of an ounce. Whereas a few big spinnerbaits have only one large willow leaf blade, most are tandem spins. The lead blade is usually a much smaller Indiana or Colorado style that adds flash, yet doesn't hinder the performance of the bigger blade. The most unique designs incorporate two large willow leaf blades. Some have an offset bend in the overhead wire shaft, which

Spinnerbaits with oversized willow leaf blades appeal to big bass. The top spinnerbait has a trailer hook.

Adding a trailer to your spinnerbait can bring on more aggressive strikes.

prevents the lead blade from slipping back and interfering with the trailing blade.

Fish spinnerbaits when bass are in shallow, visible cover, as they are during the spring prespawn and spawning periods. Plunking the spinnerbait smack on top of the bass may spook it, so cast beyond the cover and retrieve the lure to the object. If the bass are right against the shoreline, cast the lure onto the bank and gently ease it into the water. Accurate casting helps you avoid hanging your spinnerbaits in trees, bushes, and other cover, and it also lets you retrieve your lure within inches of the bass, which increases your odds for a strike. Bait-casting tackle provides greater casting accuracy and will handle the heavy lines that are often necessary when fishing spinnerbaits in dense cover. As a further aid to accuracy, opt for short casts rather than long ones.

You'll catch many more bass on spinnerbaits if you experiment with a variety of retrieves until you find one the bass want. A steady retrieve that keeps the spinnerbait within sight of the surface is a favorite of Jimmy Houston, the bass pro and host of

a TV fishing show, and one of the top spinnerbait anglers in the country. One advantage of this tactic is that you can see the bass when they strike your lure. Spinnerbaits with oversized blades, such as the big willow leaf models, will stay near the surface even with very slow retrieves. They fish especially well over thick weed beds, because they give the bass more time to intercept the lure. A steady retrieve with the spinnerbait down and out of sight will also produce, particularly when the lure is coming over submerged cover, such as weed beds or brush piles.

Purposely bumping the spinnerbait into stumps, flooded bushes, and other objects often provokes bass into striking. Another trick is to bump an object with a spinnerbait, halt the retrieve, and let the spinnerbait flutter down a few feet on a tight line. The bass may strike as the lure is dropping, or when you resume the retrieve.

Bulging the surface works especially well in clear water and can call bass up from deep water even during the hot months. Retrieve fast enough so that the spinnerbait creates a bulge on the surface, but

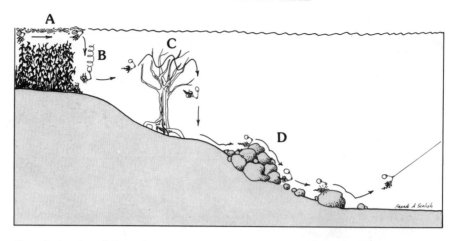

Some basic spinnerbait retrieves: A, bulging the surface (ripping); B, dropping; C, lift-drop; D, slow roll.

Mark Hicks retrieves a big willow leaf spinnerbait through holes in a weed bed.

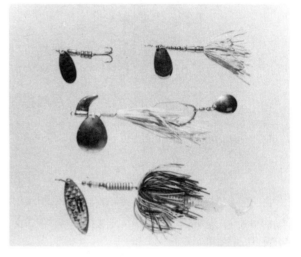

In-line spinners come in many sizes and styles.

not so fast that the blades break the water. Many spinnerbaits will roll or run on their sides when retrieved at the high speeds needed for the bulging maneuver. You can eliminate the problem by attaching a rubber core sinker to the wire shaft directly in front of the lure's lead head. For another productive retrieve, make the blades alternately

break the surface for a few feet and then drop below the surface for the next few feet.

When bass are deeper, the slow roll works well. In this method, a slow retrieve allows the spinnerbait to sink and to swim forward at the same time. Your goal should be to keep the lure swimming just over the bottom or over bottom cover, such as weeds.

During cold-water periods, single spin spinnerbaits can be fished with a lift-drop retrieve, much as you would fish a jig over submerged structure. As with the jig, the bass generally strike as the spinnerbait is falling. Scraping bluff banks with a single spin is also productive in cold water. You must cast the spinnerbait right up against the bank and let it free fall on a semi-tight line. Don't lift

Bob Tomasko and many other anglers have found that small in-line spinners are especially effective on smallmouth bass.

the lure with the rod tip; this will pull it away from the bluff and the bass. If the spinnerbait catches on a ledge, nudge it off and let it continue falling.

In-line Spinnerbaits

Relatively few bass anglers use in-line spinners, since most of these lures have exposed treble hooks that are prone to snagging. Even so, in-line spinners have their place, particularly for fishing clear lakes and streams for smallmouth bass. Few lures can compete with a small brass spinner with a squirrel-tail dressing when it comes to smallmouths. In-line spinners can also save the day when bass are feeding on tiny baitfish and refusing larger lures. In this situation, the bass are still willing to strike an in-line spinner that matches the baitfish in size and color. Light spinning tackle is the best match for these little lures.

There are also a few in-line spinners on the market that have large single hooks with some type of hook guard, such as the Snagless Sally and Meppster. These spinners will run through and over weeds with good success, and can be used in other cover as well.

Crankbaits

The term crankbait generally describes plugs that dive and wiggle when retrieved. Crankbaits are unsurpassed baitfish imitators, and some even pass for crayfish. They also lure fish with relative ease. Simply crank the reel's handle, and these lures wiggle and throb with an alluring action. Since many of the bass that strike crankbaits hook themselves, you can have success without the refined sense of touch required when fishing with jigs and plastic worms.

Use crankbaits to entice bass from weeds, and from wood and rock cover; use them also in the shallows and in depths of more than twenty feet. They consistently produce bass from spring through fall and in dingy or clear water. Because few lures cover the water as quickly and efficiently as crankbaits, they are unbeatable bass-finding tools.

Crankbait bodies are fashioned from plastic and from hard foam, and from balsa and other light woods. Most crankbaits float at rest and dive when retrieved, pulled down by a plastic or metal lip attached to the front of the lure. Other crankbait designs include suspending models that dive when retrieved, and that suspend or rise very slowly when stopped. Sinking crankbaits are also available. The most popular are the thin, vibrating shad imitators, such as the Rat-L-Trap, that have no diving lips. An angler can fish sinking vibrators either just below the surface or in deep water, depending on how long he lets them sink and the speed of the retrieve. A fast retrieve will keep them near the surface.

As a first step in becoming a skilled crankbait angler, select an assortment of lures that will run at various depths. The running depth is more important than the size, action, and color of the lure, because you simply will not catch bass unless your crankbait runs at the depth the bass are swimming.

Some anglers wisely arrange crankbaits in their tackle boxes according to how deep they run. The shallow runners include most lures that have line ties on their noses and small diving lips. They swim at depths from about two to six feet deep. Medium runners dive from six to nearly nine feet deep and are comprised mainly of small-to-medium-sized

Crankbaits have built-in actions that bring bass on the run.

lures that have line ties embedded in large diving lips. Deep divers dig to about twelve feet, and some of the super-deep divers plow to depths greater than twenty feet. Deep divers are large lures, because big bodies must offset the oversized diving lips found on these lures.

There are several ways to alter a crankbait's running depth. A short cast prevents a crankbait from achieving maximum depth, whereas a long cast lets it dive deeper. You'll gain about one foot of depth for every four pounds of line test that you eliminate. For example, a crankbait that runs at nine feet with 17-pound line will run at about eleven feet with 10-pound line. Many anglers mistakenly believe that the faster you reel, the deeper a crankbait will run. The truth is that a moderately slow retrieve gets crankbaits deepest. You'll lose as much as two feet of depth with a fast retrieve, because it pulls the lip forward and diminishes the plug's steep diving angle. If you want your crankbait to run shallower, hold your rod tip high. If you want it to run deeper, put your rod tip into the water.

Serious bass anglers have recently developed a technique, dubbed "kneeling and reeling," that drives crankbaits into depths where bass have never seen them before. The method requires a six-and-a-half- to seven-and-a-half-foot rod that has a double handle. This rod allows the angler to make longer casts; enables the angler to kneel down and push the rod tip deep into the water, which drives the crankbait deeper; and allows the angler to brace the long double handle against his or her body to relieve the strain of retrieving the big, hard-pulling crankbaits that are used with this method.

After depth, the speed of retrieve should be your next consideration. In clear water, a fast retrieve is generally more productive, since a bass can easily see your crankbait and chase it down from a distance of several feet. The fleeting lure is also harder to distinguish as a fake. In dingy water, a bass must rely on its sense of sound to home in on your crankbait, so it can't react as fast. In this case, you'll have more success with slow and medium retrieves. If your crankbait is moving too fast, the bass may not even give chase. When the water is warm, faster retrieves usually attract more active bass. In cold water, however, the sluggish bass demand slow retrieves, even when the water is clear.

Crankbait actions vary from wide slow wobbles to tight fast wiggles. Whatever their action, the steady vibrations transmitted through the rod to your fingertips will let you know if the lure is running properly and will help you detect strikes. Bass don't always belt crankbaits. They sometimes inhale them, in which case the throbbing action merely stops or falters, telling you to set the hook.

Many novice bass fishermen take great pains to keep their expensive crankbaits away from potential snags. They rarely get their lures caught in a snag, but they rarely catch bass either. Without a doubt, the most effective stunt for triggering aggressive strikes with crankbaits is to keep them bumping into things. If your crankbaits are not digging the bottom or bumping into some type of cover, they won't attract many bass. Except when you're casting for suspended bass in open water, select a crankbait that runs a little deeper than the bottom or the structure you are fishing. Keep in mind that you must cast beyond the area you want to fish in order to give the crankbait time to dive to the desired depth.

Successful crankbait fishermen purposely run their lures into the bottom, stumps, limbs, boulders, brush, and weeds. Highly buoyant, floating/diving crankbaits with large lips are least likely to

Sinking vibrators can be fished just below the surface or in deep water, depending on how long you let them sink and the speed of the retrieve.

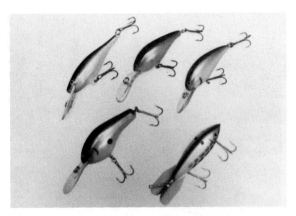

The large diving bills on deep crankbaits pull these lures to depths of about twelve feet.

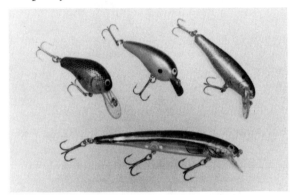

Shallow-running crankbaits have small lips and swim at depths from about two to six feet.

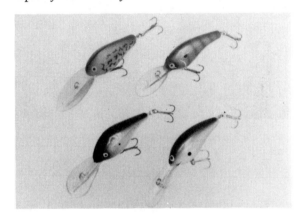

The oversized diving bills on large, super-deep divers make these lures plow down to depths of more than twenty feet.

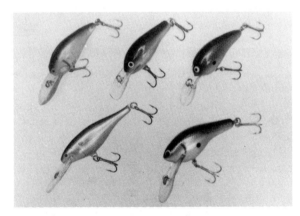

Medium-running crankbaits dive between six and nine feet deep.

get hung up. The lip is the first thing to make contact and it shields the hooks. Should the crankbait become wedged, give it slack line and it will float free. Some snagging is inevitable, so invest in a lure retriever and keep it handy. It will probably pay for itself the first time you bring it along.

When fishing in flooded standing timber, or in areas where frequent snagging is unavoidable, spool your reel with heavy line, such as 25-pound test. Your crankbaits won't dive as deep, but you'll be able to pull them free from most snags. Replacing the heavy hooks, which are standard on many large crankbaits, with fine wire trebles allows you to straighten the hooks with a steady pull and to retrieve the lures more easily. Simply bend the hooks back into shape with pliers and continue fishing. Another trick is to bend in the leading hook on the front treble, which is the one that snags most often.

When retrieving a crankbait over a relatively clean bottom, a moderate, steady retrieve that keeps the lure digging the bottom can be highly productive. You should also master the stop-and-go retrieve. Crank your lure down until it bumps

Push the rod tip into the water to make crankbaits run deeper.

If a crankbait is not running true, you can tune the lure. First point the lure toward you.

the bottom, a stump, or some other object, and then hesitate for a moment. The lure will float up, presenting an enticing target to any bass that may have been attracted by the bumping action. When you continue your retrieve, be prepared for action. When fishing a crankbait through sparse weeds and brush, occasionally try ripping the lure ahead when it comes into contact with the cover. This sudden burst of speed sometimes triggers strikes.

Try not to get too hung up on lure color. This is not nearly as important as depth, speed, and action. If you know the bass are feeding on a certain species of baitfish, try selecting a lure color that closely resembles it. Silver, and shad or natural baitfish colors and patterns generally work best in clear water. Chartreuse, bone, and white patterns are generally better in dingy water. Crayfish patterns work well over rock and pebble bottoms where bass feed on these crustaceans. They are also effective when bass are spawning. Crayfish eat bass eggs, so a crayfish-colored crankbait tends to rouse a bass when it suddenly plows through the midst of a spawning bed.

Many crankbaits have rattles and sound chambers designed to attract bass. They are especially helpful when used in stained water, where bass must rely more on sound than on sight to locate their food.

No matter which brand of crankbait you buy, you'll often have to fine-tune some lures to make them run true. Say, for example, that you have a crankbait with a plastic lip that runs to your right when retrieved. Hold the lure so that the lip is facing you and bend (don't twist) the line tie slightly to the left with needle-nose pliers. If the lure runs to the left, bend the line eye to the right. A crankbait with a metal lip will run off center when the lip becomes bent out of kilter. Simply bend the lip back into proper alignment with pliers. Most crankbaits come with O-rings attached to their line ties that allow the lures to swim with a freer action. If you have a crankbait that doesn't have an O-ring, attach one or use a snap.

Topwater

The most exciting bass you can catch is the one that slashes your lure off the surface. Bass fishing

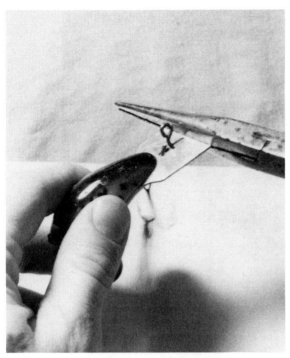

Crankbaits that have metal lips can be tuned by bending the bills back into proper alignment.

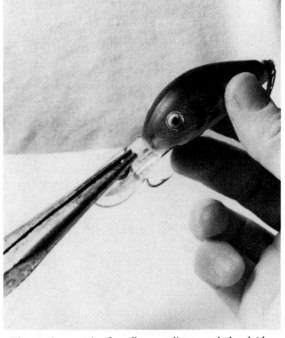

Then, using a pair of needle-nose pliers, gently bend (do not twist) the line eye to the right if you want the plug to run toward the right, or vice versa if you want it to run left.

and topwater lures were once nearly synonymous, but for awhile most bass fishermen overlooked them in favor of the many other types of lures that have proven to be so effective. In recent years, interest in all types of topwater lures has been renewed thanks to the surging popularity of the buzzbait, a lure with a large propellerlike blade that plops noisily over the surface. Bass anglers have rediscovered the fact that topwater lures provoke thrilling strikes and will sometimes hold their own against any lure.

Topwater lures are especially productive in clear-water situations where they can pull bass up from depths of twenty feet or more. Bass also strike on top in stained water, but they won't come far to take your lure. Casting accuracy can be critical, since you must work topwater lures close to or right over whatever cover the bass are using. Most anglers fish surface lures only during the prime low-light feeding periods of early morning and late evening. Overcast days often provide extended action, and bass will sometimes come up during the midday hours even under a bright sun.

Although summer fishing can yield good results, spring and fall are the best seasons for catching topwater bass. When the surface water temperature is around 60°F and the sun is less intense, bass swim in cool comfort in the shallows. Bass are also more aggressive at these times.

The Buzzbait

There are several types of topwater lures. The popular buzzbait type has two basic designs. One is the in-line model, whose hook usually has a weed guard and follows directly behind the prop-blade. It is adorned with bucktail or another dressing. Some in-line buzzbaits have a spoon or another type of body that helps them plane over the surface.

The second style of buzzbait has a wire arrangement like that of a spinnerbait. The prop-blade is attached to the top prong, and the bottom prong and the single hook are molded into a lead head. The hook rides with its barb positioned over its shank. The lead head usually sports a vinyl or rubber skirt which flares back over the hook. The blade sputters on top, and the lead head, with its undulating skirt, dances just below the surface. Both

Fishing with topwater lures is exciting and productive.

types of buzzbaits are nearly snag-free—one reason for their enormous popularity.

The buzzbait is very easy to use. Toss it out, crank it back over the surface, and the noisy prop-blade brings bass on the run. The lure also comes over most snags and weeds without a hitch. About the only variable that should concern you is the speed of retrieve. Many anglers fare best by cranking their reel handles just fast enough to keep the blade plopping on top. But some days you'll get better results with a fast retrieve that really froths the water. If you're missing strikes, add a trailer hook. You'll get more snags, but you'll miss fewer bass.

Floating Minnows

Because bass often feed on shad and other baitfish, it's easy to understand why floating plastic or balsa minnows make superb topwater lures. Casting these lures can be exasperating on a blustery day. The wind blows them off target, and their sharp treble hooks seem to impale everything they touch. They land lightly on the water, however, and won't spook bass as readily as other lures, especially when the water is calm.

The floating minnow can imitate a dying minnow like no other lure. After casting the lure and letting the surface ripples fade, pull it forward a few

Two popular styles of buzzbaits include the overhead blade (top) and the in-line model. The buzzer on top sports a rubber skirt and a plastic curl-tail grub; the bottom buzzer has a bucktail skirt and a trailer hook.

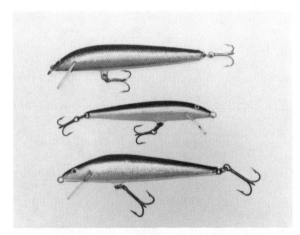

Floating minnows are unbeatable baitfish imitators.

A floating minnow lure can be made to imitate a dying baitfish, an excellent ploy for fishing big bass.

inches. The lure's small diving lip will pull it under like an injured minnow struggling to right itself. Like a real minnow, the lure will float back to the surface. This gentle twitch-and-wait retrieve can tease wary bass into striking. For a noisy retrieve, work your rod tip with a sharp jerk-pause rhythm. The minnow will pop with each snap of the rod. You can pause occasionally or use a steady popping retrieve.

Stick Baits

Stick baits look like fat cigars and are difficult to master because they have no built-in action. But a skilled topwater angler can make these lures do everything but breathe. Most stick baits are large lures, and they attract the attention of big bass.

The basic stick-bait retrieve is called "walking the dog." Learning it requires practice and dedication. After making the cast, hold the rod tip low and alternate between jerks and pauses. Take up line after each jerk, but not too much. You must leave a little slack so the lure can work properly. Each time you jerk, the stick bait will swap ends

Stick baits have no built-in action, but can be brought to life by skilled anglers. Top lures shown here have no spinners; bottom lures have spinners.

Bob Troxel prepares to "walk" a stick bait down a log, a productive tactic.

Poppers (top) have a concave face that "pops" the surface when the rod is twitched. Wobblers (bottom) have a built-in action and are effective and easy to use.

and glide. The key is to maintain an even cadence, which will make the lure sashay back and forth. By varying your rhythm and how hard you snap the rod tip, you can create everything from a slow, gentle shuffle to a fast, splashing sprint.

Propeller Baits

Propeller baits have small propellers on their tails and many models have them on their noses as well. These lures are more easily mastered than stick baits, and can really kick up a ruckus when retrieved with sharp snaps of the rod tip. They also fish effectively when worked with gentle twitches that barely spin the propellers.

Wobblers

Wobblers don't have the exaggerated walking action of stick baits, or the splash of propeller baits, but they are much easier to use. These lures have a cupped metal face or some other device that makes them wobble back and forth with an even plop-plop-plop. They'll take bass when retrieved steadily or when worked with pauses.

Ron Yurko of Conneaut, Ohio, retrieves a weedless spoon over lily pads in hopes of drawing a surface strike.

Poppers

Poppers have a concave face. When you pull them forward they "pop" the surface. The harder you twitch, the louder they pop. Sometimes you'll get more strikes by popping the lure once and letting it rest for several seconds. At other times you'll call up more bass by giving the lure several pops before letting it rest. When you really want to stir things

This bass blew up through surface weeds to nail a spoon on top. Note the buzz blade in the middle of the spoon.

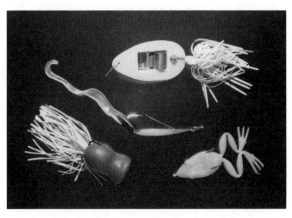

Weedless spoons (top) and hollow plastic poppers and frogs (bottom) will take bass from thick surface weeds. The spoon in the middle has been dressed with the end of a swimming-tail worm.

up, retrieve the popper at a medium speed while giving the rod short jerks. This is called chugging.

When fishing with topwater lures, keep a few basic rules in mind. Avoid bumping the boat and don't try to get too close to likely cover or you may

spook the bass. Whenever possible, cast beyond your target and work the lure past it. Plunking your lure smack on top of a bass may scare it away. Since most bass will be tight to cover, it's usually a waste of time to work a topwater lure all the way back to the boat. When your lure is out of productive water, retrieve it quickly and cast again. Finally, when a bass strikes, wait until you "feel" the fish before setting the hook. Otherwise, you may pull the lure away from it. This takes steady nerves, and you'll probably miss a number of bass before you can stifle the urge to strike too soon.

Specialty Lures

Lures That Defeat the Weeds

Big bass often lurk beneath impenetrable aquatic growth, especially in the summer when lily pads, moss, and grass form a dense carpet on the surface of the water. These aquatic jungles teem with minnows, frogs, and other things for bass to feed upon. Even though air temperatures may be broiling, the dark, shaded water under the weeds is relatively cool. With food, cover, and comfortable water temperatures, the bass that live in weeds grow fat and disregard most bass fishermen with impunity.

A weedless surface spoon is one lure that will help you get the bass out of the tangle. Its basic design features a metal spoon with a single hook and a wire weed guard, but there are also spoons molded of tough plastic. These lures wobble when fished under the surface. They have little action when dragged over matted surface vegetation, but, in many cases, that is just what the bass want. A few spoons have their noses turned up to give them a side-to-side action when skittered over the weeds.

Some spoons have buzz blades or spinner blades to provide extra action, and many come with plastic or vinyl skirts attached to their hooks. Pork rind and plastic trailers can also entice strikes.

Other deadly lures for weed-loving bass include soft plastic frogs and poppers that have snag-free hooks. These lures land on the water with a lifelike "splat," and can be hopped over the greenery like a real frog. You can fish them more slowly than weedless spoons, and that's often just what it takes to enrage a hefty largemouth.

One of the most difficult aspects of fishing with spoons and snagless lures is learning when to set the hook. All too often, the bass slashes through the weeds and the angler jerks the lure away too soon. When a bass attacks a spoon, you should either continue reeling steadily or drop your rod tip and let the spoon sink into the hole created by the bass. The best advice is to wait until you feel the weight of the bass before you set the hook. With soft snagless lures, you should drop the rod tip upon receiving the strike, take in the slack line, and set the hook hard. Use stout bait-casting tackle and heavy line for hauling big bass from the weeds.

Deep-structure Lures

When bass are deep, no lures will get down to them faster than jigging spoons, tailspinners, and vibrating blades. These metal lures cast like rockets, sink like anchors, and resemble shad and other forage fish. They sometimes produce good catches when other lures fail to get strikes, especially during cold-water periods.

Jigging spoons differ from casting spoons in both design and action. The wide, thin shape of most casting spoons slows their fall. The more concentrated mass of a jigging spoon, however, makes it sink faster. Many of them give off pulsating vibrations when pulled sharply through the water, and sink with an erratic flutter. Jigging spoons are constructed from stainless steel, stamped brass, and lead. Lead spoons come in assorted painted colors or are plated with a chrome or silvery finish. Brass spoons usually receive a plated finish.

A vertical presentation is the most efficient method for fishing with jigging spoons. Instead of casting the spoon, position your boat directly over the area you intend to fish and let the spoon sink straight down. Fishing vertically allows you to get your spoon to the fish faster and with pinpoint accuracy.

The jigging action is easy to impart, but it requires absolute concentration. When jigging a spoon on the bottom, let it sink until it touches down. Hold your rod horizontal to the water, reel in the slack, and lift the spoon with a sharp twitch of the rod tip. How high you lift the spoon depends on the activity level of the fish. In cold water where bass are likely to be sluggish, a lift of six to twelve inches may suffice. When fish are more aggressive in midsummer, you may have to snap the spoon up three feet or more. After lifting the spoon, follow it back to the bottom with the rod tip. The trick is to let the spoon fall freely and therefore resemble

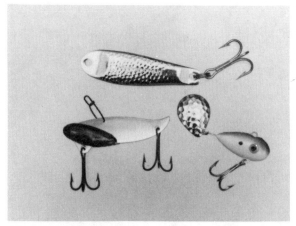

Three lures that quickly get down to bass in deep water are (clockwise from top): the jigging spoon; the tailspinner; and the vibrating blade.

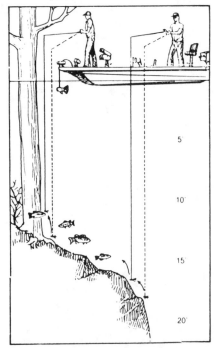

A vertical presentation is the most efficient method for fishing jigging spoons. (Courtesy American Fishing Institute of Indiana State University)

a dying minnow, yet to keep enough slack out of the line so that you can feel strikes.

Most strikes occur as the spoon is falling, so set the hook whenever you feel a slight bump or see the line twitch. Anytime the spoon stops falling before the rod tip returns to a horizontal level, it has probably been intercepted by a fish, so set the hook immediately.

This smallmouth bass went for a tailspinner that was ripped off the bottom.

Jigging spoons work well when bass suspend in deep water during the cold months.

Bass sometimes stay suspended above the bottom, especially spotted bass during the winter months. You must first find the bass with a depthfinder and then lower the spoon to the proper depth by pulling line off the spool one or more feet at a time. A piece of tape wrapped around the butt of the rod can be used as a measuring device. Once the spoon is at the right depth, simply use the jigging method just described.

Many anglers shy away from jigging spoons because they believe too many lures will be lost to snags. The bare treble hook does tend to hang up occasionally, but the compact weight of the spoon serves as its own plug-knocker. If you position your boat directly over a snagged spoon and snap your rod tip a few times, the spoon will usually drop free. You can further reduce hang-ups by cutting two hooks off the treble. In some reservoirs, bass frequent flooded trees, and vertically jigging a spoon right in the tree limbs can be highly productive. A strong rod, and line of at least 17-pound test are needed to horse bass from the trees before they can wrap the line.

Tailspinners

A tailspinner has a compact lead body with a short length of wire protruding from its tail. A spinner blade attaches to the wire with a clevis, allowing the blade to turn freely. Most tailspinners have a treble hook fastened to the bottom of the lure and a line tie located on top. The spinner blade, throbbing and flashing behind the lead body, makes the tailspinner very attractive to bass.

You can vertically jig tailspinners, but they don't come loose from snags as easily as jigging spoons do, so it's best to fish them over clean bottoms. Tailspinners are also effective when used with casting methods. When bass maraud schools of shad on the surface, you'll often scare them down and away if you try to get too close. With the tailspinner, you can stay farther away and still reach the feeding activity. Cast the lure over or into the schooling fish and retrieve it fast enough to make the spinner cut a wake on the surface.

When you want to cover a lot of water quickly, try ripping a tailspinner. Ripping works especially well when fishing a sandbar or some other structure that's relatively free of snags. Make a long cast over the structure and take up slack when the lure hits the water. Let the tailspinner fall to the bottom on a tight line. Then point your rod tip at the lure, take up the slack, and sweep your rod tip up and back. This will rip the lure about five feet off the bottom, attracting any gamefish in the immediate area. Keep a tight line as you let the lure fall back to the bottom, since this is when you'll get most strikes. Continue ripping the tailspinner all the way back, and cover the structure thoroughly by fanning your casts.

Tailspinners are also excellent tools for taking bottom-hugging bass from deep drop-offs. Position your boat in shallow water, up on a point or drop-off, and cast toward deep water. After letting the tailspinner sink on a tight line, pull it off the bottom to start the spinner turning and then use a slow, steady retrieve. Try to keep the lure swimming within a foot of the bottom. If you retrieve too fast, the lure will rise above the bottom and the fish.

Vibrating Blades

Vibrating blades have thin metal bodies shaped like minnows. The belly and head sections of these lures are molded of lead, and the resulting balance makes them wobble sharply, giving off strong vibrations. Many anglers have good success with these lures by simply casting and retrieving them like crankbaits. Because they sink so quickly, you can fish them deeper than the deepest-diving crankbait.

You can also use vibrating blades in all the situations described for tailspinners, and they are excellent for vertical jigging. Since they have two trebles, you'll hook more of the fish that strike these lures than when fishing with tailspinners or jigging spoons. That extra hook also increases your odds for snagging up, but vibrating blades can be worked free most of the time.

Chapter 5

Bass Tackle

In the not-too-distant past, a typical "bass-hound" would rely on a few pet rods and a limited assortment of lures. Now that we've learned more about bass and have invented new lures and techniques for catching them, we need a wider selection of rods. These days, the expert selects a rod for a specific fishing situation, much as a golfer chooses a particular club depending on the lie of his ball. It's common to see a knowledgeable bass angler with six or more rods at the ready, each with a different lure tied to the line. You don't need several rods to get started, but you should choose one or two that are likely to best handle the most evident fishing conditions you will encounter on your home waters.

Many fishing tackle companies now exist, and the industry benefits from space age materials, computer technology, and modern manufacturing methods. Much of the emphasis has focused on improving bass tackle, and, as a result, today's top-flight rods and reels are truly remarkable fishing tools. Bass anglers never had it so good.

Bait-casting Reels

Bait-casting tackle is still the mainstay for most bass anglers, because it provides the greatest casting accuracy. Your thumb rests directly on the spool and is used to slow and stop the flight of the lure, much as you step on a brake to stop a car. Masterful bait-casters can make a hard, low-trajectory cast and slow the lure at the last instant so that it enters the water softly and precisely on target. Bait-casting requires a higher level of skill than spinning or spin-casting tackle does.

The longstanding problem with bait-casting reels is that they can backlash, sometimes forming an impossible tangle of monofilament. In response, reel manufacturers have devised mechanical, centrifugal, and now magnetic anti-backlash mechanisms that work well. When on high settings, they virtually eliminate backlashes. Unfortunately, high settings also reduce casting distance and prevent the fine touch that allows for optimum lure control and accuracy. To get the most out of bait-casting, you must learn to rely more on your thumb. Use anti-backlash devices on low and medium settings, depending on the lure and on the wind conditions at hand. But remember that backlashes may still occur, particularly when casting into a wind.

A bait-casting reel is easy on your line, since the line flows straight onto the spool. Spinning and spin-casting reels twist the line around a bail or pin and can cause line twists and kinks. Bait-casting reels work especially well with lines of 12-pound test and up, which makes them unbeatable for fishing around cover. They perform well with lures weighing ¼ of an ounce or more, but poorly with lighter lures.

Modern bait-casting reels are lighter and more streamlined than their forerunners. Most have smooth side plates opposite the handles, which makes them more comfortable when resting against the palm of your hand. The spools are generally narrower than they were in the past, because anglers no longer need hundreds of yards of line when bass fishing. The incorporation of hard plastics, graphite, and lightweight metals have shaved ounces from bait-casting reels without sacrificing strength. Reels that have ball bearings supporting the spool shafts tend to be smoother casting and more durable. A fast gear ratio, something around five to one, works best for most bass fishing methods. Slower gear ratios sacrifice speed for more power.

Many bait-casting reels have a lever across the back of the reel that lets you release the spool with your casting hand. It's faster and more efficient than the traditional push-button spool release, but the latter is still functional and popular. Some bait-casting reels contain many more features, including miniature computers. You may find some features worthwhile and others frivolous.

Consider whether you want your crank on the left or the right side of the reel. Most right-handed anglers choose reels that have the crank on the right, but it's largely a matter of personal preference. If you cast with your right hand, you must pass the rod to your left hand in order to turn the crank on right-handed reels (and vice versa with left-handed reels). When a right-handed angler uses a left-handed reel, he or she can cast and retrieve while holding the rod in the right hand. This is more efficient, but can be more tiring. If you're unsure, consider buying a reel with a reversible handle.

Spin-casting Reels

Spin-casting reels cost less than bait-casting reels, and they are the easiest to use. The push-button line release can be quickly mastered, so that the beginner spends more time fishing than learning how to cast. Although spin-casting reels do not allow for the pinpoint accuracy that can be achieved

Modern bait-casting reels provide better cast control when using lures weighing over ¼ ounce and lines of 12-pound test or more. (Courtesy Lew Childre and Sons and Quantum)

Bait-casting reels have come a long way in recent years. This compact model has many features. (Courtesy Quantum)

Consider whether you prefer your bait-casting reel to have the crank on the left or right side.

Spin-casting reels continue to be functional introductory reels for novice bass anglers. (Courtesy Zebco and Johnson Fishing, Inc.)

with bait-casting reels, and although they are not as durable, they continue to function as good introductory reels for budding bass anglers.

Spinning Reels

Most bass anglers reserve spinning reels for light lines and lures. Because the line flows off the spool of a spinning reel with little resistance, it provides more distance and better accuracy with lures weighing ¼ of an ounce or less. Spinning reels also do a better job of handling light lines of up to about 10-pound test. Reels that have skirted spools prevent the line from sneaking under the spool and tangling. An internal bail trip, which eliminates the exposed knob found on an external bail trip, is another worthwhile feature.

Thanks to the incorporation of graphite and other new materials, spinning reels are lighter than ever and may even provide additional sensitivity. Gear ratios range from about 3.2 to 1 to about 5.4 to 1. The higher the gear ratio, the faster the reel will gobble up line, which is an advantage in most fishing situations. Ball bearings improve the smoothness and increase the life of the reel, and are worth the extra cost. Many reels convert easily to left- or right-hand retrieve, a major consideration for left-handed anglers.

If you plan on using the same reel with a variety of lines, you'll find snap-off spools to your liking. The conventional drag adjustment, located on the top of the spool, works well but prohibits the use of a snap-off spool. Many reels now have their drags and drag adjustment knobs at the rear of the reel, and these are easier to adjust while fighting a fish. The roller guide on the bail is a critical point of stress. Reels that have large line rollers will abuse your line less, especially if the rollers are made of aluminum oxide or some other super-hard material.

The bail trigger, one of the most innovative changes in spinning reels, lets you open the bail with the index finger of your casting hand. This convenient device speeds up the casting process, resulting in more casts per fishing day.

Line

Novice bass anglers commonly buy a quality rod and reel and then try to save money by purchasing cheap line. Poor quality line hampers your casting

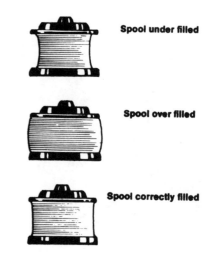

This spinning reel features graphite construction, ball bearings, and a rear drag. (Courtesy Quantum)

Top spool is underfilled, middle spoon is overfilled, and bottom spool is correctly filled.

This graphite spinning reel has its drag adjustment knob on the face of the spool. (Courtesy Browning)

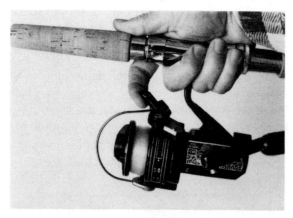

The bail release trigger on this spinning reel allows for one-hand operation.

distance and accuracy and will not hold up as well as premium line. Your line is the most important link between you and the bass. Buying cheap line is false economy.

Few bass anglers today use anything but nylon monofilament or cofilament lines. While clear, green, and other low-visibility lines are difficult for bass to see, they are also difficult for anglers to see. Many fishermen favor fluorescent lines when fishing with plastic worms and jigs. Fluorescent lines are much easier to see above the water, but are not nearly as visible under the surface. Some very thin lines are designed for extra limpness and castability. They thoroughly satisfy many bass-fishing situations and are the best choice for beginners. A few lines, made for extreme toughness and abrasion resistance, are unbeatable for standing up to heavy cover, but do not cast as well as limp lines.

Just how long your line holds up depends on how often and hard you use it, and how well you take care of it. Infrequent anglers may get by with an annual line change at the beginning of each season. Those who fish several times a week should change lines at least once a month. If you frequently fish around rock, wood, weeds, or other abrasive cover, your line will have an even shorter life. It pays to run the last three feet of line through your fingers every so often, and especially after hauling a bass out of cover. If you feel any nicks, cut off the affected line and retie. Your line is only as strong as its weakest point, and a tiny nick could cut your line strength in half.

Out of Line

I'm a fanatic when it comes to keeping fresh line on my reels, but not everyone shares my views on this subject. Not long ago, I went fishing with a friend of mine who has little regard for his line. He's out after bass at least three times a week and occasionally makes a good catch. He also has a lot of bad luck. I've often heard him lament the loss of big bass, and the culprit is usually broken line or the bass throwing the hook. We were fishing on his favorite lake that evening, and he ran the boat straight to his most productive spot.

"Right over there," he said, pointing at a fallen tree, "is where I lost a lunker just last week on a purple worm. I got my hook into him, but he spit it out when he jumped."

When my friend cast his fake crawler into the submerged tree limbs, I noticed that his monofilament line was badly coiled, a sure sign of age. Coiled line causes undue slack, and I wondered if that was the reason my friend had not hooked his bass well the week before.

"There he is!" my friend yelped. When he jerked back on his rod, an ominous swirl erupted from the tree limbs and a very large bass tailwalked on the surface. The fish was in open water and should have been landed. But when it surged for the deep water, the line popped like thread.

"I don't understand how that line could break so easily," my friend wailed. "I just put it on two months ago."

I didn't say anything at the time, but I later suggested to my friend that he could eliminate much of his "bad luck" by changing his line more often. Although monofilament will hold up for years if stored properly, it ages in direct proportion to how often it is used. A casual angler who gets out for a few hours once a week may be able to get by with the same line all season. But anyone who fishes as often as my friend, and with as much zeal, should consider changing lines at least once a month. Every two weeks is even better. I generally change lines weekly, and when I'm fishing around abrasive cover I sometimes respool every day.

—Mark Hicks

Sunlight gradually destroys nylon lines. Normal fishing conditions shouldn't do any harm, but weeks of prolonged exposure to the sun in a boat, or in the back window of a truck, will surely weaken the line. Store your rods out of the sun in a cool, dry environment. The same goes for line on bulk spools. If you notice a chalky coating on your line, it may indicate that the line is losing some of the plasticizers that help keep it soft, flexible, and easy to cast. Consider changing it at your earliest convenience.

Changing line may not cost as much as you think, because you need only replace the first forty to fifty yards of line and not the entire spool. To get the best casting performance possible, you must fill your reel's spool properly. An underfilled spool results in short, inaccurate casts, poor drag performance, and a decreased retrieve ratio. An overfilled spool causes the line to balloon off, leading to backlashes and "bird's nests." On bait-casting and spinning reels, fill the spool until the line comes to within about ⅛ of an inch of the lip, or edge, of the spool.

To avoid putting twist in the line while spooling up a bait-casting reel, put a pencil through the hole in the center of the line's spool. Have someone hold the pencil so the spool turns with uniform, minimum line tension while you crank on the reel handle. To fill a spinning reel, have someone hold the line spool or place it on the floor or the ground. Hold the rod tip three to four feet away from the spool and make fifteen to twenty turns on the reel handle. Stop and check for line twist. If the line is twisting, turn the line spool over and wind the rest of the line onto the reel. Use the same procedure for filling spin-casting reels, and remember that you must partially remove the reel cover to insure that you do not overfill or underfill the spool.

Nylon line absorbs water when in use and will "set" after it has been allowed to dry. This is normal

How to Fill Your Reel

Improper loading of your reel can cause line twist which can greatly reduce casting accuracy and distance. Worse yet, it can cause you to lose fish.

You can avoid problems by having your reel filled on a linewinding machine at your favorite sporting goods store. However, it pays to learn how to do it yourself because most line problems occur at lakeside, miles from the nearest winder.

Filling a Revolving-Spool Reel

Insert a pencil into the supply spool to allow the fishing line to feed smoothly off the spool. Have someone hold each end of the pencil while you turn the reel handle. Keep proper tension on the line by having the person holding the pencil exert a slight inward pressure on the supply spool.

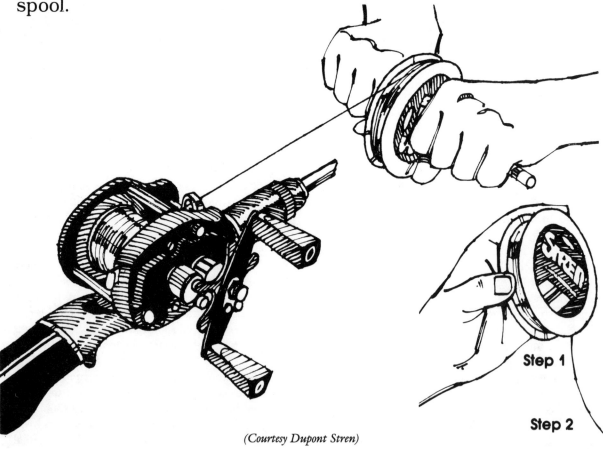

(Courtesy Dupont Stren)

Step 1

Step 2

Filling a Spin-Cast/Closed-Face Reel

Use the same procedure (steps 1 to 6) described for filling a Spinning Reel. Remember to partially remove the reel cover so you will be able to see the spool and the rotation of the pickup pin. This is critical to insure that you do not underfill or overfill the spool.

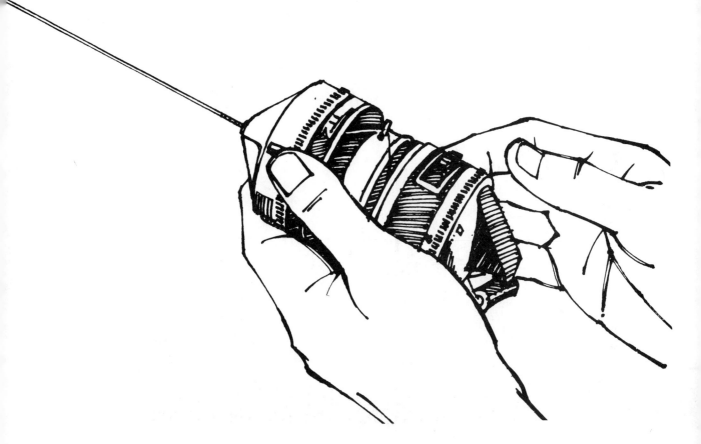

(Courtesy Dupont Stren)

Palomar Knot

This knot is equally as good as the Improved Clinch for terminal tackle connections and is easier to tie, except when using large plugs. It, too, is used by most of the pros.

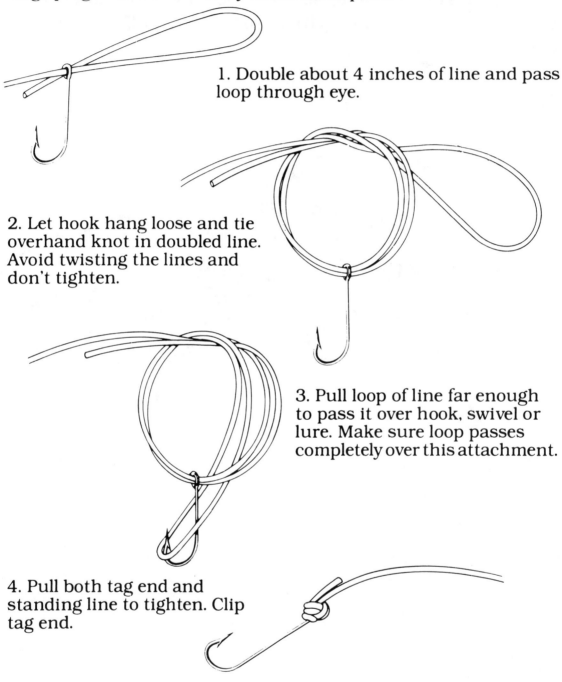

1. Double about 4 inches of line and pass loop through eye.

2. Let hook hang loose and tie overhand knot in doubled line. Avoid twisting the lines and don't tighten.

3. Pull loop of line far enough to pass it over hook, swivel or lure. Make sure loop passes completely over this attachment.

4. Pull both tag end and standing line to tighten. Clip tag end.

(Courtesy Dupont Stren)

Knots to Hold Terminal Tackle

Improved Clinch Knot

This is a good knot for making terminal-tackle connections and is best used for lines up to 20-pound test. It is a preferred knot by professional fishermen and angling authorities.

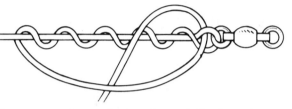

1. Pass line through eye of hook, swivel, or lure. Double back and make five turns around the standing line. Hold coils in place; thread end of line around first loop above the eye, then through big loop as shown.

2. Hold tag end and standing line while coils are pulled up. Take care that coils are in spiral, not lapping over each other. Slide tight against eye. Clip tag end.

World's Fair Knot

The winning knot in Du Pont's Great Knot Search

Created by Gary L. Martin of Lafayette, IN, this terminal tackle knot was selected by a panel of outdoor writers as the best new, easy-to-tie, all-purpose fishing knot from 498 entries in the Du Pont Great Knot Search. Martin named it the World's Fair Knot because it was first publicly demonstrated by him at the Knoxville '82 World's Fair.

1. Double a 6-inch length of line and pass the loop through the eye.

2. Bring the loop back next to the doubled line and grasp the doubled line through the loop.

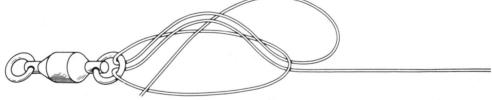

3. Put the tag end through the new loop formed by the double line.

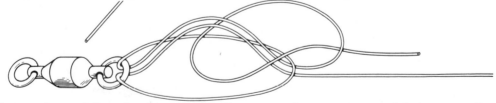

4. Bring the tag end back through the new loop created by step 3.

5. Pull the tag end snug and slide knot up tight. Clip tag end.

even for premium lines. The line regains most of its limpness once it has absorbed water again.

All your efforts in selecting and caring for your line will be in vain if you fail to tie good knots. The knot is the weakest point in the line, although some knots have remarkably high breaking strengths when tied properly. The Trilene and Palomar knots put two wraps of line around the hook eye and retain 85 to 90 percent of the original line strength. The Improved Clinch knot, which has only one wrap around the hook eye, retains up to 80 percent of the line strength.

Tie your knot carefully, and once you've made the required turns and wraps, wet the line with saliva and snug the knot down slowly with one fluid motion. Don't snip the excess line too close. Instead, leave a tag end about ⅛ of an inch long. Never melt the excess line with a cigarette or lighter; the heat will weaken both your knot and your line.

Adjust the drag depending on how and where you are fishing. When using light lines in snag-free water, or when casting lures that have small hooks, a light drag setting—maybe 25 to 30 percent of the line strength—works best. At the other extreme, when flippin' a jig into thick cover with a heavy line, you cannot afford to let the bass take any line; in such a case, you should tighten the drag to the point where it will not slip. Since bass are often hooked near some type of cover and are not noted for making long runs, a fairly heavy drag setting—something over 50 percent of the line strength—serves best for most fishing conditions.

Serious bass anglers have many different rods and use whichever one best matches the lure and conditions that confront them.

The Right Rod for the Job

Today you can select the right rod from a seemingly endless variety of rod lengths, actions, materials, and designs. Start by considering exactly how and where you intend to use the rod.

Will the rod be used to cast lures or live bait? For lures, a fast action works best for most conditions, since only the upper one quarter to one third of the rod flexes to make the cast. The rest of the rod is stiff to insure good hook-setting power and control over the fish. Many novice bass anglers make the mistake of selecting a rod that has too little backbone. Even when using a light-action rod with light line and lures, you need to have stiffness in the rod's butt. For live bait, you'll want a rod with moderate, slow, or parabolic action (which

flexes all the way down to the angler's hand), because one with fast action tends to throw bait off the hook.

How much power should the rod have? Many manufacturers list the power of their rods as ultra-light, light, medium, medium-heavy, and heavy. Another method gives the rod a numerical power rating from 1 to 9, ranging from ultra-light and to ultra-heavy. These designations are not an exact science. For example, two medium-heavy five-and-a-half-foot bait-casting rods from different manufacturers may have noticeably different actions.

For a better indication of power, check the manufacturer's recommendations for lure weight and line test. This information is usually listed in catalogs and may be found right on the butt section of the rod blank. A typical rod description might read: Medium, 8–15 lb. line, ¼ to ⅝ oz. lures.

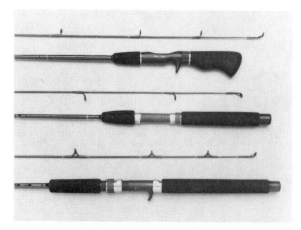

The advanced bass angler needs a wide assortment of rods to meet changing fishing conditions. (Courtesy Browning)

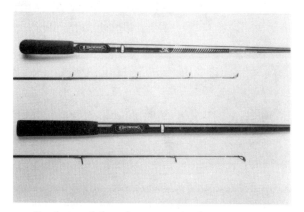

Fat-butt rods have become popular in recent years. (Courtesy Browning)

Bass anglers are using longer bait-casting rods with long handles for many fishing chores.

This particular rod will handle a wide range of lure weights and line sizes. You should avoid using lures and lines that do not fall within these specifications, or the rod's performance will suffer.

How long should the rod be? Not long ago, a five-and-a-half to six-foot bait-casting rod sporting a pistol grip was the standard tool for serious bass anglers. This type of rod is still excellent for pinpoint, close-quarter casting, but more anglers now add longer rods to their arsenals. The introduction of the flippin' rod played a major role in this trend. Bass anglers quickly learned that this beefy seven-and-a-half-foot rod has no equal when bass burrow into dense cover. It allows you to flip plastic worms and jigs into tiny openings on a short line, and to haul bass forcefully out of the thick cover.

A few enterprising anglers began experimenting with flippin' rods and discovered that they allowed for longer casts. The rods also delivered more consistent hook sets with Texas-rigged worms and hook-guard jigs, and, when the rod tip was jammed into the water, could force deep-diving crankbaits to dive deeper. But many anglers found flippin' rods to be too cumbersome for accurate casting. The natural evolution has led to specialized long rods that are destined to become prominent among bass anglers everywhere.

These specialty rods generally measure from six and a half to seven feet in length, with the rod blank running through double handles for increased strength and sensitivity. The double grips allow for powerful two-handed casting. The extended handle can be propped against your stomach or forearm for more leverage when setting the hook, or to offset the water resistance created by certain lures, such as big diving crankbaits and oversized willow leaf spinnerbaits.

Most bass anglers match long rods with bait-casting reels. They reserve spinning rods, generally five and a half to six and a half feet in length, for fishing with light lines and lures.

A major advancement in rod design occurred with the introduction of graphite, and, soon after, of boron. These materials have resulted in much lighter, faster, and more powerful rods than those made from fiberglass. Thanks to these materials, the longer, stiffer rods, now becoming so popular, are remarkably lightweight.

Equally important, graphite and boron rods offer increased sensitivity, which helps you detect subtle strikes. The most sensitive rods have a high graphite or boron content, usually well over 80 percent.

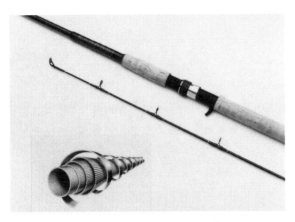

Rods that have a high graphite content and continuous strands of graphite running from the tip to the butt are the most sensitive, and therefore best for fishing plastic worms and jigs. (Courtesy Browning)

Some manufacturers build rods with 100 percent graphite fibers. Graphite and boron rods are the most expensive, but they are unbeatable when fishing with jigs, plastic worms, or anything that requires you to feel the strike before setting the hook.

Fortunately for your pocketbook, graphite or boron rods aren't necessary for all your fishing chores. When fishing with spinnerbaits, crankbaits, and other lures that do not dictate a refined sense of touch, a less costly composite or fiberglass rod will do. Most composite rods are a combination of fiberglass and graphite. The best composites meld graphite and fiberglass into lightweight rods that are more sensitive than fiberglass alone, while retaining the durability that fiberglass is noted for.

Some professional bass anglers prefer composite or fiberglass rods when fishing with lures such as crankbaits, spinnerbaits, and buzzbaits. They claim that graphite rods react so fast when you set the hook that an angler who has sharp reflexes can inadvertently take the lure away from the bass. A slower composite or fiberglass rod gives the bass a fraction of a second longer to engulf the lure, which results in more solid hookups. Many anglers also believe that a slower fiberglass rod will help prevent bass from throwing lures during the fight.

If you want a rod with maximum sensitivity, be sure the handle or reel seat incorporates graphite or exposes a section of the rod so that you can lay a finger right on the blank when fishing. As for the grip material, both cork and foam do an excellent job. The best guides are made from silicone carbide or aluminum oxide. Double foot guides give the rod more backbone, whereas single foot guides let the rod flex more freely.

The following seven outfits might provide useful sets for the typical bass fisherman who is active all across the country. For the tournament angler, all these outfits, or ones like them, come into play many times over the course of a season. Some bass anglers may require more or fewer rods than these, and at least some of their basic rods may differ. An experienced fisherman knows which type of rod works best for him or her in a given situation.

Flippin' Rod

Match this seven-and-a-half-foot rod with a light bait-casting reel. For fishing plastic worms and jig and pork combinations in and around heavy cover, use the outfit with 14- to 25-pound test line to prevent breaking off. Approach stealthily when employing the flippin' method, because you must ease your boat within twenty feet of the bass.

To make the flip cast, hold your rod tip up and let out about fourteen feet of line. Then reach up to the first guide above the reel and grasp the line with your left hand (vice versa for left-handed an-

Bob Troxel hauls a bass out of heavy cover with a flippin' rod.

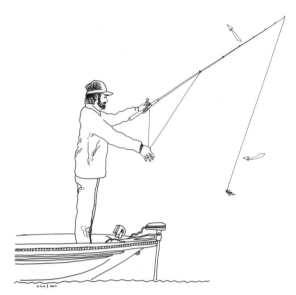

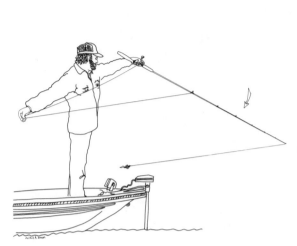

To make the flip cast, hold your rod tip up and let out about fourteen feet of line. Then hook (do not grasp) the line in the crotch between the thumb and forefinger of your free hand. Lift the rod tip and pull the line with your free hand to start the jig swinging toward you.

As the jig swings back to you, drop your rod tip below horizontal to keep the lure close to the water. Note how the rod's handle extends above the wrist. You may twist the handle inside or outside the wrist.

glers). Pull the line to your left and lift the jig to within about seven feet of the rod tip. Swing the jig back pendulum fashion and drop the rod tip just below horizontal. As the jig swings forward, raise the rod tip slightly to increase the lure's momentum and then feed line with your left hand. When done properly, the lure will stay inches above the water throughout the cast. Just before the lure reaches the intended target, snub its progress with the line in your left hand, and it will slip into the water with barely a ripple.

This soft presentation is the key to successful flippin'. Bass in shallow water sometimes spook easily and refuse to chase fast lures. You must practically put your offering into their mouths, and flippin' allows you to do just that. Once the lure enters the water, let it drop straight down to the bottom. Be alert, since many strikes come on the initial fall. In this event, set the hook immediately and force the bass into open water with the heavy tackle. If the initial fall fails to get action, work the jig slowly back to the boat by gently lifting and lowering the rod tip. Make as much bottom contact as possible and be especially alert for a strike whenever you bring the lure over an object and let it fall back to the bottom.

Although flippin' may seem tedious, it is actually a fast method of fishing a slow lure. The moment you work the lure out of productive water, quickly flip it into another bit of cover. You waste no time retrieving your lure through dead water or making long casts. Few fishing techniques rival flippin' for pure efficiency.

Most successful flip-casters search for stained or slightly muddy water where they can get close to the bass without spooking them. In reservoirs, feeder creeks and streams are good bets since silt and other sediment often discolor them. When bass are deeply entrenched in weeds or wood cover, you can usually approach them closely even in clear water. If you can't get close enough for flippin', you can usually make do with a tactic called pitching.

Pitching is an offshoot of flippin' that provides more distance. Prepare for the pitch cast by letting out line until the lure hangs down to the reel or slightly above it. Grasp the lure in your free hand, so that the hook points away from your flesh. Lower the rod tip toward the water and hold the lure below the rod. Release the lure and swing the rod tip up and out, while feathering the spool with your thumb. The lure should glide just over the water's

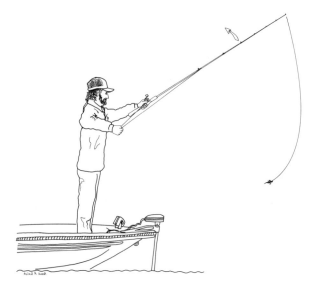

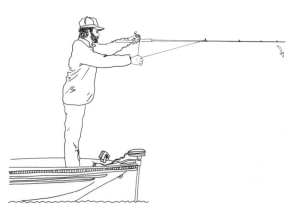

Raise the rod tip sharply and feed line with the free hand as the jig swings forward.

Lower the rod tip and feed line. Lift up slightly just as the lure reaches the target to make a soft entry into the water.

surface to distances of thirty feet or more. Pitching is nearly as accurate as flippin' and allows for a very soft lure entry. The technique works better with lures weighing ⅜ of an ounce and up, because lighter lures can't sustain enough momentum.

Deep Crankbait Rod

The next rod down the line is seven feet long and has a double handle. Although it is not as stiff as the flippin' rod, it does have a medium-heavy action. You may want to match this rod with a large, high-speed bait-casting reel filled with lines ranging from 10- to 15-pound test. Use this outfit mainly for making long casts with medium to large crankbaits. You can increase the diving depth of your crankbaits by pushing the rod tip deep into the water. Also use this rod with big spinnerbaits and other lures when long casts are necessary.

Plastic Worm and Hook-guard Jig Rod

A basic outfit for casting Texas-rigged worms and jig and pork combinations is a six-and-a-half-foot, double-handled, medium-heavy bait-casting rod with a lightweight, high-speed reel. Use 12- to 17-pound test line, depending on the thickness of the cover you're fishing. This outfit is easy to cast all day and has the backbone for penetrating hook sets.

Close Quarter Casting

For close, accurate casting with spinnerbaits, crankbaits, topwater plugs, and other lures, use two five-and-a-half-foot pistol-gripped bait-casting rods, one medium action and the other medium-heavy. Choose the rod that best matches the size of the lure you're casting, and match these rods with lightweight bait-casting reels filled with 12- to 17-pound test. For peak efficiency and close range accuracy with these outfits, it's hard to beat the side cast. The low rod position keeps the lure close to the water throughout the cast, which makes for a softer lure entry and lets you shoot your lures under overhanging branches and other cover.

Light Worm Spinning Rod

Bass sometimes prefer small plastic worms with light slip sinkers, and light jig and pork combinations which are difficult to cast with bait-casting tackle. In these circumstances, go with a very stiff, medium-heavy spinning outfit and 10-pound test line. The outfit easily handles the light lures, while providing the backbone needed for driving the hook home. It's also ideal for skipping the lure over the surface like a stone. When bass are under boat docks and other cover that can't be penetrated with regular casting methods, skipping lets you get a lure to them.

The Side Cast

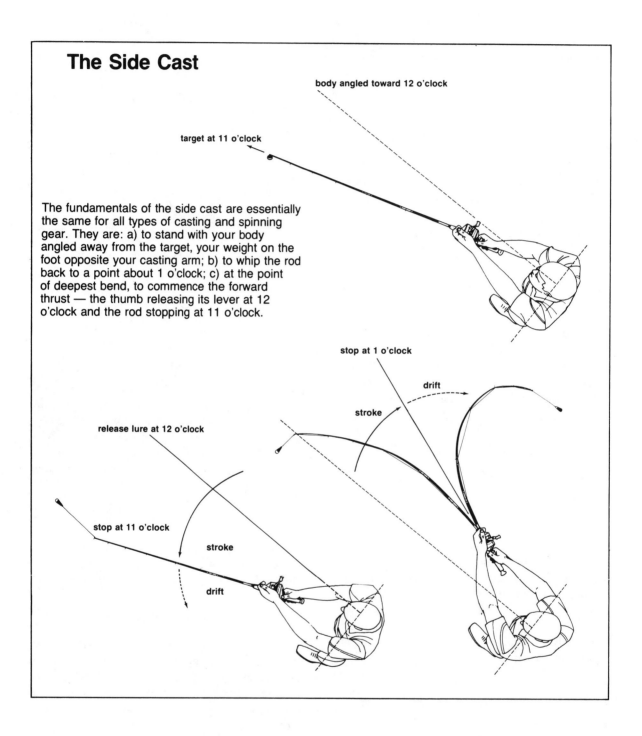

body angled toward 12 o'clock

target at 11 o'clock

The fundamentals of the side cast are essentially the same for all types of casting and spinning gear. They are: a) to stand with your body angled away from the target, your weight on the foot opposite your casting arm; b) to whip the rod back to a point about 1 o'clock; c) at the point of deepest bend, to commence the forward thrust — the thumb releasing its lever at 12 o'clock and the rod stopping at 11 o'clock.

stop at 1 o'clock

drift

stroke

release lure at 12 o'clock

stop at 11 o'clock

stroke

drift

Mark Hicks prepares to "pitch" a jig under a pontoon boat.

A long bait-casting rod with a long handle is the ideal tool for casting and retrieving big, deep-diving crankbaits.

A worm and jig rod should be sensitive and stiff enough to drive the hook home. Note the long handle for additional leverage.

Pistol-gripped bait-casting rods are ideal for making short, accurate side casts.

Tommy Simpkins is one of many proficient bass anglers who use a stiff spinning rod for casting small Texas-rigged worms and light jig and pork combinations.

When skipping worms, peg the slip sinker to prevent it from sliding up the line. The secret to the skip cast is to keep the rod tip low to the water. The casting motion, both forehand and backhand, is comparable to swinging a tennis racket. But you must put a hard wrist-snap into the cast and angle it toward the water. When zipped along at such a sharp angle to the surface, the lure will bounce off rather than cut into the water.

Light Line Spinning

A medium-action six-foot spinning outfit handles lines from 6- to 10-pound test well. Use it with lures that don't require heavy hook sets, such as small topwater minnows, light jigs that have exposed fine-wire hooks, and any lightweight lure that has treble hooks.

Chapter 6

Bass Boats

Next to his tackle, a bass fisherman most needs some kind of watercraft to carry him safely to the action. Rental boats, available on many waters, are not always practical for bass fishing and are often in poor condition. The most serious bass fisherman will eventually own a boat. Almost any craft, from a frail canoe to a high-performance fiberglass bass boat, will do, depending upon the kind of waters likely to be fished and how much the angler cares to spend.

Kinds of Bass Boats

Canoes, inflatable rafts, and small johnboats are good for fishing on rivers and small ponds. They can be transported on car-top carriers and are light enough to be carried to the water's edge. These vessels do, however, cramp the angler and can become extremely uncomfortable after several hours of fishing. The slightest breeze can cause the angler to spend more time paddling to maintain boat position than casting to catch fish. You can greatly alleviate the latter problem with the addition of an electric maneuvering motor.

The electric motor probably bears more responsibility for the surging interest in bass fishing than any other single factor. It has taken much of the

work out of boat control and has allowed for the development of large, stable, and comfortable bass boats. Precise lure presentation, necessary to catch bass consistently, requires precise boat control. With a bow-mounted electric motor, even the heaviest bass boats can be pulled about quietly and easily. Some excellent bass fishing takes place under windy conditions that are impossible to overcome without the aid of an electric motor.

Many anglers who own bass boats use foot control units that let them both steer and run the electric motor with one foot, leaving both hands free for fishing. The motor can be run while standing or sitting. Others use hand control motors, which are especially popular among anglers who always stand while fishing. An on/off foot switch is usually affixed to the floor and an extended handle guides the motor with nudges from the hands, feet, or knees.

An electric motor's power is measured in terms of thrust. Heavier boats need more thrust. Following a basic rule of thumb have five pounds of thrust for every two hundred pounds of boat, including the weight of its contents. A 12-volt motor with a minimum of twenty-four pounds of thrust will suffice for medium-sized bass boats, fourteen to sixteen feet in length. For larger boats, you need a 24-volt motor (which requires two batteries) with well over thirty pounds of thrust. Use only deep-

Sneaking Up

I made good use of a miniature pontoon boat a few years ago while fishing a strip mine pond. One side of the pond was hemmed in by a sheer high-wall, the other side overgrown with small trees and shrubs that hung out over the water, providing shade and cover for bass. The water was crystal clear and the bass were edgy. Getting a lure under the limbs and branches without spooking the fish posed quite a challenge. The little pontoon boat proved to be the perfect craft for meeting that challenge.

As I sat in the swivel seat, the controls for the electric motor were conveniently located between my knees. I flicked the switch into forward and the little boat slipped toward the overhanging cover, barely disturbing the water's surface. This sneaky approach allowed me to get close to the bass without alarming them. My profile was low, so the bass were not likely to see me. By making a low sidearm cast, I could pitch a plastic worm far under the cover. I had rigged the worm without any type of weight so that it would land softly and sink slowly.

I had fished maybe ten yards down the bank when my line twitched as the worm sank into a dark, shaded spot beneath a leafy branch. I dropped my rod tip, cranked two times on the reel, and set the hook.

The bass plowed for deep water, then reversed direction and leaped into the air. The little boat remained steady throughout the tussle and I eventually landed a six-pound largemouth.

—Mark Hicks

---

cycle marine (not automobile) batteries to power electric fishing motors. Deep-cycle batteries disburse a slow, steady flow of current for extended periods. Give the batteries a slow charge after each day's fishing. Running a battery too low or giving it a fast "hot charge" will shorten its life.

Any craft that has a bow-mounted electric motor and a comfortable swivel seat can serve as a bare-essentials type of bass boat. Miniature pontoon boats fit into this category, and they are excellent car-toppers. Many of these boats measure less than four feet wide and about six feet in length. They sport swivel seats for one or two anglers, and have a bracket for an electric motor on the bow and room for a battery behind the seat. They are hard to beat for sneaking around ponds and other small waterways.

A wide, stable fourteen- to sixteen-foot johnboat makes an ideal craft for adaptation to a rustic bass boat. (V-bottom aluminum boats may also be used, but they are not as stable and tend to be pushed around more by the wind.) Secure a wooden brace to the bow to support an electric motor and fasten slightly elevated swivel seats to the standard bench seats. In the larger johnboats, some anglers even install casting decks made from exterior grade ply-wood. Outdoor carpeting will dress up the boat, muffle noise, and make for surer footing.

Commercially made aluminum bass boats are heavier and more stable than johnboats and have more flotation. They are laid out much like fiber-glass bass boats, so they have more interior space. The smaller models generally have pedestal seats mounted on the floor inside the boat, whereas larger models have their seats mounted on casting decks. Aluminum bass boats may contain all the appointments found on fiberglass models, including live wells, rod lockers, carpeting, consoles, and many other features. Some are rated for outboards in the 50- to 80-horsepower range, and they reach speeds over 40 mph. They cost less than fiberglass bass boats, run economically, and can be towed by small cars.

At the top of the line, costly, well-designed fiberglass bass boats provide a very stable fishing platform and hold their position in the wind better than most other boats. They'll also give you a smoother ride on choppy water, and the larger models are much safer on rough water, which is not uncommon in big reservoirs.

Smaller bass boats, fourteen to sixteen feet in length, perform well with outboards in the 35- to

Even an inflatable raft can serve as a bass boat, especially when fishing ponds or slow-moving rivers.

Bill Englefield and many other anglers prefer a hand-controlled electric motor. Note the extension handle attached to the shaft of the motor.

This angler uses a foot-controlled electric motor to maneuver his boat while casting. (Courtesy Ranger Boats)

This sturdy attachment allows the angler to steer the electric motor with his foot. (Courtesy MotorGuide)

85-horsepower range, are easy to tow, and are large enough for most fishing conditions. At the other end of the spectrum, the beamy high-performance rigs that measure eighteen to over twenty feet in length can reach speeds of 55 to over 65 mph when matched with a muscular outboard of 150 horse-power or more. Professional anglers, and all anglers who need to whittle large reservoirs down to size, opt for these sleek, stable fishing machines. Whatever size the outboard, it should never exceed the boat's U.S. Coast Guard horsepower rating.

The larger rigs can cost over $20,000, so shop

Only deep-cycle marine batteries should be used to power electric maneuvering motors. (Courtesy GNB)

Miniature pontoon boats are great for fishing small waters.

A top-of-the-line fiberglass bass boat provides the ultimate in comfort and stability, and it has enough speed to cut large impoundments down to size. (Courtesy Johnson Outboards)

and compare features. Some hulls are designed mainly for speed, but lack interior space and will give you a hard ride on rough water. Slower models may offer more room and better withstand pounding waves. Many first-time boat buyers choose to go with a faster hull, but experienced anglers— even the professionals who compete on the B.A.S.S. circuit—usually opt for more weight and room and for less speed. You'll get more out of a high-performance hull if you pair it with a high-performance outboard. Almost every outboard motor manufacturer carries a special line of finely tuned motors that have been designed for bass boats.

When looking a boat over, don't be bashful about pounding on the hull. Does it feel solid? Open all the hatches. Are they securely fastened? Do they feel sturdy or flimsy? Is the interior under the rear deck lids finished cleanly, or does it reveal rough spots? Is the transom adequately braced inside? If you take time to inspect the workmanship thoroughly, you can get a good idea of the boat's quality. Always get a demonstration on the water to tell you better than words how the boat handles and rides.

Avoid any temptation to cut costs on the trailer, because this is where the boat will spend most of its time. The trailer should have bunks (not rollers) supporting the hull. Rollers can deform the hull and hurt the boat's performance. Never tow larger rigs with anything smaller than a full-sized automobile, and always protect your investment with a boat cover. A boat that is constantly exposed to the sun and to extreme weather conditions will age prematurely.

In order to achieve optimum performance, find a marine dealer who specializes in rigging bass boats.

Other Considerations

Deal with a marina that has a good reputation for rigging bass boats. They'll have a wide variety of stainless steel propellers, which is extremely important because the right prop is imperative for getting the most out of your bass boat. You should consider purchasing a jack plate, which allows the engine to be raised or lowered on the transom to fine-tune its power and control. The jack plate also sets the motor back several inches, which helps the boat get up on plane faster and allows more water to reach the prop.

Many waters have submerged hazards, such as reefs, boulders, stumps, and trees. If your lower unit hits one of these obstacles, even at slow planing speeds, the collision could throw you from the driver's seat. Whenever you are moving under the power of the gas motor, always wear a life vest that is attached to a kill switch that will stop the engine if you are jarred from your seat. Carry aboard a fire extinguisher and a distress flag. Many experienced bass anglers also bring along a tool kit for the outboard, and a spare prop.

A jack plate will help you get the most out of your boat and motor combination.

Some anglers install a foot throttle (like that on an automobile) in their bass boats, and trim switch buttons on the steering wheel. These accessories afford better speed control and let you keep both hands on the steering wheel at all times. This is especially important when boating at high speeds, or when you must slow down and constantly adjust your speed to negotiate big waves. Elastic cords and nylon straps are available to keep rods and tackle boxes in place when traversing rough water.

Every bass angler should carry one, and preferably two, anchors. A ten-pound anchor holds boats of up to about sixteen feet in length; a fifteen-pound anchor is the minimum size for larger boats. A fifty-foot length of ¼-inch diameter polybraided rope should handle most anchoring chores for bass boats. Store anchors in compartments or hook them to anchor winches.

The interest in bass boats has grown tremendously in recent years, and it shows no signs of slowing. If you like the idea of fishing in comfort, style, and efficiency, you may not be satisfied until you own one.

Chapter 7

Tackle Boxes, Scents, and Other Accessories

Tackle Boxes

Back when there were fewer bass fishermen and less wary bass, no one worried much about organizing fishing lures. Anglers would muse over a tackle box stuffed with a hodgepodge of lures until the hand finally selected a lure by reaching out with the wavering uncertainty of a pointer on a Ouija board. Then the angler randomly tried one lure after another, hoping to find "what the bass wanted."

Attaining success on today's crowded bass waters requires a more scientific approach. As we discussed in Chapter 2, you must first study the habits of the bass in order to determine their location. Only then should you consider which lures best suit the job at hand. Accomplished bass anglers regard their lures as tools and break them down into categories, as was done in Chapter 4. To help you find precisely the tool you need without wasting time, develop a tackle box system.

Which of the many types of tackle boxes are right for you? To a great extent, that depends on how many lures you have accumulated. If you're just starting out, one small or medium-sized trunk-type box with fold-out trays will probably hold all your lures with ease. Anglers who have fished bass for years and have mastered lures in all categories generally need several tackle boxes in a variety of designs. Most tackle boxes are now made of tough, lightweight plastic that is impervious to both rust and the chemical reaction to plastic worms that used to destroy early plastic boxes.

Your first trunk-type tackle box should have trays with compartments of various sizes. Long compartments are needed for plastic worms and long plugs, such as topwater minnows and deep-diving crankbaits. Shorter compartments will hold jigs, short plugs, worm hooks, slip sinkers, and other smaller items. Some boxes have trays with removable dividers, so you can alter the size of the compartments. The bottom section of the box should contain a rack for hanging spinnerbaits and buzzbaits, lures that do not fit well in regular compartments. You would be wise to purchase a tackle box that may seem larger than necessary; you'll be surprised at how fast you will fill the empty compartments.

Many anglers use a different tackle box for each lure category. Anglers who store their tackle boxes in boat lockers let the size of the lockers dictate the size of the tackle boxes.

Flat boxes with see-through plastic lids have become quite popular with bass anglers who strive for organization. The thin boxes fit into many boat compartments and hold a copious amount of lures.

This trunk-type tackle box has compartments in varying sizes. (Courtesy Plano)

Rusty Kisor uses a trunk-type tackle box that has a hanging rack in the bottom for spinnerbaits and buzzbaits.

Flat boxes store easily and their see-through lids allow you to find the right lure before you open the box. This model has movable partitions so you can accommodate lures of various sizes. (Courtesy Plano)

Hanging-rack boxes are best for spinnerbaits and buzzbaits, and they are also available for crankbaits and other plugs. (Courtesy Flambeau)

Most flat boxes also have movable partitions so that the compartments can be arranged to accommodate long or short lures. Miniature flat boxes are ideal for organizing small lures, such as jigs and plastic grubs. They easily fit into small boat lockers, and may even slip into the storage spaces of larger boxes, reserving shelf space for larger lures.

Trunk-style and flat boxes house most lures well, but hanging-rack boxes are much better for spinnerbaits and buzzbaits. The racks keep the lures in order, prevent them from tangling together, and allow the skirts to hang straight and to dry thoroughly. Some rack boxes will hold a hundred lures or more and have one or two trays with compartments for extra blades, skirts, trailer hooks, and

other paraphernalia. Hanging-rack boxes designed for crankbaits and other plugs are also available.

Although a system of small boxes is ideal for many anglers, a single big box may work best for you. If your boat has limited storage space, for example, you may have less clutter with one big box than with several smaller ones. One box is also easier to transport when fishing with someone else, and your buddy's bass boat may be too cramped for a number of small boxes. One of the most convenient large tackle boxes you can own is the drawer-style box.

Large drawer-boxes have five to seven drawers (shelves) that will hold a generous supply of lures. You can select a combination of interchangeable

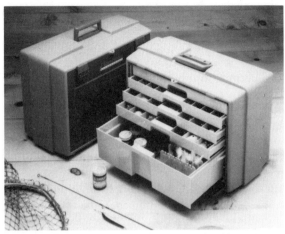

A large drawer box holds a generous supply of lures. Note the spinnerbait rack in the deep bottom drawer. (Courtesy Flambeau)

A hip-roof box has racks of trays that fold out on each side, and has ample storage room in the bottom. (Courtesy Flambeau)

This huge box has four roomy drawers plus a spacious compartment on top that has a spinnerbait rack and room for reels and other larger items. (Courtesy Plano)

possibility, the hip-roof design, opens from the middle and has stacks of fold-out trays on each side. Most have trays with compartments of varying sizes, so you should be able to find something with the right combination of shelves for your basic selection of lures. The larger models may be overwhelming, however, since a giant multishelved box may harbor enough lures to fill a tackle store. Many bass boats are too small to let you fully extend all those shelves—and doing so exposes all your lures to the elements, causing rusty hooks and mildewed lures.

No matter which type of tackle box or boxes you choose, be sure that they have sturdy latches and handles. Especially endearing are no-spill handles that prevent the lids from opening even when the latches have not been secured. Dumping the contents of a tackle box plays havoc with your organization, not to mention what it does to your disposition.

Scents

Several companies now offer scents or scented lures for bass. Do scents really help? Many bass anglers still scoff at the idea, but there is growing evidence that scents can improve fishing success. Scientific research has revealed that many fish have a highly refined sense of smell, including all the black basses. Larger bass have larger and more developed olfactory organs and may be more sus-

drawers—some that have long compartments for worms and large plugs, and shorter compartments for smaller lures; drawers with racks for spinnerbaits; even deep, open drawers to house spare reels and other large items. Some anglers reserve each shelf in such a large box for a specific lure category. Since you don't have to swing open a top, you can gain access to your lures even in cramped quarters.

A unique tackle box design that appeals to many bass anglers is the combination drawer/fold-open box. These typically have three drawers. Another

Revived by Scents

I firmly believe that applying scents to lures encourages more strikes. My good friend Bob Troxel agrees, and he would no sooner go fishing without his scent than with his favorite rod and reel. He used a scent for the first time several years ago during a championship bass tournament on the Ohio River. All of the competitors received a complimentary bottle of Fish Formula II at a banquet on the evening preceding the tournament. At the time, Troxel had little regard for fish scents, but on a lark he tossed the bottle into his boat.

When Troxel's boat number was called the next morning, he raced to a submerged rock pile that he suspected was holding a school of bass. He worked the water over with crankbaits and promptly caught three bass, two of which made the twelve-inch minimum size. Troxel continued casting a variety of crankbaits to no avail. The feeding spree was over. He backed his boat out over twenty feet of water and began fishing deeper with a plastic worm. The worm produced another keeper and two short bass. Then the action stopped.

Troxel knew more bass were around, but they had become inactive and difficult to catch. Precious hours passed as he continued probing the rock pile with worms and crankbaits. How could he make the bass strike?

He glimpsed the forgotten bottle of Fish Formula. He figured that he had nothing to lose and sprayed his worm with a good dose of the stuff. To his amazement, he began getting hits immediately and the action continued throughout the rest of the day. He didn't land every bass he hooked, but he did manage to boat three more keepers and about fifteen smaller bass. After the weigh-in the first day, he found himself leading the tournament.

He returned to the rock pile the next day and right off he began using the scent on his plastic worms. The result was enough bass to win the tournament. He won a fully-rigged bass boat worth over $16,000, armloads of fishing tackle, $1,000 cash, and a huge trophy. Convinced that the scent had helped him win the tournament, Troxel has used the stuff ever since.

—Mark Hicks

ceptible to scents than smaller bass are. Many of the noteworthy bass professionals who use scents, such as TV personality Bill Dance, claim greater success in catching big bass when using scents.

Some fishermen disregard scents because they have caught bass on lures that they deliberately doused with gasoline or some other offensive substance. But in almost every case, the bass were actively feeding when this "experiment" was conducted. When bass are aggressive, they home in on your lures mainly by sight and sound, so a scent really isn't necessary. Although bass feed with such abandon for short sprees or during prime periods within the season, most of the time they are inactive or dormant. Dormant bass won't respond to anything, but inactive bass can be coaxed into taking your lure. Scents work especially well when fishing for inactive bass.

One of the biggest misconceptions is that scents will attract droves of bass from long distances to fight over a lure. View with suspicion any scent

manufacturer who makes such claims. Inactive bass won't swim far for any offering, so you must get your lure close to them to give the scent a chance to work. This requires knowledge of bass location and skillful lure presentation. The truth is, the better the fisherman, the more success he or she will have with scents.

Inactive bass generally respond better to slow lures, such as plastic worms and jig and pork combinations, and it is with these lures that scents work best. A slow-moving lure stays near the bass longer, allowing more time for the scent to encourage a feeding response. Scents can also achieve results on other lures, such as spinnerbaits and crankbaits, especially when making repeated casts to the same cover or structure.

Say, for example, that you are fishing an isolated stump with a spinnerbait that has been sprayed with a scent. You retrieve the lure past the stump with no results, but in the process you have left a scent trail in the area. The more casts you make,

Bob Troxel sprays a scent on his worm that will mask offensive odors and give off an odor to encourage bass to bite.

Other Accessories

Sunglasses

You should never go fishing without sunglasses, because they do much more than protect your eyes. Polarized lenses, the only type you should consider, also cut surface glare and let you see into the water. When fishing in shallow water, savvy anglers are constantly looking for submerged stumps, weed lines, boulders, and other cover. Bass often hold close to such objects, and you'll overlook many of them without the help of polarized sunglasses. Occasionally, sunglasses actually help you to see the bass following your lure. If you see the bass before it sees you, you can frequently encourage a strike by changing the lure's action.

Electronic Aids

Depthfinders and temperature gauges have become standard tools for serious bass anglers everywhere, but some other electronic fishing aids have received mixed reviews. Some of the top professional bass anglers applaud color selectors and pH meters, for instance, while others claim that they are more bother than they are worth.

A color selector determines the most productive lure colors for given water conditions. A probe is lowered into the water to measure light intensity, which varies depending on the water clarity and the probe's depth. A dial then identifies lure colors that the bass will prefer. When you consider the vast array of lure colors, it's easy to see that a color selector can greatly simplify your fishing. But keep in mind that the lure's color is less important than its depth, speed, and action. A color selector does, however, give you more confidence in your lure. As a result you will fish the lure more thoroughly, which inevitably improves success.

A pH meter measures the acidity of the water. Since bass desire and seek a particular pH content, the meter can help you locate water that is most likely to harbor bass. A probe lowered into the water charts the pH level on a scale from 4 to 10. A reading of 7 indicates neutral water, which is equivalent to distilled water. Readings below 7 indicate greater acidity, while readings above 7 indicate greater alkalinity. Bass prefer a pH equivalent to that of their body chemistry—7.5 to 7.9—and will seek water closest to this optimum.

the more scent you leave, and this may eventually arouse an inactive bass. Bill Dance claims that he once saw a bass come out looking for his scent-sprayed lure several seconds after it had passed by. He believes the fish was reacting to the lingering scent trail left by his lure.

Homemade scents, which have been around for years, usually are designed to mask odors that bass find repulsive. Scientific research has shown that one of the most offensive odors to a bass is a chemical found on human hands—amino acid L-serine. Wash your hands before handling baits and lures, but use a scent for insurance. One popular homemade scent consists of mineral oil mixed with oil of anise.

Some of the most popular commercial scents contain a combination of masking scents with other scents designed to encourage a feeding response from the bass. Many are oil-based scents that can be sprayed on your lures or applied drop by drop. Scents with a gel base can be rubbed onto lures, whereas some plastic worms, crankbaits, and other lures come from the factory already imbued with scents.

Bob Dillow often takes big smallmouth bass like this one in the dead of winter. A snowmobile suit—which has become standard attire for cold weather bass anglers—keeps him warm when the temperature plummets.

Sun Protection

Dermatologists have found that prolonged exposure to the sun causes 98 percent of all skin cancers. Protect yourself with sunscreens, which are labeled numerically by their degree of protection. The higher the number, the greater the protection. Anglers should opt for a high protection level, say 15 or higher. Be sure to apply the lotion to high exposure areas such as the back of your hands and neck, and your forearms, nose, and ears. Wear a hat that shields your face, ears, and nose from the sun, and wear lightweight long-sleeved shirts and pants.

Cold-Weather Clothing

You can enjoy excellent bass fishing in cold weather, provided you can withstand the elements. Snowmobile suits have become standard attire for cold-weather bass anglers, and these garments are especially welcome when speeding over the water. Insulated rubber boots, a knitted wool cap, and fingerless gloves will also help you endure cold weather in comfort.

Rain Gear

Never leave the dock without some type of rainwear, no matter what the weatherman has predicted. Few bass anglers let rain interfere with their fishing, and many claim to have enjoyed some of their most successful outings during inclement weather. An inexpensive poncho is easy to store, but a full suit of rainwear is better, especially during chilly weather. Cheap, frail rainsuits fall apart in short order, so buy the best quality suit you can afford. Waterproof suits should be roomy enough to fit over jackets and heavy pants during cool weather. Because it lets moisture escape, the Gore-Tex material has endeared itself to many bass anglers for rain protection despite its high cost.

Chapter 8

Other Methods That Take Bass

Bank Fishing

Those who do not own boats can catch plenty of bass while fishing from the bank. A boat gives you access to larger bodies of water that can't be reached from the bank, but your feet will carry you to many excellent fishing spots that are off-limits to boats. You'll find ideal bank fishing for bass all across the country on the shorelines of farm, strip mine, and beaver ponds, rock quarries and small streams.

Stealth is one skill that successful bank fishermen possess, especially those who cast for bass holding on cover near the shoreline. Instead of marching boldly up to the water's edge and flailing away, the bank fisherman treads lightly and puts some forethought into his or her approach. He knows that bass near the bank can sense the vibrations of heavy footfalls, which will put them on the alert or send them scurrying for deep water. He also knows that if he can see bass in the water, the bass may well see him and flee or ignore his offerings.

Before approaching the water, the stealthy bank fisherman analyzes where a bass is likely to be. He then eases into the best position to cast to the spot, keeping a low profile or using shoreline cover to hide his presence if he deems this necessary. Some of the more sneaky—and more successful—bank fishermen even wear camouflage clothing so they can blend in with the background.

The skilled bank fisherman avoids casting haphazardly and has developed the ability to size up potential fishing areas. After catching one bass, he doesn't hurry to the next spot. Very often, several bass can be taken from a single small area, especially if you land the bass without making a commotion. When you catch one or more bass from a particular spot and the action stops, move on, but keep the place in mind. Chances are good that you can return there and catch bass later that day or on other outings. If the area has attracted bass in the first place, it will probably draw others.

In addition to stealth, patience, and the ability to read the water, you must have refined casting skills in order to achieve consistent bank-fishing success. Make a poor cast and snag your lure, and you will spook the very fish you are trying to catch. Since you can't retrieve snagged lures when fishing from the bank as easily as the angler in a boat can, accurate casting will also save you money. Here again, it pays to size up your target before you cast in order to insure the best presentation possible.

Making good casts from the bank is challenging because undergrowth often ensnares your rod tip when you're making an overhead back cast. To overcome such obstacles, you must develop special

The bow and arrow, or slingshot cast (top), and the underhand cast (bottom) enable you to cast from shore when impeded by heavy undergrowth.

techniques that will allow you to cast in tight quarters. When using spinning, spin-casting, or bait-casting tackle, you'll probably rely on the side cast more than any other (see Chapter 7). The side cast keeps your back cast low and your lure close to the water, so it can sneak under overhanging snags more easily. The lure also lands more softly than it does when the overhead cast is used, so you will spook fewer fish in calm water.

When there is no room for even a side cast, an underhand cast will get the job done. Begin with the rod pointing straight at the target. Snap the rod tip up sharply, halt its progress almost immediately and snap it down, stopping the rod abruptly just below the horizontal position. This should make the lure swing down toward your feet, putting a bow in the rod. As the rod tip swings back up, release the line and the lure should shoot straight forward.

The underhand cast, while effective, is difficult to master and requires a limber rod. A simple lob cast is easier to accomplish, provided you use spinning or spin-casting tackle. To make the lob cast, let three to five feet of line dangle from the rod. Raise the rod tip so the lure swings back toward you like a pendulum. As the lure swings forward, sweep the rod tip up and out and release the line. You won't get much distance with the lob cast, but in many cases a short cast is all you need.

The bow-and-arrow or slingshot cast will also work in tight quarters with spinning and spin-casting tackle. Let out a short length of line from the rod tip, and grasp the lure by the bend of the rearmost hook to avoid sticking yourself. Point the rod tip at the target while pulling the lure back, putting a tight bend in the rod. Release the lure and it will zip into spots that are too confined to reach with other casting methods.

Although the successful bank fisherman must possess many skills, the novice angler will have an easier time learning bass fishing fundamentals from the bank than from a boat. This is especially true of youngsters who generally have little patience, and soon tire when limited to the confines of a boat. The boat also confronts the young novice with many potential obstacles. He or she may feel uneasy when the boat rocks, and, if like most youngsters, may need constant reminders to stay seated, to be still, and to stop scraping his or her feet or tackle on the bottom of the boat.

When fishing from the bank, however, young beginners have fewer distractions and can put all their efforts into casting and retrieving. They are free to move about, and, if they tire of fishing, can hunt for frogs or explore their surroundings until they feel the urge to continue casting. And the skills they learn while fishing from the bank will come in handy when fishing from a boat.

Wading puts you within casting range when fishing for smallmouth bass in streams and rivers.

Wade Fishing

A special sense of adventure arises when you step into the water with a fishing rod in hand. Wade fishing plucks you out of high-tech society and carries you to the essence of the sport. Instead of a padded boat seat against your backside, you feel the slap of cool water. Your feet may have to probe for a solid base on slippery rocks or pull free of deep muck. Challenging bass while chest-deep in their environment can be hard work, but it can also yield excellent results.

Many neglected fishing opportunities exist all across the country for anglers who are willing to wade. Wading can be a productive method for fishing streams, ponds, lakes, and reservoirs. The savvy bank fisherman always catches his share, but a wading angler can fish water that can't be reached from the bank. In many cases, getting out just a little farther from the shoreline puts weed beds, drop-offs, and other prime fishing spots within range of your casts. On many waters, the cover along densely overgrown shorelines produces excellent bass fishing. Such places prove difficult to approach when fishing from the bank, but wading out only a few feet makes them more accessible to your lures.

Getting off the bank will also improve your casting by allowing you ample room for making backcasts. Wading anglers spook fewer bass than bank fishermen. Wade with stealth and you may be surprised by how close to the bass you can sneak without alerting them.

Wading is also a productive method for fishing shallow areas in ponds, lakes, and reservoirs.

Wade fishing is also the least expensive way to get off the bank and into the water. An old pair of jeans and sneakers may serve you well as wading gear when fishing streams, ponds, and lakes in midsummer. But when the water is chilly and the bot-

Getting My Feet Wet

One of my most successful wade fishing adventures took place near my home in southeast Ohio, on a stretch of a small stream interrupted by pools and riffles. Forgive me for not revealing the stream's name or location. I found it a few years ago while driving a back road on a grouse hunt. The stream is overlooked by other anglers—a good thing because it's too small to withstand much fishing pressure.

I parked my vehicle alongside a lonely gravel road, donned my waders, grabbed my rod, and began a short hike to the spot. Minutes later, I could hear the gurgling water ahead, and then the stream came into view. I slipped quietly into the water near a shallow riffle and waded against the current and over the pebble bottom to the tail of a small pool. One side of the pool had a deep undercut bank guarded by the thick roots of an aging hardwood.

I tossed a small balsa minnow upstream from the tree with my light-action spinning outfit, and reeled in slack line as the current carried the lure back. When the minnow was inches from the root system, I twitched it once and a two-pound smallmouth darted from the shadows and slashed the lure from the surface.

The bass leaped the moment I set the hook and several times thereafter. It seemed too large for the small pool, and I was lucky that it didn't part my light line when it dashed for the safety of the roots. I finally landed the bass and took a moment to admire its rich bronze coloration and tigerlike stripes. Then I held the fish beneath the surface, released my grasp, and watched it dash for the sanctuary of the root system. I have caught and released many other good bass from this unlikely little stream.

—Mark Hicks

---

tom tricky, commercial waders better suit the job.

There are two wader types to choose from: stocking-foot waders that require shoes which slip on over the wader and boot-foot waders that come with the boots permanently attached. Either will do. When shopping for a wader, consider where you intend to use it. If you will be treading on slick rocks, opt for soles made of felt or some other material that will take hold. Soles with deep rubber ripples are better when wading over sand or mud. Felt or spiked soles that strap on over rubber soles assist those who may encounter both slippery and soft bottoms. If you plan to fish in cold water, consider buying an insulated wader, or one that has ample room for thick socks and bulky clothing underneath.

Always try on a wader before purchasing it. Waders vary in cut, and a proper fit is important to your comfort and safety. A wader that is too high in the crotch will have excessive folds in the legs. The folded material will wear faster than the rest of the wader and will therefore leak sooner, and the folds may impede your leg movement. A wader that is too tight or too low in the crotch will also not allow for free leg movement and could make you stumble or fall. The better waders come with a choice of inseam lengths, allowing you to select the best possible fit. After donning a wader in the store, lift one leg up onto a chair to make sure it does not hinder leg movement.

Natural rubber is a common ingredient in most waders, so ozone cracking can frequently cause leakage. You can extend the life of your wader by avoiding unnecessary stretching and exposure to the air. These four steps will hinder ozone cracking: Make sure the wader is dry inside to prevent mildewed boot linings; loosely fold or roll the wader for storage; place the wader in an airtight container, such as the manufacturer's box; and store the container away from light and from ozone-producing machinery, such as electric motors.

Bring waders with you on fishing trips, even when you have no plans to use them. Then, if high winds make boat fishing difficult, you can fetch your waders and head for a shallow backwater that is protected from the wind and off-limits to boats. You'll catch bass while other fishermen are killing time back at camp.

You can carry a tube and waders into remote backwaters that few other anglers fish.

Tube floats let you sneak close to bass.

Tube Fishing

Bass fishing from tubes—or doughnuts, floats, belly boats, or floater bubbles—has become increasingly popular, especially with fishermen on small lakes and ponds. A fisherman can fashion these devices from an old inner tube with a seat rigged in the center so he or she can sit in the water and cast conveniently all around. Many commercially manufactured ones are also a pleasure to use.

Fishing floats begin with a standard sixteen- or twenty-inch truck inner tube, which is placed inside a cover of tough material (usually canvas, nylon, or vinyl-coated nylon) and then fully inflated. The cover protects the tube from punctures and forms a saddle seat inside the hole. Wearing chest waders, the angler sits in the middle, legs in the water, with the covered tube forming an arm rest. Zippered waterproof pockets, sewn or bonded to the cover, hold tackle, lunch, a Thermos, and other items. Some deluxe pouches also include a sort of apron to cover the fisherman's lap (for fly casting) so that the coils of loose line do not fall in the water. Other tubes include an inflatable backrest for

added comfort, and now an attachment is available that permits installation of a depth sounder.

Besides the tube, a floating fisherman must have a means of propulsion, and there are two options. The simplest way of getting about is with a pair of snorkeler's swim fins attached to the feet. Just by raising the feet and kicking stiff-legged, as when swimming, the floater travels backward. Paddle-pushers—hinged fins made of plastic that strap onto the heels—propel the tube when the angler swings his or her legs back and forth from the knees down. The paddle-pushers move you forward or sideways and provide the greater maneuverability of the two choices.

There are many good reasons for the expanding interest in float fishing. Tubes make it possible to explore ponds, swamps, and sloughs that are difficult or impossible to reach by boat. A tube opens up some spots that have never been fished seriously before. The whole outfit—tube, pump, fins, tackle—can be carried in a rucksack or daypack, on a trail bike or bicycle. And some hard-core doughnut fishermen in the South swear that the odds on catching fish are doubled in favor of anybody fishing from a tube. They insist that tubes frighten fish far less than boats and motors, and that a tube fisherman, being alone, is a more quiet fisherman.

The cost is appealing, too. A fully equipped bass boat (as described in Chapter 6) costs more than fifty times as much as the best tube outfit available. Of course, the boat owner has a vastly wider range and greater capacity. But the tube user reigns on small, remote waters.

Sitting crotch-deep in cool water can become an uncomfortable chore during spring and autumn when the tuber usually resorts to long johns and woolen pants beneath his or her waders. But in summertime, when water temperatures reach 75° and beyond, it may not be necessary to wear waders at all—just old cotton pants and tennis shoes. Incidentally, most veteran float fishermen prefer the rubber stocking type of wader worn inside oversized tennis shoes with an old pair of thick socks sandwiched in between.

To avoid tube punctures, refrain from using old, worn-out inner tubes. Always carry a spare flotation device such as a water skier's belt worn around the waist, a USCG-approved lifesaving vest, or one of the cartridge instant-inflatables that can be carried in a pocket or clipped onto a jacket.

The big plus for every tube fisherman comes at the end of the day. Now there is no heavy boat to winch onto the trailer and no need to scrub it down. Not even a small canoe or a small craft waits to be hefted onto a car-top carrier. You simply step out of your doughnut, deflate it, and toss it into the luggage compartment of your car. Then homeward bound to a fresh bass dinner.

Bass Fishing at Night

Most anglers prefer to fish during daylight hours, but sometimes the bass bite better after dark. Night fishing can be productive on gin-clear lakes throughout the fishing seasons, and is especially fruitful on most waters in the heat of the summer. Many anglers believe that bass become sluggish and feed less frequently when it's hot, and this may be true in certain shallow lakes where the bass become stressed in soup-warm water. In most lakes, however, bass feed more often in warm weather because their metabolism increases with the rise in the water temperature. The higher their metabolism, the faster they burn energy and the more food they require.

So why isn't daytime fishing better in the summer? For one thing, bright sunlight drives fish into deep water or below wood or weed cover in search of shade and cooler, more comfortable temperatures. There they are hard to reach with baits and lures. Even when you do manage to get a lure in front of them, they may be reluctant to strike due to excessive summertime boat traffic. Also, lakes and reservoirs blossom in the summer, producing an abundance of forage fish and other food sources. With so much to eat, many bass are content to wait until dark when they can ambush their prey more easily.

If you wait until dark, you'll ambush your prey more easily too. At night the bass come up from the depths and out of heavy cover to feed. They are more aggressive and more likely to be fooled by your offerings, especially when you fish with artificial lures. Under the revealing light of day, bass have less trouble distinguishing your lures as fakes. At night, however, they see a world of shadows and silhouettes and are more likely to chase your lures for the sounds and vibrations they emit. Since they can't see your lures well, they are less inclined to shy away from them.

Unless you're a veteran night fisherman, select a moonlit night and plan to quit about midnight or shortly thereafter on your first outing. (Always bring an ample supply of bug repellent, or your outing surely won't last very long.) Some anglers claim that pitch-black nights yield more action, but others believe that bright nights are just as good. Even with the aid of pale moonlight, you'll find that night fishing requires much more concentration than daytime fishing. Judging distances can be tricky. You may not know if you're on target until you hear the satisfying "splat" of your lure hitting water, or an exasperating "thunk" that says you've overshot your mark. Simple tasks, like finding lures and tying knots can become major projects.

This problem raises the question of whether to use lights at night. Tradition labels all lights taboo, but many bass anglers have been successfully using lights in recent years. Black lights have become especially popular, because they make white and fluorescent colors glow with an erie blue-violet hue. Under black light, thin fluorescent fishing lines look like flexible strands of neon rope, and you can readily see your line jump when a bass strikes. This is an invaluable advantage when fishing with jigs, plastic worms, and falling spinnerbaits—lures that bass generally strike as they are

Night fishing can be especially productive during the summer on gin-clear lakes that provide little action during daylight hours.

dropping. The light doesn't spook the fish, because it doesn't penetrate the water.

A few anglers have even begun to experiment with white lights that illuminate the bank. The lights greatly improve casting accuracy, and some anglers believe they also help bass home in on their lures. If you choose not to use night lights, you'll still need some type of flashlight to help find lures and tie knots. A penlight ideally suits these tasks, and some anglers paint the lens red since this color has the least affect on night vision. Once your eyes adjust to the darkness, you can see dim shapes well enough to feel your way around. But glance at an ordinary bright light, and you'll lose that fine edge of perception until your eyes readjust.

Excessive noise surely spooks bass at night, so take pains to be quiet. Put your gear in order so that you can find it without pandemonium. Things will go more smoothly if you rig two or three rods with different lures before you set out, so you can switch lures without rummaging through your tackle box. If you have an aluminum boat, cover the floor with carpeting or carpet remnants to deaden boat noise.

Fill reels with lines testing four to six pounds heavier than you normally use during the day. Your line will suffer more abuse at night, and heavier line will insure landing that big one when you finally get your hooks into him. Don't worry about line-shy bass; they have a hard time seeing your line at night.

Topwater plugs have long been the favorites of night bass fishermen, and, for some, a thrilling topwater strike in an inky blackness is what night fishing is all about. Whatever style the plug, you can't go wrong with the color black. Bass see surface lures at night as dark silhouettes against a comparatively light sky. Black lures make better silhouettes and are consequently easier for bass to see.

Spinnerbaits are also proven nighttime bass lures. In deep, clear impoundments, many anglers hop them slowly over submerged rocky points and down steep shale bluffs to catch smallmouth and

A bass leaping in the darkness is a thrill that keeps anglers coming back for more.

spotted bass as well as largemouths. Spinnerbaits also take bass when retrieved steadily along weed edges and close to wood cover. Spinnerbaits, nearly snag-free, are very forgiving when your casts go astray after dark. Plastic worms and jigs also make good nighttime lures, provided you have the skill and patience to fish them at night. Work them slowly and with a lot of bottom contact.

Fish a strange lake at night and you'll spend more time trying to find your way around than fishing. Your night forays will be more successful if you visit a lake that you know well from previous daytime outings. Avoid lakes or reservoirs that have dingy or muddy water. Bass living in clear water are much more active at night.

Shoreline cover near deep water makes for good fishing at night, because bass move up from deep water or out from under the cover to feed along the edges. The edges of weed beds can yield·exceptional catches. Wood cover, such as fallen logs, stumps, flooded timber, and flooded bushes can also be productive. For deeper bass, ply drop-offs along submerged points, shoals, and humps where

the creek channel cuts close. Bass move up onto these structures from the deeper water in the channel.

Trolling

Many bass anglers disdain trolling, believing that it leaves too much to chance. But as with any fishing method, the degree of its successfulness hinges on the skill of the individual fisherman. Inept trollers know little about the shape of the lake bottom, the habits of the bass, or how deep their lures are running behind the boat. They drag lures all day without rhyme or reason and rarely catch anything. When done skillfully, on the other hand, trolling can be deadly. It keeps your lures in the water and lets you cover more potential fishing area in less time. Trolling is especially productive when bass are deep and hard to catch with casting methods.

Of all the variables to consider when trolling, the most important is the running depth of your lures.

There are several ways to achieve depth control. One way is to assemble a selection of crankbaits that will dive to varying depths from shallow to very deep water, and select the one that runs at the depth you wish to troll.

Keep in mind that crankbaits dive deeper when trolled than when retrieved after a cast. Other factors also influence the lure's running depth. A light line lets the lure dive deeper than a heavier line, so you'll have more consistent results if you stay with the same pound test for all your trolling. Generally, the more line you let out behind the boat, the deeper the lure will dive. There is a point, however, at which too much line causes the lure to lose depth. Also, although it may seem that a fast trolling speed will pull your lures deeper, a slow speed actually allows for the greatest depth.

It takes trial and error to determine how deep a given crankbait will run, but this information is crucial to successful trolling. An easier way to govern trolling depth is with the Spoonplugging system devised by Buck Perry, who many regard as the father of structure fishing. Perry designed four unique metal lures, called Spoonplugs, that run at predictable depths (from four to fifteen feet deep) when trolled.

A bait-casting outfit should perform well when you are trolling with monofilament line. The rod ought to have enough backbone to compensate for the stretch in monofilament and to help set the hook when a bass strikes. A stiff rod also does a better job of transmitting vibrations to your hand, which will tell you if your lure is running properly or if it has become fouled. Experienced trollers learn the intricacies of a lake's bottom faster than casting anglers do, because they can tell when their lures are digging into soft or hard bottoms, and when they are clipping weeds or bumping wood cover. As they troll, they actually "feel" the bottom of the lake.

Someone who trolls extensively relies upon contour maps and depthfinders. Knowledgeable anglers study their depthfinders constantly as they troll in order to keep their lures swimming over a specific bottom depth, along submerged weed lines, timber lines, creek channels, and other structures. They will sometimes see bass on their depthfinders, especially when the fish are suspended above the bottom, and the running depth of the lures can be adjusted to intercept them.

The super-deep diving crankbaits dig thirty feet or more when trolled with monofilament lines, but in some waters bass reside in depths of fifty feet or more. This is the case in a number of clear California reservoirs that have been stocked with the Florida strain of largemouth bass. Innovative anglers have found that they can reach the bass by trolling with lead-core line. The method has dredged up some enormous bass, many over ten pounds and a few over fifteen pounds. Trolling with stainless steel wire line also gets lures down fifty to seventy feet deep. This method is currently used on the central basin of Lake Erie to take big smallmouth bass during the summer and fall.

When trolling with lead-core or stainless steel wire, you need a trolling reel matched with a long rod, say seven-and-a-half to eight-and-a-half feet in length, that has a forgiving tip. Some anglers use downrigger rods. They need the flexibility because lead-core and wire lines have no stretch and will rip the hooks from the mouths of bass when used with stiff rods.

Another way to get lures deep is by employing some type of sinker. The standard method is to attach a keel or oblong trolling sinker three to six feet ahead of the lure. Be sure to use swivels on the sinker to prevent line twist. The more refined sinkers can walk over boulders, limbs, and other snags. They have a V-shaped wire, similar to that of a spinnerbait, with a lead weight molded to the bottom prong. The top prong has a swivel to which you tie the drop-back line for your lure. The rod line attaches to the loop in the center of the V. Because the sinker is almost snag-free, it lets you troll your lures tight to the bottom. Walking sinker weights range from about ⅝ of an ounce to ten ounces, so they can be used to troll anywhere from the shallows to depths of sixty feet or more.

Downriggers

The most exacting way to control your trolling depth is with a downrigger. Downriggers, used most frequently on big waters for lake trout and salmon, are also employed by a few bass anglers who fish large, deep reservoirs. The heart of a downrigger is a large spool that holds a steel cable. An arm, called a boom, extends from the spool over the side or transom of the boat. The cable runs from the spool, over a pulley attached to the end of the boom, and down into the water. A round or bullet-shaped weight, usually seven to ten pounds, attaches to the end of the cable.

Before hooking up to a downrigger, drop your

lure into the water behind a moving boat and let out the desired amount of line, up to about one hundred feet. Next, place your line in the release mechanism located on the downrigger weight or just above it. Lower the weight into the water. A footage counter on the downrigger tells you when the weight reaches your chosen depth. In addition to getting your lures down where deep bass live, downriggers allow you to use light tackle. Your line snaps free of the line release when a bass strikes, so you can thrill to the battle without additional weight on the line. Inexpensive miniature downriggers are available for use on small boats.

Some anglers just don't care to fish unless they're casting. But if you want to catch bass consistently all season long, no matter how deep they may be, trolling will get action when casting methods fail.

Trolling lets you cover more water in less time and is especially effective when bass are deep.

Float and Camping Trips

No special fishing techniques, other than those already described elsewhere, are involved in camping trips or in float trips on rivers, but both have important roles in catching more bass.

Float Tripping

With modern boats, rafts, canoes, and outboard motors, today's fishermen have covered just about every square foot of fishing water that exists on bass lakes everywhere. Of course, some lakes are pounded harder than others, but all get fished to some extent. Today the only relatively undisturbed places remaining are parts of streams and rivers beyond easy walking distance from highway bridges, or waters beyond the marinas and public docks from which boats can be launched.

Float trips have provided me with good bass fishing, plus solitude and complete escape, even though I could occasionally hear the noise of traffic on busy highways nearby or the sound of a farmer's tractor in a hayfield. Most of these trips were on Midwestern rivers—far from the bridges and popular fishing holes that other fishermen frequent. It's something that almost any angler in America can do at almost any time.

Except in a few regions such as the Ozarks and parts of the Southeast, float tripping for bass is a

The most accurate way to control trolling depth is with a downrigger. Small models like this can be rigged on bass boats. (Courtesy Cannon Downriggers)

forgotten art, despite its simplicity and productivity. Too many fishermen miss this chance to enjoy good sport, sometimes spectacular sport, only a few hours from home. Consider a trip that a friend and I took on a Midwestern creek that passes almost through the state capital and that actually is heavily fished. We had high adventure; we caught fish, and we saw sections of the stream that few sportsmen ever see.

We launched a canoe at a bridge just southeast of the city, after making arrangements for a pickup the next afternoon where our river joined another. We carried plenty of tackle (which is possible when you're boating rather than wading), a small explorer tent, a cooler full of ice, a trotline, and even a seine to gather bait.

A good way to find solitude—as well as good bass fishing—is to take a float trip.

It was the most leisurely sort of trip downstream. During the morning I paddled while my friend cast into pockets and eddies along the way. In one stretch of water, where the paths along the banks had completely run out, he caught a pair of fat smallmouths and four rock bass. We ate them for lunch on a sandy bar—along with several ears of sweet corn apiece, which we had purchased from a farmer along the way. In this topnotch agricultural country one can buy anything from fresh eggs and frying chickens to fresh butter or carrots while traveling downstream.

That night we camped on a peninsula formed by a long bend in the river. While I built a fire my partner unfolded the seine and collected a buck-

etful of crayfish and hellgrammites for bait. At night, after dinner, we stretched the trotline across the river at a point just below a shallow riffle. Then we baited up with the crayfish Lew had collected. When we "ran" the trotline first thing in the morning, we found our breakfast in the form of two channel cats.

A river trip is an easy venture to organize. You simply get a boat (of almost any type), collect the gear you need, and push off downstream. Nothing could be simpler. You can float for one day or for two weeks, depending on the time you have to spare or on the length of floatable water.

For two-man trips, I prefer a canoe because it's easier to handle, easier to move through dead water, and easier to carry over shallow places and deadfalls. I have an eighteen-foot canoe for larger, rocky streams and for longer trips. My thirteen-foot aluminum canoe is perfect for short trips on slow, mud-bottomed streams. It isn't wise, though, for beginners to take canoes on turbulent or dangerous waters. It isn't comfortable either.

In those regions where float tripping is popular, professional outfitters invariably use long, sturdy, square-ended boats—johnboats, usually—because of their extreme safety and comfort. A fisherman can move around and stretch in most of them without turning the boat over. The johnboat handles sluggishly in dead water, however, and it's completely out of the question for a fisherman who must depend on car-top delivery to and from the river. The most important requirement in *any* float boat is a shallow draft and fairly rugged construction. Until recently all of them were of wooden construction, but nowadays there are some splendid aluminum and fiberglass models on the market.

Check the distances to be traveled before starting downstream. On an average stream in mid-America, a party can cover ten miles per day rather easily. Figure on less if you want to stop frequently to fish—or more if the current is swift and the actual trip is more important than the fishing.

The best way to plan a trip is to use two cars with car-top carriers or boat trailers. Park one car at the end of the trip and drive to the starting point with the other. Two cars also make it possible to leapfrog from bridge to bridge, ending the trip whenever the mood strikes.

Float trippers can fish the back country with almost the same comforts and conveniences of an average fishing camp. Take a large tent, for example, and erect it each night on an air-conditioned (by nature) gravel bar. Safari cots come in handy too. Take all the cooking utensils you need to make every meal a pleasant experience. While traveling, all this gear can be completely stored away with no trouble at all.

An enterprising traveler can almost live off the country while traveling downstream. Besides the bass he catches, freshwater crayfish are delicious (and hard to tell from shrimp) when boiled and served like shrimp. Often it's no problem to gather frogs or catch a snapping turtle for soup. If the rivers run through limestone country you will find watercress for salad, and in springtime, morel mushrooms grow along wooded banks; look for white button mushrooms in farm meadows during early fall. Other wild edibles a floater might find are cabbage palms, wild asparagus, any of the wild greens (dandelion, dock, lamb's quarter, mustard, horseradish, poke), walnuts, hickory nuts, and paw-paws; there's no end of them.

Every drifter should take some precautions. For instance, do not drink the river water or use it for cooking. If it's absolutely necessary, boil it first and dissolve iodized tablets into it. Always carry an emergency kit containing first-aid materials, plenty of insect repellent, waterproof matches, lighter fluid (for starting a fire quickly), a flashlight, and, if your boat is made of rubber or canvas, a patching kit.

Floating is made to order for bass fishermen who are limited to weekend fishing. They can avoid the heavy concentration of anglers and boating fans on most impounded waters on those busy days. It's a good family activity too, and high adventure for small children just learning to fish. It's also a good way to stay off the highways—and to use the weekend for unwinding rather than for developing *more* tensions.

But probably the best reward of all for the float tripper, no matter where he lives, is the new and lively brand of fishing in places that less adventuresome anglers seldom see. Since many streams, even in highly developed states, are seldom fished in an entire summer, float tripping can be like discovering virgin bass waters—and, sometimes, you actually might.

Camping

Strange as it may sound, camping—either with tent or recreational vehicle—is another way to catch bass. It places an angler at water's edge when fish are striking and at the same time it saves a long drive from home. This becomes especially important for daybreak fishing. A camper can roll out of bed, brew a pot of coffee, and be casting after a minimum of effort and a maximum of sleep. In addition, camping is simply a wonderful experience that goes hand in hand with fishing.

Thanks to the vast variety of fine camping gear that's available nowadays—everything from tents that "spring" open to effective insect repellents—you can live outdoors inexpensively and with all the comforts of home. I know families who spend almost the entire summer camping on various lakes while the breadwinner commutes from work to camp. When vacation time comes, all pack up and

Your parked recreational vehicle becomes your fishing camp.

travel to Canada, where they set up camp again on a good bass lake. The number of fish they catch in a season's time sounds almost fictional.

The new RVs, compact units on the road that open up into roomy living quarters, are made to order for vagabonding fishermen. They make comfortable fishing camps wherever you park them, and eliminate the need for long drives in predawn chill to start a day of bass fishing.

Chapter 9

Live Baits for Bass

Not too many bassers nowadays use live bait, because artificials serve very well. Those who use live bait find that minnows, crayfish, and nightcrawlers are effective; but a bass may tackle anything that moves, native to the water or not, and a wise live-bait fisherman considers other possibilities. Some of the lesser-known baits can do quite well. The following information may help you decide which ones to try.

Alewife: Also called killifish, the alewife are sometimes found landlocked in smallmouth lakes, although it is a saltwater species. They may migrate into freshwater coastal streams to spawn. Caught, kept, and hooked in the same manner as minnows, they make fair bait.

American brook lamprey: Found in the mud bottoms of streams, brook lampreys are harmless members of the family to which the parasitic sea lamprey belongs. In areas where brook lampreys live, they can be dug from the muck with a hay fork in fairly shallow water. These tough and long-lasting baits can be hooked in various ways: through the tail so that the lamprey continues to swim freely; through one of the gill openings; or strung on the hook like a worm. Anglers especially favor them for largemouth bass.

Australian cricket: This wingless cricket, accidentally introduced into the United States, makes good bait and has been grown commercially.

Bee: You can use adult bees for catching bass. More frequently, the grubs of bees, hornets, and wasps are used as bait. Use great care in handling.

Beetle larva: Beetle larvae, called grubs, make excellent bait for bass. One of the most popular of the grubs is the meal worm. Other grubs can be dug from rotting logs and stumps, from beneath tree bark, grass roots, or manure piles. It is best used for fishing through the ice.

Black-nosed dace: A small minnow common in cold, preferably fast-moving waters. It is dark above and white below, with a dark stripe down the side; sometimes the dark line will appear to be yellow or tan, and the sides are often blotched. Maximum size is about three inches.

Blacknose shiner: One of the many shiners used as bait. See Golden shiner.

Bloodsucker: See Leech.

Bluntnose minnow: One of the most popular for pond propagation. It has a prominent spot at the end of a lateral line, just in front of the caudal

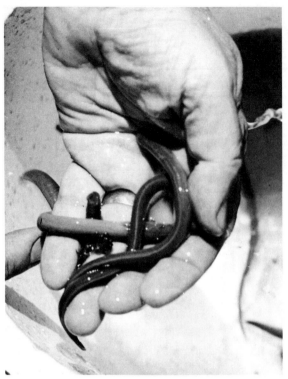

Brook lampreys are little-known, nonparasitic creatures that make excellent bass bait.

fin. The head is broad, blunt. Maximum size is about three inches.

Brassy minnow: A common bait minnow in the Midwest, found in creeks and ponds. It gets its name from the brassy color of the large scales along its sides.

Bream: Bluegill; the name also refers to one of the various shiners used for bait.

Brindled madtom: Madtoms are the smallest of the catfishes; distinguished by continuation of the adipose fin into the caudal fin. Generally five inches or less in length, they prefer swift waters and are frequently found under rocks. They have poison glands at the base of each spine and can inflict painful injuries. Better bait for bass than is generally known. Durable on hook. Clip their spines for safety.

Bullfrog: Frogs, because they are lively and will attract a fish's attention, often catch fish where other baits fail. The leopard frog, the pickerel frog, and the green frog are favorites, although small bullfrogs also make good baits; tadpoles, too, can take fish. You can catch the frogs by

hand or with a scoop net; at night, blind them with a flashlight. They can be kept in a large wooden cage partly submerged in the water if you provide them with rocks or pieces of wood for resting places. When you go fishing take them in a small container filled with damp grass and leaves.

Bullhead: Bullheads make good bait for bass when they are five inches or less in length. The horns on the pectoral and dorsal fins are generally clipped so that the bait is more attractive and less dangerous. Young bullheads can be seined from ponds and quiet backwaters and can be kept for long periods of time in bait buckets. They also live for a long time on the hook.

Caddis worm: Caddis worms, the larvae of small, winged insects belonging to the same order as the dobson fly (adult hellgrammite), live in the water and are generally encased in portable protective sacks made of sticks, leaves, stones, and other material that they cement together with secretions from their mouths. You can catch caddis worms by hand as they crawl about on the bottom. Removed from the case and strung on a hook, they are excellent bait for bass. Sometimes more than one can be used on a hook.

Carp: Carp are the largest members of the minnow family and were introduced to this country in the 1800s as a food and forage fish. Their closest relative, also an introduced species, is the goldfish. Both are good baits, but should not be placed in waters still free of them. State laws frequently ban the use of goldfish or carp as bait.

Caseworm: See Caddis worm.

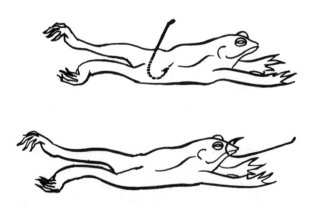

For still-fishing, hook the bullfrog through the back. For casting, the bullfrog should be hooked through the lips.

Catalpa worm: The catalpa worm is the caterpillar or larval stage of the sphinx moth. It sometimes reaches a length of three inches and can be found only on the catalpa tree, its sole source of food. Harvest these worms by shaking the tree and picking up the worms that fall to the ground. You can keep them alive in a cage, feeding them catalpa leaves; or you can save them in corn meal in the refrigerator. They can be housed in ordinary coffee cans, provided they have leaves to eat. No holes need to be punched in the cans, as the empty space provides plenty of oxygen. They can be strung on the hook like a fishing worm, or the heads can be cut off and the soft body inside shucked from the skin, to make a possibly more appealing bait.

Catfish: See Bullhead.

Chub: Chubs are stocky, hardy minnows with big heads and large scales. Generally caught in gravel-bottomed areas of creeks and large streams, they often reach a length of eight inches or more. They are sometimes caught on hook and line for sport. Small ones make excellent baits for bass.

Chub sucker: See Sucker.

Cicada: Cicadas (seventeen-year locusts) make good bait for bass during years of abundance. Actually, they are found in all years, but particularly at seventeen-year intervals.

Clipper: See Hellgrammite.

Common chub: See Chub.

Common shiner: See Golden shiner.

Common white sucker: See Sucker.

Conniption bug: See Hellgrammite.

Corn earworm: See European corn borer.

Crawdad or *crawfish:* See Crayfish.

Crawler: See Hellgrammite.

Crayfish: Also called craw, crab, crawdad, crawfish. The crayfish, which looks like a miniature lobster, is another excellent bait that bass cannot resist. A number of different species live in swamps, brooks, streams, rivers, and lakes. They come out of hiding mostly at night, but during the day they can be caught by hand or with a small net under stones or in weedbeds. Minnow traps baited with dead fish or meat scraps will often catch them if the funnel openings are wide enough for them to enter. For a day's fishing you can keep them in damp weeds or moss in almost

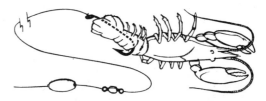

The best way to hook a live craw. Leaving hook point on top helps prevent hangups, while the slip-sinker rig lets skittish bass pick up craw without feeling resistance.

Crayfish tails, unpeeled (left) and peeled (right), are great bass catchers. Note how the entire hook is threaded through the tail.

any container. The best crayfish for bait are those that have shed their hard shells and are soft and helpless. Tie these to a hook with fine thread and fish them for trout, black bass, walleyes, catfish, carp, and large panfish. To use hard-shells, break off the large claws and hook them through the tail or back. The tail alone often makes a good bait. Frogs and crayfish require plenty of water and space, and it's not practical to try to raise them in small numbers. You can catch more than you need for yourself in most lakes or rivers.

Creek chub: See Chub.

Cricket: Catch crickets from under leaves and stones by hand or with a small net. Keep them in a box of grass during trips. For fishing, fine wire hooks are best. Run the point under the collar carefully so it doesn't kill the cricket. Good bait for bass, the two common species are gray and black. They are easily grown.

Dace: See Black-nosed dace.

Damsel fly: See Nymph.

Darter: Also called Ohio log perch, sand pike, and zebra fish. This smallest member of the perch family was named because of its habit of rapidly moving from place to place, then pausing. Found principally in and below currents.

A variety of live baits can be used for either smallmouths or spotted bass in limestone streams such as this.

Catch it on hook and line, or seine. It makes good bait.

Dewworm: See Nightcrawler.

Dobson fly: The adult stage of a hellgrammite.

Dragonfly nymph: Dragonfly nymphs, often called perch bugs, ugly bugs, and bass bugs, live in ponds, lakes, and quieter stream sections. They hide in mud, vegetation, and debris, where they can be caught in seines or dip nets. Bringing debris from the bottom with rakes and examining for nymphs is also productive. It's good bait for black bass.

Earthworm: While the common earthworm will take bass, the nightcrawler makes better bait due to its larger size. Success with nightcrawlers begins with learning how to obtain and care for them. The bigger and more lively your crawlers, the more bass they'll catch. A dehydrated, listless nightcrawler will not draw nearly as many strikes as a fat, squirming one will. The crawlers you want are often called Canadian nightcrawlers, and are available at most bait shops. They don't come only from Canada, but are the same big earthworms that you can capture at night in your own backyard.

You may be able to save money if you buy nightcrawlers in large quantities, say five hundred or more. Most bait shops purchase their crawlers in quantity and package them in small containers holding one to three dozen at a time. You pay more per dozen when buying these containers. Buying in bulk eliminates the packaging cost and should result in a substantial discount.

You can save even more money by catching your own crawlers from lawns and golf courses. Chemical fertilizers kill nightcrawlers, so search for your bait only in grass that receives organic fertilizers. Since dry soil drives crawlers deep, wait for a good soaking rain to bring them up. Soaking your lawn thoroughly will also bring them up. If the ground is especially dry, this may take several days.

As the name implies, nightcrawlers come out at night, and this is when you must collect them. They are very sensitive to ground vibrations, so tread lightly and wear soft-soled shoes, such as tennis shoes. Nightcrawlers are easy to spot under the beam of a flashlight, but will slip back into their holes if the light is too bright. You can avoid this problem by taping red or yellow cellophane over the lens of your light.

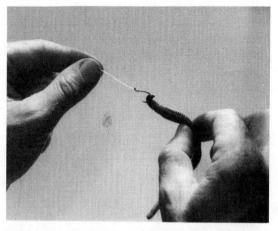

You'll get more action from your crawlers if you impale them once through the tip of the head with a small hook.

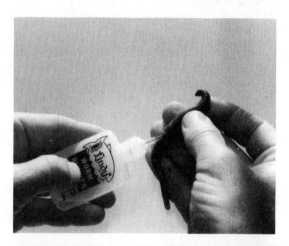

Injecting air into a crawler makes it float higher off the bottom.

Don't bother snatching up undersized crawlers. When you spot a nice crawler, ease close and grab fast, but avoid a tug-of-war that may injure the crawler and eventually kill it. One end of the crawler will usually be near or in its hole. Remove it by placing your thumb over the portion of the crawler nearest the hole and applying firm pressure. At first, the crawler will contract as it attempts to return to its hole. When it relaxes momentarily, extract it without a fight.

Once you've obtained a good supply of nightcrawlers, you'll want to keep them healthy. Many fishermen kill their crawlers with too much moisture. They can live in moist soil for awhile, but it eventually does them in. Coffee grounds also make poor bedding. You can keep your crawlers indefinitely with a relatively dry bedding, such as sphagnum moss or dead leaves lightly sprinkled with water. There are also a number of excellent commercial beddings that you mix with water. Chlorinated water may kill the crawlers; rain water or lake water will do fine.

A Styrofoam cooler makes an excellent container for worm bedding because it breathes. Your bedding should be no more than four inches deep. After adding water to a commercial bedding, wait a day or two before using it. The water sets off a slight chemical reaction that generates heat, which could be harmful.

Place your crawlers on top of the bedding and let them work their way into it. The healthy crawlers soon burrow into the bedding, while those that are dead or dying remain on top. Check the container for the next few days and remove those still lying on top of the bedding. If you fail to remove dead crawlers, they will generate heat and bacteria as they deteriorate. This could kill some of the healthy crawlers, creating a chain reaction that will eventually kill them all.

Store the crawlers in a basement or some other cool place at a temperature of 40° to 60°, and avoid exposing them for any length of time to higher temperatures. The ideal storage place is an old refrigerator turned up as high as it will go. Some fishermen keep them cool by placing picnic ice (wrapped in newspaper) on top of the bedding every day.

Make note of how moist your bedding is when mixed initially and try to maintain that level of moisture. If it becomes too dry or too wet, your crawlers could be doomed. One way to maintain moisture in the bedding is to place damp (not dripping wet) newspaper over it and to put a lid on the cooler. When returning unused crawlers to the cooler after a day of fishing, don't dump the wet bedding in with them, since it will add unwanted moisture. A fifteen-by-fifteen-inch cooler supports up to three hundred crawlers indefinitely, provided you use an appropriate bedding and store the container in a cool place.

If you would like to turn your crawlers into the fattest, juiciest live bait you've ever used, prepare a batch of them about four days ahead of time. Fill a small carton, such as that used for cottage cheese, about halfway with very wet bedding and then add about eighteen crawlers. Place a mound of crumpled, wet newspaper on top of the bedding and push the lid onto the container, compressing the newspaper. Store them in a cool place. When confined in such a tight space, the crawlers absorb the moisture. When you open the container days later, they will appear twice as plump and will be so lively that you'll have trouble getting a hook into them. Eventually, the moisture in the cartons will kill the crawlers, so return the leftovers to their dry bedding after your fishing trip. If you head out on a spontaneous fishing trip and don't have time to prepare your crawlers ahead of time, put them in ice water. They will plump up fast and will be full of life.

Successful nightcrawler fishermen have learned that the key to success is in making the most natural presentation possible. They never use snaps or swivels and opt for 4- to 6-pound test line which the bass is less likely to see. They also use a fine-wire Aberdeen hook, sometimes as small as a No. 10 size. They use the lightest weight necessary to keep the crawler near the bottom where the bass are, and in the shallows they may not use any weight at all. To get deeper, they'll fish small split shot or a walking sinker about eighteen inches or more above the hook. The proper weight depends on how deep they are fishing.

Nightcrawler experts never gob their bait onto the hook. They thread the small hook through the tip of the crawler so that it swims straight and is free to wriggle, expand, and contract with irresistible action. When a bass strikes, they give free line for several seconds to insure that the bait is taken. Then carefully they take up slack line and set the hook hard.

The crawler must be replaced whenever it becomes damaged or grows listless, because bass prefer a healthy bait. Many anglers inject air into their crawlers just above the sex band with a hypodermic needle or a special plastic bottle designed for this purpose. Injecting a bubble of air will make the crawler float just above the bottom where it is more visible and alluring.

Eel: See American brook lamprey.

Fairy shrimp: A transparent, freshwater crustacean that grows to 1½ inches, and is found in streams, ponds, potholes in grass, weedbeds, and edges. They can be caught with a "drag"

The Lively Nightcrawler Catches the Fish

Relatively few bass anglers these days use night-crawlers, but they have come through for me on many occasions. One notable time I was fishing a middle-aged natural lake in Ontario, Canada, north of Minnesota. A steady breeze blew that day, so I elected to let the boat drift over likely feeding areas while bumping a night-crawler rig over the bottom.

I rigged up a walking sinker with a six-pound test leader about eighteen inches long and tied a small Aberdeen hook to the end of the leader. Then, turning to my container, I fetched a crawler that was so lively that I had trouble holding onto it as I ran the hook one time through the very head of the bait. Hooking the crawler in this fashion would make the bait glide straight in the water and give it full freedom to squirm and wiggle enticingly.

The morning sun had barely crested the pines when I made my first drift of the day over an underwater point comprised of rock and gravel. I started out fairly shallow, four to six feet deep, and my crawler failed to encourage a single bite. On my next pass, I moved out to about ten feet of water. This time I soon felt a bass tugging at my bait.

I was using a spinning reel with the bail open and the line resting over my forefinger. The moment I felt the strike, I released the line and let the fish take the bait for several fidgety seconds. Then I closed the bail on the reel and slowly took up the slack. When I began to feel the weight of the fish, I slammed the hook home. A dandy smallmouth bass stripped line and then cleared the water with three consecutive jumps. The bass continued battling with characteristic fervor, and more than a few minutes passed before I could lead it into my net. I made several drifts over the same area, and— still fishing with the lively and irresistible night-crawlers—managed to catch my limit of small-mouths before lunch.

—Mark Hicks

---

bucket of closely woven wire mesh, or seined, and make excellent bait.

Fathead minnow: Also called blackhead minnow, they are among the most popular and the most easily raised minnows in ponds. They rarely exceed three inches in length and can be caught in many streams, ponds, and lakes.

Field mice: See Mouse.

Fish (as bait):   Strips of fish, particularly belly meat, with the skins attached, are trolled for bass occasionally.

Frog: See Bullfrog.

Garden hackle or **garden worm:**   See Earthworm.

Garter snake: See Snake.

Gizzard shad: Like the alewife, the gizzard shad is a member of the herring family. It is also used for bait.

Golden shiner: The golden shiner is one of several species of shiners that make the finest of bass baits. Their bodies are compressed to form a sharp lid on the belly just behind the pelvic fin. Shiners are generally found in the shallower parts of lakes, ponds, and in slow-moving streams. They can be raised successfully in ponds for bass bait.

In Florida waters, no lures or live baits can compete with the golden shiner when it comes to catching trophy largemouth bass of more than ten pounds. Quality bait is imperative to success. Guides and serious shiner fishermen claim that big shiners seven to eleven inches long consistently catch the biggest bass, and that wild shiners are livelier and therefore more effective than hatchery-raised shiners. Many anglers capture their own shiners with cast-nets and other methods, because they cost from $7 to $12 per dozen. They keep the shiners alive in large aerated tanks.

When fishing big golden shiners for trophy bass, you must use much heavier tackle than

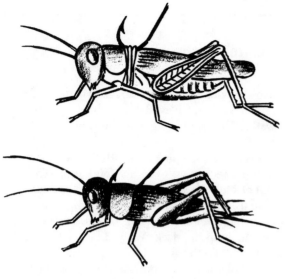

How to hook grasshoppers.

normal, especially when fishing near typically heavy aquatic growth. Use stout six- to eight-foot baitcasting rods with 17- to 40-pound test, the line size depending upon the thickness of the cover. Large 5/0 to 8/0 hooks are also needed. Secure the boat in place with two anchors to prevent drifting. Shiners are usually fished under floats, but are sometimes allowed to swim free. Anglers often coax free-swimming shiners beneath floating mats of vegetation where heavy largemouths lurk.

Goldfish: This species of minnow, *not* a carp, is successful for bait production in ponds. It is very prolific and hardy. Do not use *ornamental* goldfish for bait.

Grasshopper: Like crickets, grasshoppers can be caught in fields and gardens and can be kept for long periods of time in containers before actually being used on a fishing trip. They're hooked in much the same manner as crickets.

Harvest fly: Another name for cicada.

Helldiver: Another name for hellgrammite.

Hellgrammite: This popular water insect bait, also known by other names—such as alligator, water grampus, conniption bug, snipper, flip-flap, and helldiver, to name a few—is the larval form of the big, winged insect known as the dobson fly. It is black or dark brown with two sharp pincers, six legs, and numerous "appendages" on both sides of its long body. Hellgrammites live under rocks in the riffles of streams and rivers. They

can be caught by turning over the rocks and holding a wire screen or net below the rocks. Keep them in damp leaves or grass in a cool spot. They make a tough bait and can be hooked under the collar, in the tail, or turned inside out after cutting the head off. It's a great bait for spotted and smallmouth black bass, especially in rivers, but it will often take largemouth bass as well.

Hog sucker: See Sucker.

Horned chub or horneyhead chub: See Chub.

Horned dace: See Black-nosed dace.

Horned pout: See Bullhead.

Katydid: Like the grasshopper, fish in the same manner as the cricket.

Lake emerald shiner: See Golden shiner.

Lamprey eels: See American brook lamprey.

Leech: There are many species of leeches (also called bloodsuckers), varying in size from less than an inch to several inches in length when stretched out. They belong to the same group as the earthworm, but most of them have a sucking disk at each end of the body and live by sucking blood from various animals. They can be caught in traps baited with blood or meat. Sometimes fishermen rub liver or bloody meat across their waders and then wade through a mucky pool where leeches will attach themselves to the waders. Leeches can live a long time without food, so can be easily kept in aquaria. They are very durable baits for bass.

Leopard frog: See Bullfrog.

Locust: See Cicada.

May fly: Also called Willow fly or Canadian soldier, adult and immature May flies are important

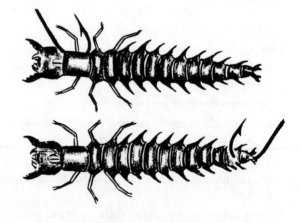

How to hook Hellgrammites.

fish food. The immature or nymphal stage of May fly is often used as bait. Adults and nymphs are often copied in fly patterns and used by trout anglers. Capture nymphs by scooping up muck and mud from the bottom of streams and pools, then draining mud away from the insects. They can be kept in aquaria where water is well aerated and the bottom covered with debris similar to that from which they were taken.

Meal worm: Large numbers of meal worms are easily raised in a large washtub or box filled with alternate layers of burlap and chicken mash or other grain meals. This container, which should be stocked initially with a few hundred meal worms, will need a sprinkling of water every day or so; you can add some raw carrots or potatoes to provide the necessary moisture. Keep the container covered with wire screen to prevent the meal worms and the adult beetles from escaping. Used for bass fishing through the ice. See Beetle larva.

Minnow: Most freshwater fish like minnows, and so they are a popular bait with anglers. There are many kinds, such as the bluntnose, fathead, and the various chubs, dace, and shiners. These small bait fish can be caught in most freshwater streams, lakes, and rivers with seines, drop nets, minnow traps, and tiny hooks baited with bread, dough, or bits of worm. They can also be bought from bait dealers. In minnow buckets, which keep the water cool and fresh, minnows will live for days if not too crowded. For longer periods keep them in "live boxes" submerged or floated in clean, cool water. Minnows from one and a half to ten inches long are usually used for bait, depending on the size of fish sought. They can be hooked through both lips or the back for still-fishing and "sewed" on the hook for casting and trolling. Minnows can also be raised, but if you need only a small number during the fishing season it is cheaper and less trouble to buy them or seine them from a pond or a stream. To raise them in large enough quantities to supply several anglers, or to raise them for sale, you need one or more ponds or tanks. Since there are many kinds of minnows that can be raised and since different methods are called for in different parts of the country, consult your state conservation or fish and game department for information on raising minnows in your area. It can supply the necessary literature on construction or selection of ponds, species, proper breeding, feeding, control of diseases, and handling.

Mouse: Both field mice and house mice can be used as bait for big bass. They are frequently tied onto the hook with wire or thread.

Muddler: See Sculpin.

Mud minnow: This small, hardy bait fish lives a long time on a hook.

Newt: Newts and salamanders are amphibians, sometimes found near rocks and logs and damp places near the water. They must be grabbed by their heads or midsections because their tails break easily. Care for them in the same manner

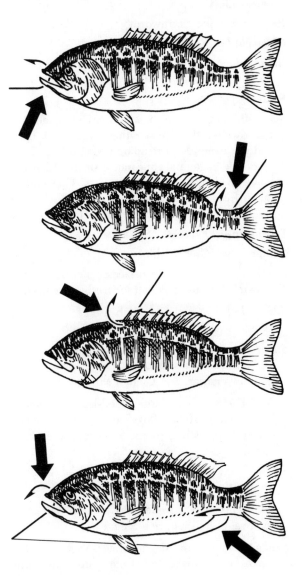

How to hook minnows, dace, chubs, shiners, or any other small fish used as bait.

as frogs and hook them through the tail or through one of the feet. Also called waterdogs.

Nightcrawler: See Earthworm.

Nightwalker: See Earthworm.

Peeler: A crayfish that can be peeled when its hard shell loosens. See Crayfish.

Perch: See Yellow perch.

Rainworm: Another name for nightcrawler. See Earthworm.

Redfin: A bait minnow popular in the Southeast.

Red horse: A member of the sucker family caught on hook and line when fully grown and used as bait while young.

Redworm: See Earthworm.

River chub: See Chub.

River shiner: One of the shiners commonly used as bait. See Golden shiner.

Salamander: See Newt.

Sculpin: The sculpin, or muddler, is a small bottom-dweller that has a rather large black head and permanently protruding pectoral fins. They resemble in general appearance small catfish and make good and hardy baits for bass. They can be taken from streams by turning over rocks and catching them as they wash down into a net.

Seventeen-year locust: See Cicada.

Shiner: See Golden shiner.

Shrimp: A saltwater crustacean similar to the prawn, often used as bait for freshwater bass.

Silver chub: A common chub used for bait, also known as the Storer's chub. See Chub.

Silverside: A long, thin minnow sometimes used for bait. This is also another name for the shiner minnow or friar. See Golden shiner.

Slug: The slug is a large, shell-less land snail, found under stones, logs, and in other damp places, especially gardens. Slugs can be used as bait for bass.

Smelt: Smelt are small fish found in lakes and are frequently used as bait for smallmouth bass.

Snail: The snail is sometimes used as bait after removal of its shell. See Slug.

Snake: Many of the smaller snakes such as garter snakes, green snakes, and small water snakes can be used as bait for larger carnivorous fish such as bass.

Snipper: See Hellgrammite.

Spottail shiner: Common shiner used as bait. See Golden shiner.

Spring lizard: See Newt.

Stone cat: See Brindled madtom.

Stone pike: See Darter.

Stone roller: A minnow found in streams, it is hardy on the hook.

Striped dace: A dace often used for bait. See Black-nosed dace.

Sucker: The sucker is a bottom-feeding fish with thick, protrusible lips. There are several species, all of which may be used as bass bait when small.

Sunfish: Small sunfish, particularly with their spiny dorsal fins trimmed, are sometimes used as bass bait.

Tadpole: The tadpole is the immature, water-dwelling stage of the frog, sometimes good as bait. See Bullfrog.

Toad: Small toads, like frogs, are good bait on occasion. They are especially abundant near water during the dry season.

Tuffy: See Fathead minnow.

Ugly bug: See Dragonfly nymph.

Water dog: Another name for certain salamanders. See Newt.

Water grampus: See Hellgrammite.

Water snake: See Snake.

White sucker: A member of the sucker family. See Sucker.

Worm: See Earthworm.

Wriggler: Another name for the May fly nymph. See May fly.

Yellow perch: A small perch sometimes used as bait for larger fish, with the spiny dorsal fin often cut away to make the bait more attractive. Strips of perch belly with the fins attached are also used for trolling and skittering.

Zebra fish: See Darter.

How to Use Live Bait

There are so many potential and proven live baits that describing how to use all of them would require a library of information. Some general points, however, apply to nearly every type of live-bait dunking.

Since the only reason for using live bait instead of artificials is that live bait has an appeal and an "action" impossible to duplicate, use live bait in the freest and most unhampered manner possible. That means an absolute minimum of sinkers and bobbers, preferably none at all.

Probably the ideal live-bait tackle is a light or medium spinning outfit; with it, a crayfish, for example, can be hooked in the tail and cast, without sinker or float, exactly like a plug to a productive spot. The crayfish then swims to the bottom and behaves as a crayfish naturally would until a bass comes along and nails him. The minute this happens the fisherman flips open the bail on his spinning reel and allows the bass to run with the bait with virtually no suspicious drag at all because the light line is pulling easily off the end of the spool. When the bass pauses to swallow the crayfish the angler closes the bail, gently gathers slack line, and then strikes.

This live-bait/spinning combination works equally well in lakes and running water. Critters like leeches, hellgrammites, and large grasshoppers as well as crayfish can be allowed to drift with the current in a completely genuine manner. This is an effective technique, particularly on a rising water level or when a stream is somewhat roily from rains.

Of course, there are times when it is impossible to do without a sinker or a float—either to get a bait closer to the bottom or to keep it from burrowing *into* the bottom. In that case, use the smallest and lightest sinker possible. Often a single split shot will do the job. Or when using a float, a small sliding, thumb-sized cork with a matchstick to fit in the core will suffice. With this simple kind of float, it's easy to adjust lure depth. In any event, remember that the larger and more buoyant a float, the more "drag" is evident to a fish taking the bait.

It is not necessary to use large hooks in live-bait fishing, either. Only rarely will you need anything larger than No. 8, and usually No. 10 is good enough. You can get much more mileage out of the bait, too, with a small fine-wire hook.

Too many bass fishermen cast a live bait and then allow it to soak for much too long in one place. It is much better to move it often, to test different depths, to thump it along the bottom, and to toss it into likely "edge" just as you would a plug. And always try to keep a *fresh* bait on the hook. Now-

adays it isn't difficult to carry a large supply of bait on any trip and to keep it lively for a long time, thanks to the many new containers and devices that are available.

One of the best methods for fishing nightcrawlers, minnows, and other live baits is called backtrolling—essentially, trolling in reverse. The technique is used with small fishing boats having tiller outboard motors no greater than 25 horsepower. When in reverse, the motor pulls the boat rather than pushes it, allowing for more responsive steering. Because the transom generates wind and water resistance, backtrolling also lets you run at much slower speeds than trolling forward does; this is preferable with live bait.

For the most control, always backtroll into the wind. If you want to stop or to hover over a particular structure, simply shift the outboard into neutral and let the wind halt your progress. On windy days, water may splash over the transom. Anglers who frequently backtroll attach splashguards to the boat's transom to shield themselves from the waves. These devices can be fashioned from plastic or rubber, or they can be purchased.

The angler generally backtrolls with a spinning outfit that has a walking sinker rig just heavy enough to keep the weight on the bottom. With this rig, leave the bail open and hold the line with your forefinger. When you feel a take, release the line and shift the outboard into neutral. Give the bass a few moments to engulf the lure, then take up slack and set the hook.

Backtrolling is one of the best methods for fishing many forms of live bait, especially crawlers and minnows. Note the splash-guards that prevent waves from washing over the transom.

Live bait is most important for winter fishing—and essential in fishing through the ice. Fishing through ice requires that you keep the bait relatively stationary. Live bait appeals to bass when fished in this manner. Lures do not. It may surprise some fishermen to learn that bass *can* be taken through the ice with some regularity. Strangely enough, ice-caught bass are usually big ones, and a former Ohio record largemouth was a nine-pounder taken in a frozen lake near Youngstown. Nor is it unusual to make good catches at other frozen lakes in the Midwest.

Chapter 10

Fly-rodding for Bass

Too much has been written about the difficulty and problems of fly-fishing for bass, but not enough about the pleasures and numerous advantages. Bass bugging—casting small surface bugs or plugs—is a splendid, exciting sport. And to tell the truth, the fisherman needs no hefty fly tackle to cast hummingbird-size bass bugs. Today, hundred-pound tarpon and sailfish are being taken on fly rods once considered ideal for bass! Maybe that's why too many anglers have unconsciously balked at bass fly-rodding. That heavy-gauge tackle just didn't fit the fish for real enjoyment.

If you choose to specialize in big Southern bass and feel the need to power those hawgs out of dense cover, go ahead and use a 9- or 10-weight rod. But that is not where the charm of fly-rodding for bass really lies.

The Practical Fly Rod

A glass, bamboo, or graphite fly rod, seven and a half to eight and a half feet, is a practical outfit for bass bugging. The newer graphite rods are especially suitable because they are powerful and light-weight. The rod action should be such as to cast an appropriate level or weight-forward fly line

twenty-five to fifty feet. Use a line one weight heavier than the rod maker recommends, primarily because bass fishing is usually done at close ranges, with wind-resistant flies and limited false casting. A little heavier line works the rod more and the angler less.

If you expect to concentrate on bass with bass bugs and streamers, try an eight- to eight-and-a-half-foot rod for a 7-weight line. For small flies, stick with the No. 7 line, but use an 8-weight for flies larger than size 6.

An all-around rod for average-size bass is the System 6. It makes taking a 2-pounder a real thrill, and yet a truly big largemouth or smallmouth can be handily subdued with this tackle if you play it carefully.

Reels to Do the Job

Two reel designs, single-action and automatic, are considered practical for bass. Most fly fishermen prefer the lighter, more versatile single-action reel. It is less trouble, more fun to play a fish on, and is usually far better for dealing with a fish that is strong enough to run for cover by taking line off the reel.

The automatic reel is twice as heavy, more me-

Most fly fishermen prefer the lighter, versatile single-action reel.

chanically complicated, lacks the versatility of a single-action design, and does not have the sensitive drag of a single-action reel. Thus if you hook a strong fish, you either have to strip off line by hand to let it run, or else rely entirely on the leader's strength. There is also the hazard of accidentally pressing the trigger on an automatic and then watching the fly rip off your rod guides.

Yet some bass fishermen swear by an automatic reel. It allows casting with one hand, and controlling the boat with a paddle in the other. When a fish is hooked, the automatic will zip up the slack line and maintain tension until the boat is maneuvered away from the cover. Then the angler puts the paddle aside for two-handed fighting and landing of the bass.

The Best Fly Lines

Floating and Wet Tip Hi-D lines are the most useful in the majority of bass-seeking situations. The floating line is practical when fish are feeding on the surface or when you are casting over water three to five feet deep. A level floater works well for short casts and quite well with large, wind-resistant flies; but it does not allow for delicate presentations and long casts.

The special weight-forward *bass bug taper* developed by Scientific Anglers is, perhaps, the ultimate bass-fishing fly line. Its design makes for trouble-free delivery of flies in all sizes. It casts well in the wind with heavy flies at short or long range with a minimum of false casting.

This line also allows you to cast a fly with extreme accuracy. Using a tight loop cast, the fly can be rifled low or high into the narrowest target paths— even exceeding the accuracy of an expert bait caster. Sidearm skip casting under and behind obstacles is almost effortless; right- and left-curve casts behind stumps are a breeze.

The same bass bug taper on a Wet Tip Hi-D line extends the depth range of your fishing. It casts well and can be used with all sorts of flies, from

The most efficient leader for bass fishing is, like the one shown here, knotless, tapered, and about 7½ feet long including tippet.

topwater divers and crippled minnow bugs to bottom-crawling eelworms, crayfish imitations, and spinner-fly combos. It fishes especially well down to ten feet deep, because the tip sinks quickly. You don't have to wait and wait while the fly sinks on its own. By varying the speed of retrieve, rod angle, fly weight, and leader length, you can fish from top to bottom with very little effort.

For depths past ten feet, the Wet Head, Wet Belly, and full sinking Wet Cel Hi-D's let you work a fly down to thirty or forty feet. However, fly-fishing at these depths for bass begins to become more work and less fun. Other methods, such as bait casting, are more practical and effective.

Leaders and Tippets

The final links in the tackle chain between you and the bass fly are the leader and its tippet. While they can be heavier and less invisible than those used to fish for trout, their design, length, and durability are indeed important.

The most efficient bass leader for a floating line is a knotless tapered leader, seven and a half feet long, with a twelve- to twenty-four-inch tippet. The best taper designs—heavy butt, magnum butt, or salmon—are all two to three thousandths larger in diameter than standard tapered leaders with similar-size tips.

A *knotless* taper is especially important. Hand-tied knotted leaders cause problems in most waters where bass swim. The knots hang and tangle in the heavy cover a bass may dive into when hooked, and they pick up algae and vegetation. Of course, you still have to tie the tippet to the leader, but by using a closely trimmed double surgeon's knot, you practically eliminate this "knotty problem."

Leader tip and tippet should test from 6 to 15 pounds for most bass flies and fishing situations. Eight-pound is ideal for small-to-medium-size flies (10 to 4) in fairly open water. For larger flies (2 to 3/0), a 10-to-15-pound test tippet will turn the fly over better and allow the hook to be set firmly without risking a breakoff.

Use stronger tippets when fishing really heavy cover. Bass are not polite. They will use every trick in the book to foul your leader on underwater obstacles. A strong tippet increases your odds for holding and landing a good fish under these conditions. Always use the toughest, most durable tippet material you can find—not necessarily the smallest diameter-to-strength ratio, as this soft kind of tippet wears out very fast in bass cover.

How to Cast

Probably the best place to begin fly-casting is on smooth-cut grass. Stand in the middle of an open space about eighty feet long. Lay the assembled outfit flat on the grass with the reel handle up and walk away from it with the fly until you have pulled about thirty feet of line out of the guides.

Hold the rod pointed down the line toward the fly. Your grasp of the grip should be *firm* but not tight. Most good casters extend the thumb toward the tip on top of the grip—the side opposite the reel. Keep guides and reel down. Hold the line firmly in your left hand between the reel and the first guide.

Your feet should be separated by a comfortable distance, both quartering to the right. (This is written on the assumption you're right-handed. A southpaw would reverse the angle.) In other words, instead of facing squarely toward the line stretched out on the grass, which is the direction in which you're going to cast, your feet should be at about a forty-five degree angle in relation to it. You are about to make a back cast, and you stand in this position so you can watch the line over your right shoulder.

You are standing angled to the right, with your right elbow about three inches in front of your belly, and your forearm and rod pointed straight down the line. Your wrist will necessarily be bent down. It will remain in this position until the back cast is nearly made. Your left hand, holding the line, should be out toward the rod grip.

The back cast is made with the elbow and shoulder; the wrist remains locked in the position previously described. Start the line coming toward you on the grass by raising the elbow to lift the rod. The movement is up and back, accelerating smoothly and rapidly. *Hold the line firmly with your left hand; don't let any of it slip out through the guides.* As the rod approaches vertical, pull the line down sharply about a foot.

By the time the rod reaches the eleven-o'clock position, the line will be coming toward you in the air. Bring the shoulder into play to move the entire rod back about eighteen inches; at the same time, pivot the elbow until the rod is vertical, and stop dead. The stop is accomplished by tensing your forearm, wrist, and hand, and then immediately relaxing.

The whole movement is brisk and continuous. Don't simply sweep the rod through the air. Make it bend. Then permit the rod to tip back to one o'clock by bending the wrist. This doesn't contribute to the back cast, however, but puts the rod into position to start the forward cast. *If you have done everything properly, the line will fairly hiss out behind, passing above the rod tip, and straighten.* It will run parallel to the ground and as high above it as the rod tip at the conclusion of the backward movement. Watch it over your shoulder.

When you've made a good back cast, with the line out straight behind and tugging against the rod, you're ready to make the forward cast. Your right hand will be a few inches higher than your shoulder and somewhat behind it. Your left hand, holding the line, will be up toward the right shoulder.

Now without changing the angle of your wrist, bring the entire rod forward, still in its one-o'clock position. This is a full-arm movement by both shoulder and elbow, made somewhat as though you were pushing a weight along a shoulder-high table. Accelerate smoothly. Keep the reel above your shoulder; don't lower it.

As your arm approaches straight out in front, tip the rod forward to eleven o'clock by tipping your wrist and again come to a dead stop by tensing your arm muscles and then immediately relaxing. *Learning to stop dead at the end of a back cast and a forward cast is the most important part of fly-casting.* The stop forces the tip over extremely fast, increasing the speed of the line. Simultaneously, lower your left hand—yes, it's still firmly holding the line—about a foot. Again, the entire rod arm makes a brisk, pushing movement, with the turn of the wrist coming at its conclusion. The rod stays in the same vertical plane, both back and ahead. Let the line straighten, then fall to the grass, at which point you lower the rod and arm as it does.

Practice, resting occasionally, until you can make both the back cast and the forward cast perfectly. Remember, the line must straighten behind in the back cast before you can make a good forward cast. This is why we suggested standing so you could watch it. There must always be a pause while the loop unfolds and the rod drifts back. At first, you'll have to watch to tell how long to give it; later, this timing will become completely automatic. You won't even have to think about it, much less watch. And, of course, with the same power, it takes the same length of line just as long to straighten in the back cast as it does in the forward cast.

False Casting

You are now ready to start false casting, so called because the fly doesn't touch the water (in this case, grass) on the forward cast. We false cast to work out more line, to change direction, or to whip the water out of a dry fly so it will float.

Make the first back and forward casts just as before. When the forward cast straightens out, however, don't let it fall to the grass. Instead, start the back cast immediately. You will find this is actually easier than starting the back cast from the grass.

Following a false cast, with the line higher out in front, the back cast is more a horizontal movement. Normally angled only slightly upward, it is made very much the same as the forward cast, but in the opposite direction.

Don't let the rod drift down farther than ten o'clock on the forward cast; start the line back as soon as it is straight. Watch your back cast until you can make it straighten properly every time, and until timing the necessary pause becomes automatic.

The beginner's most common fault at this point, next to waving his rod rather than accelerating it briskly, is to let line slip out through the guides at the start of both the back cast and the forward cast. Guard against this. If you hold the line *tightly* in your left hand and pull a little each time, as we advise, this won't occur.

Instead of attempting to cast farther and farther, continue practicing with thirty feet of line past the rod tip. Actually, these thirty feet, plus an eight-foot rod and a seven-and-a-half-foot leader, make more than forty-five feet. You'll seldom want to cast a bass bug that far. So you are already casting far enough to catch fish, and in the long run maintaining perfect control at this distance will do you far more good than straining to cast twice as far.

Actual Fly-Fishing

When bass are in the cover of fairly shallow water, the fly rod becomes the most effective of all methods with the least time wasted between casts. You can comb productive pockets without cranking in over barren water, as must be done with bait-casting and spinning lures.

Casting to bass usually involves "target shooting" to a prechosen spot. False casting is not necessary in most cases, nor is it practical with large, wind-resistant bass flies. Pick the fly up off the water, and with one back cast, place it in the same spot or in a new one. The special bass bug taper line greatly enhances this one-cast presentation.

In order to place the fly accurately into prime cover spots, you should develop a tight-loop, high-line-speed delivery. A big, sloppy, slow-moving loop will not provide the reluctant bass flies with enough authority for a pinpoint cast. What's more, the wind, overhanging branches, and other gremlins will frustrate the big-loop caster.

By using mostly three-quarter to full sidearm casts, you will also keep the rolling line loop at the lowest angle and out of trouble. Your retrieves will be fairly short. This is especially true when using topwater bugs, which are seldom worked more than a few feet. Swimming or bottom-crawling flies are worked farther, usually about half to three-quarters the distance back to the rod.

Two types of retrieves are particularly effective. The first is extremely slow to almost dead still. The other is a short, rapid, erratic retrieve.

The first retrieve suggests a helpless, vulnerable prey. Cast to or just beyond a pocket you think has a bass hiding in it. Then let the fly float rest or slowly sink without any animation or retrieve for thirty seconds to several minutes. Then work the fly just a little and very slowly at first. Most strikes come before or immediately after these initial moves.

The second retrieve suggests a crippled or escaping prey to the bass. Whereas the first method works on the bass's nerves and territorial rights, the second works on his response as a predator: first to attack and kill, then to investigate. Make your cast and immediately begin a fast, erratic,

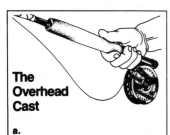

The Overhead Cast

a.

The fly rod must be held as shown in order to perform correctly. With your fingers, take a "suitcast" grip on the handle. Line your thumb up with the rod and place it as near the top as you comfortably can. (It is in this position that the thumb will brake the rod in the back cast; apply pressure for the forward cast.) Bend your wrist until the rod becomes a parallel extension of your forearm.

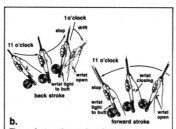

b.

The perfect casting stroke takes place between 11 o'clock and 1 o'clock. Since the angle of the cast is a relatively small 30 degrees, there may be a temptation to let the wrist do all the work. Resist it, or suffer an exaggerated, crooked arc. Instead, study the relationship of the wrist to the rod in these illustrations. Note that the entire hand must travel in a nearly straight line, with a slight upward lift through the back cast; a slight overhand on the forward cast.

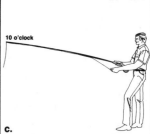

c.

By way of practice, pull some twenty feet of line from the tip of your rod and let it lie on the ground. Leave a little slack between the reel and the stripper guide and take it in your free hand. This will serve to "anchor" one end of the line while the rest is in the air. Now stand easy, with your bodyweight on the casting arm side.

d.

Begin your back cast with a smooth, even lift-off. Don't jerk. A hard, ripping pull not only scares fish but improperly sets the line in motion. Raise the rod until the leader is almost clear of the ground. A slow-starting, rapidly-accelerating movement will smoothly pick up the line.

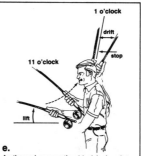

e.

As the rod passes the 11 o'clock point, speed up the backward motion and flip the line up and back, stopping the rod hard at 1 o'clock. Immediately open your wrist enough to allow the rod to drift back with the weight of the line.

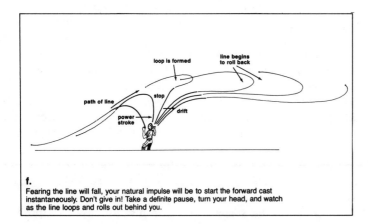

f.

Fearing the line will fall, your natural impulse will be to start the forward cast instantaneously. Don't give in! Take a definite pause, turn your head, and watch as the line loops and rolls out behind you.

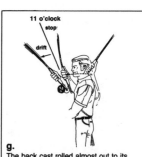

g.

The back cast rolled almost out to its end, begin the forward cast. Move the rod smoothly, closing the gap between rod and wrist as you do so. Stop the action hard at 11 o'clock. Give it that final little flip that results in extra footage, and let your hand follow through with the casting stroke.

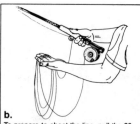

The Line Hand

a.

As your casting skills develop, the line hand will play an increasingly important role. It serves as part of your line retrieval system. It helps to maintain tension during the strike. It holds the slack line with which you will "shoot" for longer casts.

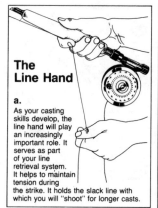

b.

To prepare to shoot the line, pull the 20 or 30 feet you have been used to from the tip of the rod. Now increase the length of your "anchor loop" between the reel and stripper guide by another 10-15 feet. Take this additional line across the palm of your line hand in long, loose loops. Keep the loops separate and in order, the last one lying nearest the tip of the fingers.

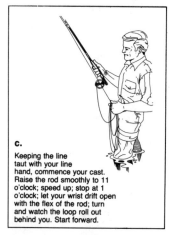

c.

Keeping the line taut with your line hand, commence your cast. Raise the rod smoothly to 11 o'clock; speed up; stop at 1 o'clock; let your wrist drift open with the flex of the rod; turn and watch the loop roll out behind you. Start forward.

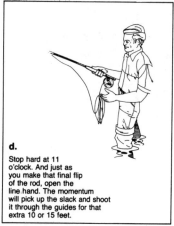

d.

Stop hard at 11 o'clock. And just as you make that final flip of the rod, open the line hand. The momentum will pick up the slack and shoot it through the guides for that extra 10 or 15 feet.

e.

The line hand also comes into play during the "false cast". The false cast is an incomplete cast which is repeated again and again — either to dry out a water-logged fly or to extend the reach of the line. In the latter instance, the line hand's work is coordinated with the back-and-forth strokes, continuing to free-up additional line until the target is reached.

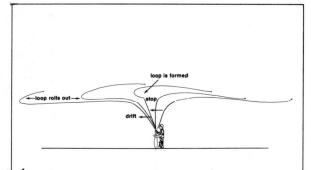

f.

Each time the 11 o'clock position is reached on the forward cast the line hand lets a few feet of line shoot out; then tightens up again. A new back cast is started as soon as the forward loop has rolled out and before it has a chance to fall to the water. When you have reached your target, or have as much line in the air as you can handle, go ahead and complete the cast.

The fly rod is ideal for fishing smallmouth bass in shallow streams.

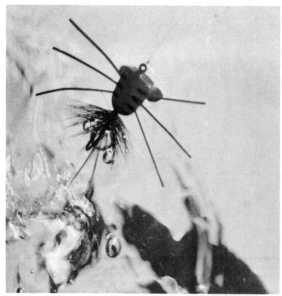

Cast your bug toward the target, then gently pop or jiggle it to attract bass.

One good way to fly-fish around small lakes and ponds is from a light, maneuverable canoe.

Fly Fishing on Dog Lake

My father has been an avid fly fisherman since before I was born, and, under his tutelage, I cut my fishing teeth on a fly rod. Although I rely mainly on bait-casting and spinning tackle when fishing for bass today, I'll pick up a fly rod when I want to derive the most pleasure and excitement from each bass I hook.

My most thrilling bass fishing experience took place when I was a teenager while fly-fishing with my father and my younger brother Lon. We were on our annual fishing vacation, but this trip was our first to Canadian waters. With great anticipation we had traveled northwest from Ohio to Dog Lake, Ontario. We had planned the trip months beforehand and had spent many winter evenings at the kitchen table tying flies in preparation. Most of our creations were bulky deer-hair bugs and streamers that we hoped would appeal to the big smallmouth bass that lived in Dog Lake.

The first few days on Dog Lake were anything but spectacular. We flung our offerings to pine-studded islands, huge granite boulders, windfalls, and reeds without even seeing a smallmouth. We did enjoy occasional frenzied moments when a pike would nail one of our flies, but most of them bit the line in two before we could boat them.

I was more than a little discouraged by the third day when we pulled into a secluded cove under the soft glow of the late evening sun. The bank was lined with reeds and boulders and we cast hair bugs close to the cover. One of my father's casts dropped his bug tight to an isolated boulder. He let the ripples fade and twitched the bug. It suddenly vanished in a large swirl. When my father set the hook, a three-pound smallmouth leaped high out of the water, displaying its vivid dark stripes. The bass completely circled the boat, jumping three more times in the process. When we finally had it safely in the boat, our excited voices must have been audible more than a mile across the calm water.

The first bass proved to be an indication of things to come. The cove was loaded with hungry smallmouths, and they belted our bugs with abandon over the next two hours. The feeding frenzy was sheer exhilaration, and I can still remember how hard each bass pulled against my long, limber fly rod.

—Mark Hicks

showy retrieve. Also try "pounding" the same spot with many casts before moving on. This technique is especially effective in hard-fished or murky water. Retrieve the fly only a few feet, pick up, and cast back as fast as possible. Bass often go into a frenzy after a dozen or more "pounding" casts.

Study and learn how the various natural prey available to bass react in the water. Frogs, mice, little snakes, moths, aquatic insects, minnows, etc., have individual behavior characteristics you can mimic to draw strikes. So much of the charm in bugging for bass is playing master puppeteer.

The Approach

The best way to approach smallmouth bass cover is by wading quietly. However, deep water or an unwadeable bottom sometimes makes this impossible. Where you can't wade, use a float tube and fins or a canoe. Any boat higher or larger than a canoe will diminish your ability to sneak up on bass. Whatever craft you use, nothing beats the quiet efficiency of good paddle, pole, or oar work.

Wading will let you maintain absolute line- and fly-position control on a lake or river. The float tube is the second best method for control on a lake, because you can hold a fairly steady position with your swim fins. A canoe or boat should be used with a sea anchor when it's necessary to slow or stop the wind or current drift.

Here's another trick that pays off: When you find particularly good cover—a cypress stump, pad bed, or fallen tree—vary your approach and casting angles as much as 180 degrees. The best approach is not always the obvious one. A different approach may well produce more strikes because it hasn't been used by other anglers at that spot.

Inches Make the Difference

Successful fly-rodding for bass depends upon the ability to place and fish the fly within inches of an obstacle or surface spot. Therefore, pinpoint casting is essential; and again, absolute fly control is a must.

You can complement your presentation by using snag guards on your bass flies. Then they can be cast or pulled into those critical "inch" areas without hang-ups or loss, and without spoiling a good spot by retrieving a snagged fly. An effective snag guard is formed by a stiff monofilament loop attached at the hook bend, extending below the hook

point and up through the hook eye. It is simple and in no way affects the fly's action or hooking efficiency.

Thoughts on Bass Flies

Bass are susceptible to both imitative and attractor-type flies. A lot of action—either built in with materials like marabou and rubber hackle, or given to them by stripping, twitching, or jerking the fly line—especially interests the bass.

Fly texture or "feel" is best when it resembles the natural food that bass eat. Most cases call for a soft texture, particularly when flies are fished slowly or on subsurface retrieves. Most bass quickly expel lures if they don't "feel" right.

A selection of typical bass flies and bugs, most of which have soft bodies and texture.

If you retrieve a streamer or bug rapidly, bass usually strike viciously and are less apt to spit out the fly even if it is hard. They often hook themselves then, too. However, experience has proved that soft-textured flies consistently get more strikes and hook better than similar hard ones.

A useful selection of bass flies runs from sizes 8 to 3/0. Color patterns that imitate frogs, mice, crayfish, sculpins, minnows, shad, and aquatic and terrestrial insects are always needed. Unnatural colors also produce: red, white, bright yellow, blue, purple; fluorescent red, yellow, green, and orange—in solid colors or combinations.

Bass are usually far less predictable than trout and favor different flies almost daily, even hourly, with little or no obvious reason. Therefore it's always wise to have a wide range of patterns and different hook sizes at hand.

Once you are really into bugging for bass, you will find there's something unique about bass flies. The hair bugs and poppers particularly have personalities all their own. It is easy to get attached to them. In fact, you may even "retire" those that have been especially good for you. And when you go over those old battle-scarred veterans, they will recall many an exciting memory.

Bass bugging can become a fascinating year-round pastime. On cold winter nights you may spend profitable hours in a basement workshop building and designing new bugs for next summer's use. Many companies sell kits or supplies for making bugs, but it isn't even necessary to buy elaborate materials. One of the best bugs I ever owned was fashioned from the cork of an empty bottle of bourbon and from hackle feathers picked up in a chicken coop. Any bass fisherman who also hunts

A selection of surface bass bugs, some homemade and some manufactured.

Mark Hicks lands a hefty bass that went for a popping bug.

can easily save a few squirrel tails or bucktails and the skin from a pheasant or a grouse. Of course, any of these materials are also suitable for tying up a supply of streamer flies.

The body materials of today's bugs run from deer hair to cork to plastic, with an increasing trend to plastic, particularly in the bugs designed to imitate crippled minnows (bullet-shaped heads) or poppers (with dished-out heads to make a popping sound on the retrieve). The plastic bodies are far more durable, and most cast more easily than cork and much more easily than deer hair. The deer-hair bugs have a slight edge in Northeastern (New England) smallmouth fishing, but their casting difficulty and susceptibility to waterlogging are disadvantages.

Some bugs now have rubber-band legs. This may seem like gilding the lily, but it has made the bugs more deadly in many situations.

Quite a number of weedless devices have been built into some bugs, and nearly all are valuable in

thick vegetation or where other sunken obstacles are numerous. The turned-up (rather than turned-down) hook is the best of these, but it does miss good strikes occasionally. A better hooker, but heavier and therefore slightly more difficult to cast, is the bug with a weed guard of fine piano wire. It's excellent for casting among pads, bonnets, or some of the smartweeds.

Still other fly-fishing lures on tackle shelves today include everything from small spinners and spoons to "fly-rod size" editions of larger casting plugs. Again, nearly all of these will take bass, but few really suit fly rods as they do the new light-spinning gear that handles them much better.

Bass Streamer Flies

Here follows a list of streamer flies and their dressings that a fly-tying bass fisherman can make at home. Most require only a few inexpensive materials. Others are a little more elaborate, but all are very effective. By no means is this list complete.

Beltrami No. 13: A strange creation developed by George Herter and named after Beltrami County, Minnesota. It was meant for big brook trout, but it works well on brown trout and bass too. Body: oval silver tinsel. Hackle: about eight lengths of white rubber band tied on as a throat. Wing: barred orange topped off with black-bear hair. Head: coated with waterproof cement and covered with finely chopped-up black hair. Shoulder: flat plastic yellow and black eyes—or jungle cock.

Black Dazzler: Wings: black bucktail or tail of black phase of a grey squirrel. Tail: same. Head: black with a small wiggling disc attached. For the body, cut some blue and clear cellophane strips about $\frac{1}{16}$ inch wide. Tie these alternately along the full length of the body as you wind it with black silk. Strips should be crinkled and trimmed so that the projecting bits are about $\frac{3}{8}$ inch long, forming a body that looks "bushy."

Bumblepuppy: An old trout streamer designed by the legendary Theodore Gordon almost eighty years ago, it is said to be a fine clear-water streamer. Tag: silver and red silk. Tail: Scarlet ibis, two mated feathers back to back. Butt: red or yellow chenille. Body: full with white silk chenille and ribbed with flat silver tinsel. Hackle: badger—large, long, and lots of it. Wings: strips of white swan or goose over white-deer hair or goat hair. Sides: jungle cock. Head: black.

Burlap Fly: A western pattern originated for steelheads by Wayne Buszek, but with splendid potential for bass. Tail: a stiff bristle of deer hair tied to the flair. Body: a piece of burlap tied full. Hackle: soft grizzly. Wing: none.

Chief Needabeh: Body: medium thick made of flat silver tinsel. Wing: four yellow neck hackles. Shoulder: jungle cock. Hackle: red.

Golden Dustman: Originated by, and one of the favorites of, Dr. James Henshall. He considered it best on dark days. Body: peacock herl. Hackle: golden yellow. Wings: bronze (from a wild turkey if possible, but a domestic turkey is suitable). Tail: fibers from a golden-pheasant crest.

Golden Pheasant: An old English wet pattern that somehow, and with some revision into a streamer, will catch smallmouths in small rivers. Body: orange chenille with gold tinsel ribs tied medium fat. Tail: strands of black feather. Wing: two golden-pheasant feathers. Hackle: red.

Hot Orange Marabou: A great pattern for roily water and midsummer stream fishing. Use No. 4 or No. 6 streamer hooks. Wings: bright orange-dyed marabou feathers topped with several strands of peacock herl. Body: a clear strip of cellophane wound until it's about three times the size of the hook shank. Shoulder: jungle cock.

Irish Iron Blue Dun: A real antique among trout flies, but good for bass when tied as a streamer on a long-shanked hook. Tail: fibers of red feather from the breast of a golden pheasant. Body: fur from the belly of a muskrat ribbed with about five turns of silver tinsel. Hackle: dark gray. Wing: gray squirrel tail.

Mickey Finn: A well-known streamer developed by John Alden Knight. Head: black. Body: medium thick made of flat silver tinsel and ribbed with oval silver tinsel. Wing: a small bunch of yellow bucktail; then a medium bunch of red bucktail on top; then a medium bunch of yellow bucktail on top of it all. Shoulder: jungle cock.

Moose River: Body: thin, made of flat silver tinsel. Head: black. Wing: a small bunch of white bucktail with peacock-eyed tail fibers tied above as a topping. Cheek: golden-pheasant tippet.

Oriole: A streamer version of one of Dr. Henshall's favorite old patterns. Body: black chenille tied thin with gold tinsel ribbing. Tail: a sliver of black feather above a thinner sliver of white feather. Hackle: black. Wings: two long white hackle feathers dyed bright orange; long golden-pheasant feathers can be substituted. Use a No. 6 long-shanked hook.

Parmachene Belle: An old, old pattern. Head: black. Body: yellow chenille ribbed with flat silver tinsel. At rear of the body put a ruff of peacock-eyed tail fibers. Wing: two white neck hackles tied between two red ones. Shoulder: jungle cock. Hackle: one red and one white tied together.

Red Angel: Developed for fishing West Virginia streams. Wing: angel hair dyed crimson tied long and sparse. Body: flat silver tinsel. Tail: black bear or squirrel hair. Head: black with a black wiggling disc. Tie on a No. 6 long-shanked hook.

Shenandoah: Originated by smallmouth fishermen in the Blue Ridge Mountains region, it could be good elsewhere, too. Wings: black bucktail or tail of the black phase of a gray squirrel. Tail: same. Body: black chenille tied fat. Head: black with a small wiggling disc attached. Tie on a No. 4 or No. 6 long-shanked hook.

Smelt Marabou: A good one for New England and New Brunswick smallmouths. Wings: pale green marabou topped with two strands of peacock herl. Body: black and thin-ribbed with silver tinsel. Eye: jungle cock.

Warden's Worry: Head: black; red eye with white-painted center. Tail: a small section of red goosewing feather. Body: rear half flat silver tinsel; front half yellow seal fur-ribbed with gold tinsel. Wing: natural brown bucktail with several yellow polar bear hairs tied on top. Shoulder: jungle cock. Hackle: yellow.

Yellow Marabou: The same as the Hot Orange Marabou except substitute yellow marabou feathers.

Zebray: A surface bass bug rather than a streamer, designed by Art Kade of Sheboygan, Wisconsin, and easy to tie. Tail: yellow Asian goat hair. Body: alternate black and white bars of bucktail deer hair, shaped wide at the rear or bend of the hook and tapered toward the front; the front end is shaped deepest below the wings with a lift line to provide easy lifting from the water; the body is shallow above the hook to provide sufficient clearance for hooking fish. Wings: divided, spent wings of bright orange, Asian goat hair. Head: black silk waterproofed. Hook: a hollow-point No. 4 Sproat with a turned-down eye.

Chapter 11

The Southeast

This is the most important and productive bass fishing region in the world. An angler can find himself anywhere in the Southeast and practically never be more than a few minutes away from good bass waters—and from big bass. A state-by-state list of the best and best-known bass waters follows.

Alabama

As with all states in the Cotton Belt, Alabama has no shortage of bass fishing—and most of it is good fishing. One of the top three reservoirs, determined by a census of 88,000 angler hours of fishing, is Eufaula (or Walter F. George) Reservoir near Eufaula. One of the best year-round largemouth lakes, it has produced several fish weighing over thirteen pounds. The other two top reservoirs are Jordan near Montgomery, and Miller's Ferry Lake near Camden. West Point Lake ranks with Eufaula for producing bass of five pounds and larger.

Fishing is gaining popularity at Lake Harris, a new reservoir above Lake Martin on the Tallapoosa River; at Columbia Reservoir downstream from Eufaula, a small but good largemouth producer in spring; at Demopolis Reservoir, near Demopolis; and on forty-eight miles of Tombigbee and Black Warrior Rivers in western Alabama. Bankhead

Lake near Gorgas and Hueytown can provide excellent largemouth fishing, especially in spring. Holt Reservoir, near Tuscaloosa, also has good largemouth fishing. Other bass waters include Lake Jackson, near Coffeeville, which is good for largemouths in spring; Guntersville Reservoir, near Guntersville; Claiborne Lake, near Monroeville and Grove Hill; and Lake Harding (Barlett's Ferry Reservoir), near Phenix City.

The Alabama Department of Conservation intensively manages twenty-two public ponds, ranging in size from 13 to 184 surface acres, that produce a large number of bass five pounds and larger.

Wilson Reservoir, near Sheffield and Florence has good largemouth and smallmouth fishing. Pickwick Lake, below Wilson Reservoir, is excellent for smallmouths. The lower part of Sipsey River, from Grayson downstream to Lewis-Smith Reservoir, is an unsurpassed float stream with spotted bass fishing. Little River from DeSoto State Park downstream to Highway 35 west of Blanche also provides good floating. Both Tallapoosa River, near Embry, 250 miles downstream to its juncture with Coosa River, and Cahaba River, east of Birmingham downstream to Centerville, are good for spotted bass.

More information is available from the Alabama

Department of Conservation and Natural Resources, Game and Fish Division, Fisheries Section, 64 North Union, Montgomery, AL 36130.

Arkansas

Arkansas is another of the great bass fishing states. The large reservoirs can provide phenomenal fishing. Norfork Lake near Mountain Home has long been a hot spot. At times Bull Shoals, on the Missouri border, has had even better trophy fishing. Lakes Hamilton and Catherine near Hot Springs are both reliable. In truth, it is hard to go wrong with Arkansas bass lakes.

Upper Table Rock Lake near Eureka Springs has largemouths and spotted bass. Greer's Ferry Reservoir, near Heber Springs, and Lake Greason, near Kirby, are good for all bass species. For largemouths, fish Lake Ouachita, near Hot Springs; Nimrod Reservoir, near Plainview; Lake Atkins, south of Atkins; the Arkansas River; and the lower White River from Clarendon downstream. Millwood Reservoir, near Ashdown, is an excellent lake, as is DeGray Reservoir, near Arkadelphia. Lake Conway, near Little Rock, has many lunker largemouths. Gilham Reservoir, near DeQueen, contains largemouths and smallmouths, as do Dierks Reservoir, near DeQueen; Lake Overcup, near Morrillton; and Blue Mountain Reservoir, near Booneville.

Other excellent bass waters include the Buffalo River near Ponca for smallmouths; Lake Chicot near Lake Village, for largemouths; and Felsenthal Reservoir near Crossett, south of the Felsenthal National Wildlife Refuge. Ouachita River has all species. Lake Dardanelle (near the Arkansas River) contains largemouths.

More information is available from the Arkansas Game and Fish Commission, #2 Natural Resources Drive, Little Rock, AR 72205.

Florida

Florida is so choked with good bass waters that even to catalogue them is next to impossible. Besides the good fishing everywhere, communities on every bit of choice fishing water have adequate accommodations.

Florida Panhandle

The two best fisheries in this region are Lakes Talquin and Jackson near the city of Tallahassee—both great in the spring for catching trophy bass. The lower fifteen miles of the Apalachicola River, near the city of Apalachicola, also has prime bass fishing.

South Florida

Some of southern Florida's best bass fishing is on Lake Okeechobee. On the southern part of the lake, Moonshine Bay's aquatic hayfields attract many bass anglers. Try weedless spoons, plastic worms, and topwater plugs. Near Naples, the Alligator Alley canal system, through Conservation Area Three, is good, particularly the western end. Lake Trafford also produces big bass.

Central Florida

The premier bass resources here are Lake Kissimmee, Lake Tohopekaliga, the Lake George area of the St. Johns River, and Orange and Lochloosa lakes near Gainesville. These lakes are noted for producing trophy bass. Other good bass waters include the Withlacoochee River, between the Rutland Bridge near Bushnell, and Ross Bridge, between Ocala and Hernando. The phosphate pits in Polk County and in the Tenoroc Management Area at Lakeland are outstanding for big bass. Also try Lake Istokpoga in Highlands County between Lakeland and Lake Okeechobee; Santa Fe River and Lower Suwannee River and the St. Johns River area from Lake George to Green Cove Springs; Ochlawaha River from Silver Springs downstream to Rodman Reservoir; Lake Seminole, near Chattahoochee; and Lake Kerr and Salt Springs Run, near Silver Springs and Salt Springs. Salt Springs Campground is ideally located between the latter two and anglers bring in many big bass there. You'll also find good fishing at Lake Tsala-Apopka, near Dunnelion; the sandhill ponds of Ocala National Forest, near Ocala, Salt Springs, Palatka, and Leesburg; and the Clermont chain of lakes near Clermont. Homosassa River, near Homosassa Springs, and Crystal River, near the town of Crystal River, produce some top bass fishing in late February and early March.

There are many hundreds more bass waters in Florida. More information is available from the

Big Bass in the Bulrushes

I've fished few places in North America that compare to Lake Okeechobee, Florida, for sheer numbers of bass. I first got a sampling of what this massive, shallow lake has to offer while fishing with Bill Englefield of Thornville, Ohio. Englefield is a highly successful tournament bass angler who frequently fishes Okeechobee. He took me on a tour of the lake that included stops in many of the areas that are famous for producing trophy largemouth bass, including the Monkey Box, Moonshine Bay, the East Wall, the West Wall, Coot Bay, and Ritta Island.

At first I was overwhelmed by the vast acreage of dense aquatic vegetation that was passable only by narrow boat lanes. In many areas you could not see over the towering bulrushes, so at times it was like fishing in the middle of a cornfield. Englefield's knowledge of Okeechobee proved extensive, as we caught bass almost everywhere we stopped. The action was especially good when we pulled into Kreamer Island on the southern end of the lake. The area had lily pads, bulrushes, Kissimmee grass, pepper grass, and other varieties of vegetation.

"This looks good," said Englefield. "You generally do better when you can find a mixture of different types of weeds."

Englefield chucked a large plastic worm into the dark pocket formed by a cluster of bulrushes and held the rod-tip high as the worm sank. A bass nabbed his offering before it even reached the bottom. Englefield grunted as he reared back on his stout rod. The water churned, the weeds parted, and a respectable largemouth was soon flopping in the bottom of the boat. The fish's back and sides were very dark, as is often the case in weed-infested waters.

Over the next hour about fifteen bass inhaled our worms, and we saw other anglers in the area also catch several bass. We didn't hook a trophy fish, but many weighed three to four pounds. Our largest bass of the trip weighed over seven pounds. In most places, they'd mount a bass that big, but it was almost commonplace on Okeechobee where nothing less than a ten-pound bass can get local anglers excited.

—Mark Hicks

Florida Game and Freshwater Fish Commission, Farris Bryant Building, Tallahassee, FL 32399.

Georgia

Georgia also has more excellent bass fishing than can be listed here. In the middle section of the state, significant erosion causes some streams continually to run red with silt, but there are fine bass waters to the north and south. The world's record largemouth came from Oxbow Lake of the Ocmulgee River near McRae in the south.

Walter F. George Reservoir, near Fort Gains, is excellent for largemouths and spotted bass, especially early in the year, and often has lunker bass above ten pounds. Clark Hill Reservoir, near Clark Hill, South Carolina, has a very stable bass population. Altoona Reservoir, near Cartersville, is at times among the best largemouth lakes. Hartwell Reservoir, near Hartwell, is often good for largemouths and spotted bass, and excellent for striped bass and white-bass hybrids. Blue Ridge Reservoir, near Blue Ridge, has good smallmouth fishing. Chatuge Reservoir, near Hiwassee, is a fair to very good smallmouth lake. Jackson Lake, near Covington, could be the most consistent largemouth lake in Georgia. Lake Sidney Lanier has mainly spotted bass in the lower section and good largemouth fishing in the upper. Nottely Reservoir, near Blairsville, has both largemouths and smallmouths. Patrick's Fishing Paradise, near Tifton, is a commercial bass lake. (Man-made lakes, small in size, charge modest fees.) Lake Seminole near Bainbridge, a very good largemouth lake, often produces bass weighing above five or six pounds. West Point Reservoir near LaGrange is now producing trophy bass due to a sixteen-inch minimum size

Even an airboat can serve as a bass boat in weed-choked southern waters.

limit. Some consider Lake Sinclair near Milledge-ville to be a sleeper trophy bass lake. Carter's Lake near Calhoun is a reservoir with good redeye-bass fishing.

The Chattahoochee River below George Reservoir is a very good largemouth bass stream. Also try Flint River near Thomaston (north end) and from Newton to Bainbridge (south end), the Altamaha River, and the Ocmulgee River. Fair bass fishing exists in the St. Mary's and the more celebrated Suwannee Rivers that drain Okefenokee Swamp. Guides can be contacted at Folkston, Fargo, or Waycross.

More information is available from the Georgia Department of Natural Resources, Floyd Towers East, Suite 1358, 205 Butler Street S.E., Atlanta, GA 30334.

Kentucky

Every season is bass-fishing time in Kentucky, with fishing conditions to suit any angler. Kentucky has more navigable water than every state except Alaska. An immense amount of bass fishing opportunities are available in its 14,000 miles of streams and rivers, over 600,000 acres of lakes, and over 50,000 acres of farm ponds.

Herrington Lake, an 1,800-acre impoundment in the heart of the Bluegrass (Mercer, Boyle, and Garrard Counties) has produced more pounds of bass per acre than any other Kentucky reservoir. Herrington is the oldest and deepest lake in the state and offers superb bass fishing in the spring and fall. Taylorsville Lake in central Kentucky, completed in 1983, is highly fertile and productive

Jim Bryant Jr., of Bassmaster Boats, fishes a rocky point at Herrington Lake, Kentucky.

for trophy bass. Kentucky Lake, the largest man-made reservoir in the world, and its sister Lake Barkley, are two other top bass lakes. Both are relatively shallow and yield good fishing for largemouth and spotted bass.

For smallmouth, Dale Hollow Lake in south-central Kentucky offers the best opportunities for big fish. The world record smallmouth (11 pounds, 15 ounces) was taken from the Kentucky side of Dale Hollow. Paintsville Lake and Cave Run Lake in northeastern Kentucky are also excellent for smallmouths and have been specifically managed for this species.

Possibly the best lake for all three species of black bass is Lake Cumberland, a 50,250-acre impoundment in south-central Kentucky. Anglers have taken more state record fish from Lake Cumberland and its tailwaters than any other lake in the state.

Generally speaking, bass fishing is better in Kentucky's central and western lakes, where you'll find more agriculture. In many of the state's eastern lakes, spotted bass comprise over half the total bass population.

Kentucky also has good stream fishing for bass, particularly in the fall. Elkhorn Creek, a ninety-nine-mile stretch of water, is the best. The Kentucky River and its major tributaries are also good.

More information is available from the Kentucky Department of Fish and Wildlife Resources, #1 Game Farm Road, Frankfort, KY 40601.

Louisiana

The state has approximately 8,000 miles of freshwater rivers, and, although all contain bass, many are lightly fished. Since many of the main river systems—the Mississippi, Red, Atchafalaya, Ouachita, Sabine, and Pearl—flow at a higher level (inside dikes and levees) than their drainage plains, they form numerous bayous, lagoons, and oxbows, all full of bass. There is actually more bass-fishing water in Louisiana than anyone could explore. Much of it exists so deep in remote, swampy sections of the state that it is practically virgin.

Trees, shrubbery, and vines close in on these dark waters and lend an air of what might be called brooding mystery. Cypress trees stand in the shallows, trailing moss. Their roots form underwater hiding places and obstacles, and grotesque "knees" thrust their rounded tops above the surface. Tupelo gums, pines, palmettos, and other growth crowd the water's edge.

Straddling Louisiana and Texas, Caddo Lake (northwest of Shreveport), long noted for its bass, is an excellent example of the lonely, haunting swamp lake. Some other Louisiana largemouth waters are located at Sabine Refuge Freshwater Pools near Hackberry; Penchant, southwest of Houma; Chicot, north of Ville Platte; Claiborne, ten miles southeast of Homer; D'Arbonne, southeast of Farmersville; Nantachie, southeast of Verda; Vernon, near Anacco; False River, near New Roads; St. John, north of Ferriday; Spring Bayou, near Marksville; Turkey Creek, west of Wisner; Indian Creek, west of LeCompte; Bistineau, near Minden; Old River, east of Innis; Bussey, near Bastrop; Bundicks, northwest of Dry Creek; and Toledo Bend, located along the Louisiana/Texas border near Logansport-Leesville (see Texas).

More information is available from the Louisiana Department of Wildlife and Fisheries, P.O. Box 15570, 2000 Quail Drive, Baton Rouge, LA 70895.

Mississippi

Within Mississippi boundaries lie many U.S. Corps of Engineers lakes, but old Ross Barnett Reservoir is probably the best bet for heavy largemouth bass, probably because of the constant year-round water

Impoundments in the South can produce good winter bass fishing.

level in its 33,000 acres. Other worthwhile destinations for a basser are: Grenada Reservoir, near Grenada, for largemouths and spotted bass; Sardis Reservoir, near Sardis; and Pickwick Reservoir, near Luka, for all bass species. Okatibbee Reservoir, near Meridan, is excellent for largemouth bass. Enid Reservoir, near Enid, makes an excellent largemouth lake with some spotted bass. Also try Archusa Reservoir, near Quitman; Little Black Creek Reservoir, near Purvis; Maynor Creek Reservoir, near Waynesboro; Lake Lamar Bruce, near Tupelo; Chotard Lake, north of Vicksburg; and Bogue Homa Lake, near Laurel.

The impoundments of the Tennessee-Tombigbee waterways have provided some of the best bass fishing in the state, particularly in Columbus and Bay Spring Lakes. Tippah County Lake is also worth visiting. It produced the state record largemouth of 14 pounds, 12 ounces.

More information is available from the Mississippi Game and Fish Commission, Box 451, Jackson, MS 39205.

North Carolina

The productive angling of North Carolina's coastal region is enhanced by the freshwater streams, lakes, and sounds nearby. In the coastal region, the famous bass fishing in Currituck Sound has suffered from saltwater intrusion. Renewed high stream flows could reverse this trend and restore the locale to prominence. The Chowan River near Edenton and the lower reaches of many of the coastal rivers still provide excellent fishing, particularly in the spring. Phelps Lake (east of Plymouth) probably has replaced Lake Mattamuskeet as the best of the natural lakes on the coast.

In the Piedmont region, Lake Wylie near Charlotte may be the state's best reservoir for largemouth bass, followed closely by nearly all of the Yadkin River Lakes. Tuckertown Lake (near Albemarle) and the falls of the Neuse Lake (near Raleigh) are managed with a twelve-to-fourteen-inch slot limit for larger bass. Many small (200-to-1,500-acre) city water supply reservoirs and numerous small ponds provide outstanding bass fishing in the area.

In the mountain region, Lake Chatuge in the southwest corner of the state is the best for largemouth bass. For smallmouth bass, Lakes Chatuge, Hiwassee, and Fontana are the best. The New River in the northwest portion of the state provides excellent river fishing for smallmouths. There is little spotted bass fishing available in North Carolina; W. Kerr Scott Reservoir may offer the best of it.

More information is available from the North Carolina Wildlife Resources Commission, 512 N. Salisbury Street, Raleigh, NC 27611.

Oklahoma

Once one of the most naturally bone-dry states, Oklahoma is a bass fisherman's paradise because today the state contains the second-greatest concentration of impounded water in the nation, with over 600,000 acres of reservoirs. Another 500,000 acres of farm ponds, plus 23,000 miles of rivers and streams, also help to make bass fishing here a year-round proposition, and now a big business.

Not long ago visiting sportsmen had trouble finding suitable accommodations in Oklahoma, but that also has changed. Nowadays there are excellent resorts, cottages, boat docks, and bait shops around every major lake. In addition, the state's Tourism and Recreation Department has installed a system of inns and resorts designed for outdoor families.

Although big reservoirs absorb about 95 percent of the bass fishing pressure, there are other possibilities. Take a float trip along the beautiful Illinois River above Tenkiller. Long stretches of this river are seldom disturbed, and the bass unsophisticated.

Located in picturesque Cookson Hills northeast of Tulsa, Tenkiller Lake contains 12,900 acres and is an extraordinary place to prospect for largemouth, spotted, and smallmouth bass. Other top reservoirs in the northeast region include Grand near Grove; Fort Gibson near Wagoner; Spavinaw near Spavinaw; Skiatook near Skiatook; and Birch near Barnsdall.

One of Oklahoma's largest bodies of water is Texoma Lake, a reservoir of 89,000 acres located midway between Oklahoma City and Dallas. Except during times of seasonal high winds, which can keep fishermen off the lake, Texoma is one of America's great bass fishing holes. Eufaula Reservoir, near Eufaula, is among the largest largemouth lakes in the southeast region and is red hot in the spring. Broken Bow Reservoir is popular for its "schooling" largemouth bass. Other bass hot spots in the southeast region include Sardis near Clayton; Pine Creek near Valliant; Arbuckle near Sulphur; Konawa near Konawa; and Dripping Springs near Okmulgee.

Fuqua Reservoir near Ducan in southwest Oklahoma also produces top bass.

More information is available from the Oklahoma Department of Wildlife Conservation, 1801 North Lincoln, Oklahoma City, OK 73105.

South Carolina

South Carolina, with a foothold in the mountains and a beachhead on the Atlantic, contains more varied bass fishing than native anglers manage to use in a year's time. Much good water lies untried and untested from year to year. A good example is the maze of moss-hung waterways and tributary streams in the lowlands from Charleston to Georgetown. An angler with a car-top boat or canoe could spend season after season exploring these places deep in the boondocks and seldom see another fisherman. Any visiting fisherman should contact the local game wardens here. All are friendly, helpful, and know the region well.

Most local fishermen concentrate on the big reservoirs of the state. The largest and most productive of these is the Santee-Cooper Reservoir, which flooded 170,000 acres of Santee River swamps to form two giant lakes—Moultrie and Marion. Bass fishing is great in both, but especially in stump- and tree-filled Marion. You'll find plenty of accommodations around Moncks Corners and Manning. Information is available from Santee-Cooper County, Box 12, Santee, SC 29142.

Other South Carolina reservoirs include Wateree, 14,000 acres near Camden; Lake Murray, 50,800 acres near Columbia; Clarks Hill Lake, 78,500 acres near Aiken; and Lake Greenwood, 11,800 acres near Greenwood.

Fishermen have greatly neglected South Carolina's rivers, though all have bass. Also, most are fine for leisurely float tripping. Here are some excellent rivers to try: Edisto, Combahee, Santee, Wateree, Witheree, Salkehatchie, Ashepoo, Cooper, Black, Waccamaw, Pee Dee, Little Pee Dee, and Congaree. To these, add the thousands of farm ponds where anglers take many bragging-size largemouths every year.

Lake Hartwell and 25,000-acre Keowee Reservoir have good largemouth bass. The latter is especially productive in late winter.

More information is available from the South Carolina Wildlife Department, Box 167, Columbia, SC 29202.

Tennessee

Tennessee has widely contrasting waters—from giant reservoirs to shallow, eerie earthquake ponds such as Reelfoot Lake. But except for the cold mountain streams in between, few waters do not contain bass. All three species of bass live in Tennessee waters, the largemouth being the most common black bass in ponds and lakes. Some larger, slower rivers also provide largemouth fishing from March to November. Originally the smallmouth was almost exclusively a stream fish in Tennessee, but with the impoundment of smallmouth streams into lakes, the species has adapted well. The smallmouth lives in many streams throughout that part of Tennessee east of Kentucky Lake. You'll find other good streams in middle Tennessee. Among the eastern Tennessee streams providing better smallmouth fishing are the Powell and Clinch Rivers, above Norris Lake; Holston River; Little River;

Television personality and bass pro Bill Dance catches bass the year around on Tennessee impoundments.

and several smaller streams in Monroe County. The larger streams on the Cumberland Plateau also support some smallmouths. In middle Tennessee almost every clean stream that flows year-round is inhabited by smallmouths. Among the better ones are the Elk, Upper Duck, Lower Duck, Caney Fork, Collins, Stones, Harpeth, and Buffalo Rivers, plus many of their tributaries.

For larger smallmouth, some weighing from five to ten pounds, the fisherman should go to Dale Hollow and Center Hill Lakes, which have produced many outstanding fish. The best smallmouth fishing, on either streams or lakes, comes during the spring and fall months.

Spotted bass are less abundant than the other bass species, but fairly common in the clearer streams of western Tennessee, such as headwaters of the Obion, Hatchie, Loosahatchie, and Wolf Rivers; these bass can be found as far east as Norris Lake, north of Knoxville.

Chickamauga Lake, on the Tennessee River near Chattanooga, covers 34,500 acres; largemouths predominate. Cherokee Lake, a storage lake on the Holston River, near Morristown, covers 31,000 acres of excellent bass water. Douglas Lake, on the French Broad River, covers 31,000 acres near Dandridge, where the principal fish is the largemouth.

Fort Loudoun Lake, on the main channel of the Tennessee, covers 14,500 acres. Nickajack is prime bass water below Fort Loudoun.

Kentucky Lake, which extends from near the Mississippi state line entirely across Tennessee to Gilbertsville, Kentucky—a distance of 184 miles—covers 158,300 acres and has a ragged shoreline of 2,380 miles. It leads the state in the production of largemouth bass and has established a very substantial smallmouth fishery in its lower end: excellent bass water. Norris Lake, first of the TVA-created lakes, is north of Knoxville; it is easily accessible and is fished for bass year-round. Pickwick Lake extends 53 miles on the Tennessee from the dam at Pickwick Landing to Wilson Dam in Alabama. Largemouth bass are the chief attractions, but these waters also yield many trophy smallmouths.

Watts Bar Lake covers 38,000 acres—74 miles of largemouth bass fishing. Fontana Lake, in a wooded mountain region on the Little Tennessee, 68 miles from Knoxville, has smallmouths. Dale Hollow Lake covers 40,000 acres and provides some of the best-sustained bass fishing in Tennessee. To form Reelfoot Lake, the great earthquake of 1812 caused forest lands to sink beneath the surface, and the Mississippi River poured in, bringing almost every variety of fish known to inland waters. Many of the submerged trees died, and the resultant stumps formed one of the finest natural fish hatcheries in the world. The lake has largemouth bass along with twenty-seven other species.

Center Hill Lake, a 40,000-acre impoundment on the Caney Fork River, near Smithville, has largemouths and smallmouths. South Holston Lake is a good bass lake near Bristol. Watauga Lake covers 6,400 acres, in Cherokee National Forest, near Elizabethton.

Cheatham Lake, just west of Nashville, has numerous boat docks and other facilities. It is not fished heavily, and has an excellent largemouth population. The 12,000-acre Normandy Lake, near Shelbyville on the Duck River, is probably second only to Kentucky Lake for largemouth bass production per acre. Old Hickory Reservoir covers 25,000 acres on the Cumberland River, east of Nashville. Woods Reservoir is located near Estill Spring. Boone Lake provides good bass water in the northeastern corner of the state. Bedford Lake, covering 47 acres in Bedford County, is noted for large bass; two largemouths weighing more than thirteen pounds each were taken there. Brown's

Creek Lake, in the Natchez Trace Forest, covers 167 acres.

More information is available from Tennessee Wildlife Resources, Ellington Agricultural Center, Nashville, TN 37204.

Virginia

Some of the best trophy largemouth fishing in Virginia probably occurs in the 51,000-acre Kerr or Buggs Island Reservoir, near Clarksville. Big bass are also taken regularly from 9,600-acre Lake Anna located northwest of Richmond. And don't overlook 20,000-acre Lake Gaston which straddles the border of Virginia and North Carolina. A highly regarded reservoir for largemouth and smallmouth bass is 20,600-acre Smith Mountain Lake southeast of Roanoke. Philpott Reservoir also yields good largemouth and smallmouth fishing from its 2,800 acres. For smallmouths only, you'll enjoy 2,800-acre Lake Moomaw in the George Washington National Forest near Covington.

Bass fishermen favor Claytor Lake, near Pulaski, because largemouth, smallmouth, and spotted bass swim in this 4,500-acre reservoir. Facilities are available at Claytor State Park.

Good bass fishing exists in other reservoirs of the state: Chickahominy in New Kent County; Carvins Cove in Roanoke County; South Holston Reservoir in Washington County; and Lake Cahoon and Lake Prince in Nansemond County. Chickahominy, southeast of Richmond, is particularly good in June, or at night later in the year.

Largemouths are common in many brackish rivers at tidewater. Among these are Chickahominy River, James River, Appomattox River, Mattaponi River, Piscataway Creek, and Piankatank and Pamunkey Rivers.

Smallmouths swim in all the larger rivers in the Piedmont and mountain sections. The best smallmouth waters are the New, James, Shenandoah (both forks), Holston, Rappahannock, Jackson, Back Creek, Cowpasture, Maury, and Little Rivers.

Back Bay, in Princess Anne County near Virginia Beach, was once one of Virginia's very best fisheries for largemouth bass. In recent years the bass population has declined drastically due to the intrusion of salt water, which has killed the once abundant vegetation. With steps intended to restore the bass fishing, Back Bay may eventually regain its former status as a haven for bass anglers.

More information is available from the Virginia Commission of Game and Fisheries, 4010 West Broad Street, Box 11104, Richmond, VA 23230.

West Virginia

West Virginia's mountain streams and lakes offer a wide variety of fishing opportunities to the fisherman for largemouth, smallmouth, and spotted bass. Flowing northeast through the eastern panhandle are the Cacapon, South Branch, and Shenandoah Rivers, which offer excellent smallmouth fishing. Through Clay and Braxton Counties of central West Virginia winds the Elk River, a top-notch bass producer.

Another smallmouth river is the New River, which originates in Virginia and rushes northward across West Virginia. Long stretches of this river run far from highways and deep in rocky gorges.

Perhaps the loveliest of all West Virginia rivers is the Greenbrier, good for floating in a canoe as well as for wading. Good bass water runs downstream from Marlinton. The river flows alternately through lush bluegrass valleys, rhododendron jungles, and rocky hemlock canyons. The entire setting of Greenbrier County is beautiful. For fly fishermen who like background and atmosphere with their sport, this region is hard to beat.

Favorite largemouth bass lakes are Plum Orchard, Stone Coal, Burnsville, Sutton, R. D. Bayley, and Bluestone. The largemouth is also one of the most important sport fish in small public impoundments and farm ponds. Significant populations of largemouths inhabit the deep, slow-moving waters of the Ohio River, backwater areas of the Ohio, Kanawha, and Monongahela Rivers, and large deep pools of every warm-water stream.

Summersville Lake near Summersville, encompassing 2,700 acres, is the state's premier smallmouth impoundment. Tygart, Sutton, Stone Coal, and Bluestone Lakes also have smallmouths.

Spotted bass are native to the Ohio River drainage and they live in several reservoirs, particularly Sutton and Bluestone.

More information is available from the West Virginia Department of Natural Resources, Wildlife Division, 1800 Washington Street East, Charleston, WV 25305.

Chapter 12
The Midwest

Except for the Southeast, the land of the largest bass and the most bass, a fisherman's best bet may be the Midwest. This is a fertile region, generally, with both natural and man-made waters. The man-made waters, usually large water-supply reservoirs, are located close to centers of population. Natural waters become more numerous the farther north you travel.

This is also the region of the Great Lakes, which contain the very best smallmouth fishing holes. Smallmouths grow larger in a few southern reservoirs; but in quantity of smallmouths, the Great Lakes are unsurpassed.

So in the Midwest, an angler is never far from good bass-fishing waters, and in no other region are facilities so numerous. That includes everything from motels to tackle shops, bait stores and boat docks, to the thousands of outfitters or camp owners from Missouri to Minnesota who cater to bass fishermen.

Illinois

An agricultural state, Illinois is extremely level in terrain and fairly well endowed with bass fishing waters. The best fishing occurs in lakes, and accommodations exist near all of these—if not on the

lake itself, in the adjacent communities.

The largest largemouths are probably found in five lakes of southern Illinois: Lake-of-Egypt, Crab Orchard, Devil's Kitchen, Rend, and Newton. Other largemouth waters include Grass Lake, east of Spring Grove; Deep Lake, northeast of Lake Villa; Lake Shelbyville, near Shelbyville; Carlyle Lake, northeast of Carlyle; Sanchris Lake, west of Kincaid; Lake Jacksonville, southeast of Jacksonville (a recently rehabilitated lake); Ramsey Lake, northwest of Ramsey; Greenville City Lake, northeast of Greenville; Lincoln Trail Lake, south of Marshall; Otter Lake, west of Girard; Gillespie New City Lake, near Gillespie; Red Hills State Lake, northeast of Summer; Dolan Lake, southeast of McLeansboro; Dale Lake, northwest of Johnsonville; Randolph County Lake, near Chester; Baldwin Lake, north of Baldwin; Kinkaid Lake, northwest of Murphysboro; Mermet Lake, west of Mermet; Cedar Lake, southwest of Carbondale; Clinton Lake, east of Clinton; Fox Lake, near Fox Lake; Glenn Shoals, north of Hillsboro; Heidecke Lake, east of Morris; Lake Springfield, south of Springfield; Sam Parr Lake, northeast of Newton; Mississippi River Pool 13, north of Fulton. Good smallmouth waters include Prairie Creek–Kankakee River, northwest of Wilmington; Forked Creek–Kankakee River, northeast of Wilmington;

Casting for bass can provide good action on many Midwestern waters.

and Kankakee River in Will County near Wilmington.

More information is available from the Illinois Department of Conservation, Division of Fisheries, 524 South 2nd Street, Springfield, IL 62706.

Indiana

Somehow the Hoosier state escapes recognition as a good bass-fishing state, although the northern portion is full of good bass waters. These are natural lakes scooped out by glaciers in prehistoric times. Elsewhere in the state, artificial lakes take up the slack.

Several of Indiana's streams have great potential for float tripping, and on the Tippecanoe River, at least, outfitters have facilities for visiting fishermen. Though quite often roily, the Wabash River is good for floating too.

Monroe Lake, near Bloomington, is the state's largest and best for big bass. But lunkers are occasionally caught in coal strip pit lakes of the South.

Other worthwhile largemouth bass waters include J. C. Murphey Lake near Morocco; Turtle Creek Reservoir near Sullivan; Patoka Reservoir in Orange and Crawford Counties; the Ohio River along the southern border of the state (for largemouth and spotted bass); West Boggs Creek, near

Loogootee; Monroe Reservoir, near Bloomington; Reservoir 26, near Dugger; Lake James, near Angola; Willow Slough, near Morocco; Bruce Lake, near Rochester; Cataract Reservoir, near Cloverdale; Mansfield Reservoir, near Ferndale; and Hardy Lake, near Austin.

For smallmouth bass try Lake Maxinkuckee, near Culver, and the St. Joseph River in Elkhart and St. Joseph Counties.

More information is available from the Indiana Department of Natural Resources, 607 State Office Building, Indianapolis, IN 46204.

Iowa

This fertile state contains 80,000 acres of farm ponds, 90,000 acres of natural and man-made lakes, over 200,000 miles of boundary rivers, and over 19,000 miles of inland streams. The bass fishing here is excellent. Only catfish surpass bass in popularity with the state's 500,000 licensed resident anglers. The state has provided and developed access sites and boat-launching facilities to supplement private installations at all major bodies of water.

Largemouth bass abound in the southern Mississippi River in Pools 17–19, particularly in the Big Timber, Burnt Pocket, and other backwater complexes. You'll also find plentiful smallmouths in the Boone, Cedar, Chariton, Des Moines, Iowa, Maquoketa, Raccoon, Shell Rock, Skunk, Volga, Wapsipinicon, West Fork Cedar, and Winnebago Rivers.

As for lakes and reservoirs, in northwest Iowa you can take smallmouths and largemouths from Spirit Lake, near Spirit Lake, and West Okoboji, near Arnolds Park. Snyder Bend, near Salix; Clear, near Clear Lake; and Briggs Wood, near Webster City, all have good largemouth fishing.

Largemouths can be taken in the southwest region from Badger Creek, near Van Meter; Cold Springs, near Lewis; DeSoto Bend, near Missouri Valley; Green Valley (smallmouths and largemouths), near Creston; Hickory Grove, near Colo; Icaria, near Corning; Lake Ahquabi, near Indianola; Lake Anita, near Anita; Little River, near Leon; Nine Eagles, near Davis City; Prairie Rose, near Harlan; Rock Creek, near Kellogg; and Twelve Mile, near Creston.

For largemouth bass in southeast Iowa consider Coralville Reservoir near Iowa City; Lake Darling, near Brighton; Lake Fisher, near Bloomfield; Lake Keomah, near Oskaloosa; Lake Miami, near Lovilla; Lake Wapello, near Drakesville; Pleasant Creek, near Palo; Rathbun Reservoir, near Centerville; and Red Haw, near Chariton. Volga Lake, near Fayette, is a top bass producer in the northeast region.

For more information contact the Iowa Department of Natural Resources, Wallace State Office Building, East 9th and Grand Ave., Des Moines, IA 50319.

Kansas

Flat, often dry Kansas depends on impoundments for bass fishing because of great fluctuations in river water levels. Here is a list of the best lakes.

In the north-central region, Glen Elder Reservoir (also called Waconda Lake) near Beloit is good for largemouths. Milford Reservoir, near Junction City, and Wilson Reservoir, between Russell and Salina, both have largemouths and smallmouths. Reservoirs in the southeast region that produce good largemouth fishing include Big Hill, near Cherryvale; Hillsdale, near Paola; and La Cygne, near La Cygne. Largemouth and spotted bass swim in Bourbon State Fishing Lake, near Elsmore; Crawford S.F.L., near Girard; and Woodson S.F.L., near Toronto. El Dorado, near Dorado in the south-central region, has smallmouth and largemouth bass.

More information is available from the Kansas Fish and Game Commission, Pratt Headquarters, Route 2, Box 54A, Pratt, KS 67124.

Michigan

Michigan attracted fishermen before many other territories attracted settlers. The state has been in the holiday business since before the Civil War, thanks to its mixed pine and hardwood forests, its lakes formed by glaciers, its beaches and waterways, and most of all its splendid fishing.

The lower half of the state contains the prime bass fishing, and you could fill a book with the names of good waters from this region. There are over 3,000 miles of shoreline along four Great Lakes alone, plus thirty major river systems with highly rated bass fishing. Within easy reach of Detroit and the other motor cities rest Gun and Thorn-

apple Lakes in Ottowa County. The Irish Hills lakes have good fishing early in the spring. Lake St. Clair, between Lake Erie and Lake Huron, may be number one in the state for both largemouth and smallmouth bass.

The lake "areas" containing bass extend from Lapeer to Hillsdale, near Flint, and Coldwater, and from near Greenville to the Indiana line. For smallmouth, the best rivers are the Grand, Kalamazoo, St. Joseph, Thornapple, Flat, and Muskegon. The drowned river mouths of the Grand, Muskegon, and Kalamazoo also are very good for largemouth. And do not forget the Saginaw Bay area, which provides outstanding smallmouth fishing around Grindstone, the Charity Islands, and the Rifle River area, and top quality largemouth fishing around the weedy west and south sides of the inner bay.

The upper half of the Lower Peninsula probably produces the greatest number of big smallmouths and also has some good largemouth fishing. By Wilderness State Park (Emmet County), the Beaver Island Group and East Arm of Grand Traverse Bay, Lake Michigan, are excellent for smallmouth. Inland waters of the area that produce trophy smallmouth include Burt Lake, in Cheboygan County; Lake Bellaire, Elk River, and the Elk, Torch, and Intermediate Lakes, in Antrim County; Leelanau, Glen, and Lime Lakes, in Leelanau County; and Mio Pond, in Oscoda County. For largemouth, some of the better areas are Houghton Lake, and Lakes Mitchell and Cadillac at Cadillac; Sanford Lake, Midland County; and Wixom Lake, Gladwin County.

The Muskegon, Manistee, and Au Sable rivers are known as top-notch trout streams, but the lower reaches contain smallmouths.

In the Upper Peninsula, none of the Lake Superior waters have bass, and more than half of the lakes and three quarters of the streams do not have bass. That is because they are cold-water bodies—primarily trout and whitefish waters. The Lake Michigan and Lake Huron shorelines of the Upper Peninsula, however, have excellent smallmouth bass fishing, as do some of the tributary streams into which the bass run in the spring to spawn. A fair number of the inland lakes are productive enough to produce some good largemouth bass fishing. Most of the bass lakes, however, are relatively infertile and produce bass in limited numbers. In some areas, such as the Sylvania Tract, the bass must be protected by no-kill regulations lest they be fished out. These lakes do produce a few big bass, however.

The first tourists at the first resort on the Upper Peninsula traveled by horse and carriage from St. Ignace to jewel-like Brevoort Lake. Accommodations now are more modern, but the lake is as lovely as ever—and it still has bass. Farther west are the Manistique Lakes. Near the Mackinac Straits, Mackinac County includes a number of islands— Mackinac, Bois Blanc, and Les Cheneaux. The waters around Bois Blanc have plenty of bass, and it is hard to match the smallmouth fishing around the Cheneaux Archipelago.

Offshore and to the east lies Drummond Island, surrounded by some of the most fertile fishing water for smallmouths. Good fishing waters also surround Neebish and Sugar Islands.

Some of the best fishing occurs in the Manistique Lakes; and this is country that an adventurous bass angler with a car-top boat or trailer can explore much further than most. West along Lake Superior is Alger County and the spectacular Pictured Rocks country.

The largest lake in Marquette County is Michigamme, which has good bass fishing. Other bass waters include Ives and Independence Lakes (near Big Bass), Goose, Teal, Bass, Kawbowgam, Deer, Silver, Mountain, and Pine Lakes. There is excellent fishing for bass in the Princeton, Gwinn, and Little system of lakes. Budget-priced accommodations are available at most lakes, with a public campsite located on the nearby 333,000-acre Escanaba Game Area.

Baraga County includes the Keweenaw and Huron Bays of Lake Superior. The best bass fishing is in Vermillac, King, Drummond, Ned, Fence, and Cliff Lakes. In Houghton County, Portage Lake, near Chassell, is good. Other bass waters include Perch, Bob, Otter, Gerald, Roland, Rice, Norway, and Mud Lakes.

Keweenaw County, almost surrounded by Lake Superior, nonetheless contains 125 lakes and 275 miles of streams. Lac La Belle produces bass and so do Fanny Hooe, Manganese, Breakfast, and Schlatter Lakes.

In Ontonagon County you'll find the best of the bass fishing in Lake of the Clouds, Gogebic, Mirror, and Bond Lakes, waters that produce all summer long, since they remain cool even during the dog days. There are 1,200 miles of streams and over 400 unnamed lakes in Gogebic County. In June, bass are taken in lakes like Tamarack, Duck,

Crooked, Sucker, Cisco, and Lac Vieux Desert. Gogebic Lake, an especially fine resort and cottage area with public campgrounds, also has bass.

In the Crystal Falls District, which includes Iron, Dickinson, and Menominee Counties, there are good bass waters. The Lower Paint and Lower Michigamme Rivers, and areas of the Menominee, provide good smallmouth fishing. The rest of the streams are primarily for trout.

Escanaba is well known for Big and Little Bay de Noc, both of which contain smallmouths. Boats, motors, guides, and all sorts of accommodations are available out of Escanaba, Gladstone, Rapid River, Stonington, Nahma, Sac Bay, Garden, and Fairport.

More information is available from the Fisheries Division, Department of Natural Resources, P.O. Box 30028, Lansing, MI 48909.

Minnesota

It is nearly impossible to list all the bass opportunities in this land of sky-blue waters. Equally difficult is the task of selecting Minnesota's *best* bass-fishing waters. The nod probably should go to the Mississippi River for its full length, but mostly upstream from the Twin Cities. It contains unlimited bass fishing, and to get the details, simply stop at any tackle store or contact any crossroads "expert" along the way.

Premium bass fishing also exists in lakes of the Quetico-Superior wilderness along the border near Ely. Typical of these is McNaught Lake (actually in Ontario), near Ely. Basswood Lake is great in springtime, through the summer. This Quetico-Superior country is completely roadless and wild. To fish there is to go by canoe. Outfitters can completely arrange trips of any length or duration. They rent everything from canoes and car-top carriers, to tents, food for a planned daily menu, sleeping bags, utensils, and even waterproof route maps of the country. There's great adventure here as well as great bass fishing.

Other lakes most often considered among the best in Minnesota include Brule, East Bearskin, Greenwood, Little Vermilion, Loon, Rainy, Saganaga, and Turtle, all in the norhtern half of the state. The following regions (grouped according to general locality) have at least fair bass fishing: Grand Marais, Gunflint Trail, Ely; Tower, Whiteface River; Alden Lake, Cloquet, Cotton; Finland,

Two Harbors, Hibbing; Virginia; Biwabik, Deer River; Grand Rapids; Nashwauk, International Falls; Little Fork, Cook, Baudette; Lake of the Woods; Northwest Angle, Red Lake; Blackduck, Bemidji; Cass Lake, Leech Lake; Hackensack, Brainard; Whitefish Lake Chain; Emily, Little Falls; Motley, Bay Lake; Deerwood; Aitkin; Mille Lacs Lake, McGregor; Arlton, Moose Lake; Barnum, Park Rapids, Detroit Lakes, Fergus Falls; Pelican Rapids; Henning, Alexandria; Glenwood; Osakis, Appleton; Ortonville; Morris, Willmar; Litchfield; Hutchinson, Paynesville; Richmond; St. Cloud, Annandale; Buffalo, Pine City; Mora, Cambridge; Princeton; Elk River, Center City; Forest Lake, White Bear Lake, Redwing; Wabash, Winona, Fairbault; Mankato; New Ulm. The Metro Lakes within the Twin Cities have excellent bass fishing.

More information is available from the Minnesota Department of Natural Resources, Box 12, 500 Lafayette Road, St. Paul, MN 55155.

Missouri

Bass fishing is traditional in Missouri, which isn't hard to explain when you consider the abundance of fine waters—impounded and flowing—especially in the Ozark region, which includes that portion of Missouri south of the Missouri River. In this area alone, there are about 16,000 miles of streams and 200,000 acres of impounded waters.

In a resort area in the northern part of the hill country is Lake of the Ozarks. Its coves, peninsulas, and rocky outcrops form a shoreline of 1,372 miles—one of the longest in the United States. Fish caught in its 60,000 acres of water include largemouth black bass, and spotted bass in the rocky coves.

In the southeastern area of the Ozarks, Lake Wappapello also attracts bass fishermen. Clearwater Dam, on the Black River in Reynolds County, has created Lake Clearwater.

In southwest Missouri Lake Taneycomo, in Taney County, has Branson, Hollister, Forsyth, and Rockaway Beach on its shoreline. There are recreational facilities and a number of fine Ozark streams in the immediate vicinity. Created by a dam in Arkansas, Norfork Lake backs up into Missouri for about eight miles. Bull Shoals Lake extends into Ozark and Taney Counties and has an area of 45,000 acres. The lake replaces the portion

of White River below Lake Taneycomo. About 15,000 acres of coves, arms, and deep water lie in Missouri, including some of the best bass areas. Table Rock Lake, and specifically the James River arm, is Missouri's top spot for trophy largemouths. It produced the state record in 1961.

The water systems of the White, Eleven Point, Current, Black, Gasconade, Meramec, and St. Francis Rivers are the major Ozark bass streams. The numerous springs of this region, coupled with vast areas of forest, make these waters ideal for smallmouth bass.

Float-trip fishing, which originated in the Missouri Ozarks at the turn of the century, is still popular. This unique method of going after fish attracts fishermen from everywhere. You can float for half a day or a week—and commercial guides will do all the paddling, campmaking, and cooking. But if you are an experienced river traveler, you can float the streams yourself. There are some twenty-five popular float streams in the Missouri Ozarks, and they're all cold and clear, curving and bent back on themselves. Rapids and "white water" give way to long, deep pools, and bold rock cliffs are succeeded by gently sloping gravel bars. The scenery equals any in the nation, and you can drift along at the current's speed all day long and still be near where you started that morning.

Where a number of boats constitute a large float-trip party, a "commissary" boat—loaded with camp and cooking gear—will accompany you. The commissary crew will have the lunch camp set up in advance of your arrival; at dusk, tents and overnight camp will be ready when fishing is done.

All the fisherman needs to bring along is his tackle. Outfitters usually supply the camp with equipment, food, and other essentials. The cost per person for a float trip averages about twenty-five dollars to sixty dollars per day, but for exact costs and information write to outfitters.

On the following major Ozark streams many such floats are conducted, or experienced fishermen float themselves: Beaver Creek, Big Piney River, Big River, Black River, Bourbeuse River, Bryant Creek, Courtois Creek, Crooked Creek, Current River, Dry Creek, Eleven Points River, Elk River, Flat Creek, Gasconade River, Huzzah Creek, Indian Creek, Jacks Fork, James River, Kings River, Long Creek, Meramec River, Niangua River, North Fork (White River), Osage Fork, Osage River, St. Francis River, Swan Creek, and White River.

The individual taking a float trip should keep the calendar in mind when making plans, so that appropriate clothing will be available. The weather will likely be rather cool at night during spring and fall months. Also, spring rains can suddenly roil rivers and make them unfishable.

More information is available from the Missouri Department of Conservation, Box 180, Jefferson City, MO 65102.

Nebraska

Nebraska, one of the drier plains states, is far from a great bass fishing state. Its still considerable bass water attracts comparatively few bass fishermen.

Many of the flood-control structures in eastern Nebraska have only a limited amount of quality largemouth bass fishing. The intense fishing pressure from the metro areas, and the deterioration of fish habitats, have taken their toll. However, good bass fishing in the western two thirds of the state can be found in Red Willow and Swanson, west of McCook; Valentine Wildlife Refuge Lakes, south of Valentine; and Calamus Reservoir, northwest of Burwell. There are many private ponds in Nebraska, but permission from the landowner is required in order to fish.

More information is available from the Nebraska Game and Parks Commission, 2200 North 33rd Street, P.O. Box 30370, Lincoln, NE 68503.

North Dakota

Bass fishing in this prairie state is very spotty and unpredictable. Nearly all waters are shallow and cold; they are subject to roiliness until late summer, and then to winterkill.

The following lakes either contain bass now, or have contained them in the past: Dickinson Reservoir, Heart Butte Reservoir, Welk Lake, Lake Elsie, and Sweetbriar Dam west of Bismarck; and the East and West Park Lakes north of Bismarck. Lake Nelson in Oliver County may be the most consistent for medium largemouths. Frequently no accommodations exist nearby.

More information is available from the North Dakota Game and Fish Department, 100 North Bismarck Expressway, Bismarck, ND 58505.

Ohio

It is hard to imagine, when passing through Ohio on high-speed turnpikes, that this is even a fair bass-fishing state. But success is considerable despite the most intensive farming, industrialization, and heavy population. There are over ten million resident fishermen.

Today there is ten times the amount of impounded water that existed originally, thanks to a network of lakes built for flood control, recreation, water supply, industrial supply, or a combination of these. A good network of rivers exists also, but far too many of these have been badly polluted.

Accommodations of all types exist on or very near every one of Ohio's public fishing lakes. Detailed maps of most (available from the Division of Wildlife) show underwater contours, stump areas, channels, locations of roads, docks, concessions, and launching sites. Listed in alphabetical order, the lakes are: Adams Lake, Adams County; Allen Lake, Hardin County; Atwood Lake, Carroll and Tuscarawas Counties; Bass Islands area, Ottawa County (among the best smallmouth areas in America). The best time is May or June, but fishing is good all summer; Put-in-Bay and Sandusky are centers of operations; Bellevue Reservoirs 1, 2, 3, and 4, Huron County; Bellevue Reservoir 5, Huron County; Berlin Reservoir, Stark, Mahoning, and Portage Counties; Blue Rock, Muskingum County; Brush Lake, Champaign County; Buckeye Lake, Fairfield, Perry, and Licking Counties (good in early spring); Burr Oak Lake, Morgan and Athens Counties; Caesar Creek, Warren and Clinton Counties; Caldwell and Stewart Hollow Lakes, Ross County; and Charles Mill Reservoir, Richland and Ashland Counties; Chippewa Lake, Medina County; Clearfork Reservoir, Morrow and Richland Counties; Clendening Lake, Harrison County; Clouse Lake, Perry County; Clyde City Reservoir, Sandusky County; and Cowan Lake, Clinton County.

Decker Lake, Miami County; Delaware Reservoir, Delaware County (good fishing and not too heavily fished by bass anglers); Delta Reservoirs 1 and 2, Fulton County; East Fork, Clermont County; East Harbor, Ottawa County (excellent in May but slumps later); Findlay Reservoirs 1 and 2, Hancock County; Forked Run Lake, Meigs County; Grant Lake, Brown County; Griggs Reservoir, Franklin County; Guilford Lake, Colum-

Kirby Stanforth hefts one of many big bass taken from Midwest farm ponds every year.

biana County; Hargus Lake, Pickaway County; Harrison Lake, Fulton County; Hoover Reservoir, Franklin and Delaware Counties; Hope Lake, Vinton County (a good camping area); Indian Lake, Logan County (good in April and May); Jackson Lake, Jackson County; Jefferson Lake, Jefferson County; Kelley's Island area, Erie County.

Kiser Lake, Champaign County; Knox Lake, Knox County; Lake Park, Mahoning County; Leesville Lake, Carroll County; Loramie Lake, Shelby and Auglaize Counties; Lost Creek Reservoir, Al-

len County; Madison Lake, Madison County; Metzger Lake, Allen County; Milton Lake, Mahoning County; Mogadore Reservoir, Portage County; Mosquito Reservoir, Trumbull County (excellent spring bass fishing in large stump areas); Mount Gilead Lakes, Morrow County; Nettle Lake, Williams County; Nimisila Reservoir, Summit County; O'Shaughnessy Reservoir, Delaware County; Oxbow Lake, Defiance County; Paint Creek Lake, Highland County; Piedmont Lake, Belmont, Guernsey, and Harrison Counties; Pleas-

Spring in the Shallows

The western basin of Lake Erie, billed as the walleye capital of the world, comes closer to being the smallmouth capital in May. That's when gangs of smallmouth bass move to shallow water and feed ravenously prior to spawning.

My wife Debbi and I enjoyed Lake Erie's springtime smallmouth fishing once as a guest of Rick LaCourse, who charters his Formula 4 out of West Catawba Marina. Also along were Ottie and Vicki Snyder, fishing friends from Columbus, Ohio, who had instigated the outing. The cold, rainy weather didn't dampen our spirits, especially when LaCourse told us that his party had landed more than eighty smallmouths weighing one to four pounds just the day before.

After boating to one of the Bass Islands, LaCourse idled his twenty-seven-foot cruiser upwind of a reef that extended south from the shoreline.

As we cast and retrieved jigs with profound anticipation, I turned to my friends. "Any bets on who'll catch the first . . ."

"Got one!" shouted Vicki. Her ultralight spinning rod bowed violently. Before I could begin to feel grateful for not placing a first-fish bet, a smallmouth belted my jig.

Moments later, both bass were beating a tattoo on the deck. They weighed about one and a half pounds each, typical Erie smallmouths. Their colors were rich brown, and their bodies were thick and heavy—unlike the lean smallmouths of the streams. We ended the day with fifteen bass all weighing between one and three and a half pounds. That would have made an excellent catch in most smallmouth waters, but was only a mediocre showing for Lake Erie in the spring.

—Mark Hicks

---

ant Hill Reservoir, Richland and Ashland Counties; Portage Lakes, Summit County; Punderson Lake, Geauga County; Pymatuning Reservoir, Ashtabula County; Richwood Lake, Union County; Rocky Fork Lake, Highland County; Ross Lake, Ross County.

Sandusky Bay area, Ottawa, Erie, and Sandusky Counties; Schoonover Lake, Allen County; Seneca Lake, Guernsey and Noble Counties; Spring Valley, Greene and Warren Counties; St. Mary's Lake, Mercer County; Stonelick Lake, Clermont County; Tappan Lake, Harrison County; Van Buren Lake, Hancock County; Van Wert Reservoirs 1 and 2, Van Wert County; Vesuvius Lake, Lawrence County; Veto Lake, Washington County; Lake White, Pike County; and Zepernick Lake, Columbiana County.

Ohio's best bass streams include the following: in northwestern Ohio, Maumee River (especially Maumee Rapids above the Toledo area) for smallmouths; Tiffin, Auglaize, and Blanchard Rivers, Sandusky River from Old Fort to Upper Sandusky, Huron and Vermilion Rivers, near Norwalk, in early spring; in northeastern Ohio, the Grand River, Ashtabula County, and the Chagrin in Geauga County. The Grand can be float-tripped.

Central Ohio is probably Ohio's best region for stream smallmouth fishing. Good waters include the Scioto River north of Columbus, Big and Little Darby, Big Walnut, Whetstone, Deer, and Blacklick Creeks; also the Olentangy and Licking Rivers. The Kokosing and Mohican are possible float-trip rivers, with a few campsites along the way.

In southeastern Ohio the Muskingum River, plus the tributary Wills Creek, and Tuscarawas and Walhonding Rivers, have bass fishing. Add also Leading Creek and Shade River, in Meigs County; Symmes and Indian Guyan Creeks, in Lawrence County; Hocking River, above Athens. In southwestern Ohio the best bets are Stonelick Creek, East Fork of the Little Miami River, Todd Fork, White Oak Creek, Caesar Creek, Rattlesnake Creek, Compton Creek, Rocky Fork Creek below Rocky Fork Lake, Sunfish Creek (for spotted bass) in Pike County, and Paint Creek.

The Ohio River, which borders southeast and southern Ohio, offers good fishing for largemouth and spotted bass with some smallmouths in addition.

More information is available from the Ohio Division of Wildlife, Fountain Square, Columbus, OH 43225.

South Dakota

Although South Dakota is not known as a great bass-fishing state, largemouths have been stocked and distributed statewide, and smallmouths have been stocked in selected waters. The better largemouth waters are the many small public lakes and private stock dams of the western and central regions of the state. Some of the larger lakes include Angostura (good for largemouths and smallmouths), Newell, Durkee, Owen, Lemon State Lake, and Curlew. Shade Hill and Orman Dam offer moderately good smallmouth fishing.

One of the best smallmouth and largemouth bass fisheries is 35,000-acre Lake Lewis and Clark in southeast South Dakota at Fort Randall. Other bass lakes in the region include Lake Vermillion and Lake Carthage, and, in the northeast, Big Stone Lake (a border lake between South Dakota and Minnesota), Clear Lake, Pickerel Lake, Mina Lake, Richmond Lake, and Elm Lake.

Smallmouths are being stocked into the massive reservoirs of the Missouri River system. They appear to be doing well and may provide a viable fishery in the future.

More information is available from the South Dakota Game, Fish, and Parks Department, 445 East Capitol, Pierre, SD 57501.

Wisconsin

Any bass angler lucky enough to find himself in Wisconsin will see a beautiful state full of pine, balsam, and birch trees; it contains 14,927 lakes and enough waterways to stretch around the earth. Bass swim almost everywhere.

There are all kinds of lakes—deep ones like Big Green, which drops off to 236 feet; big ones like Winnebago, with its 137,708 surface acres; small, clear "kettle" lakes located in terminal moraines; and lakes with rocky shorelines and gravel bottoms. Maps showing size, depths, bars, weedbeds, and principal roads are available for about 800 lakes. They can be obtained from the Department of Natural Resources and are certainly worthwhile.

Many of Wisconsin's wonderful streams are great for float tripping. The Chippewa is excellent, as is the entire Chippewa Flowage-Hayward lakes region. So are the Flambeau, the Wisconsin, the Fox, Wolf, Black, St. Croix, and the Namakagon. Autumn floating may mean carrying across shallow riffles, but it is a productive, magnificent experience when the weather and the color are at their best. The Mississippi River from La Crosse to Red Wing, Minnesota, also makes outstanding bass water.

For large smallmouths, anglers might consider the lower Wisconsin River above Prairie du Chien. But better by far are the Door Peninsula and Washington Island. Lake Michigan and Green Bay waters here are good in spring and again in October. The biggest largemouths seem to be in the backwater sloughs of the Mississippi, pools 7, 8, and 9.

Northern Wisconsin counties with the greatest number of good bass lakes include Ashland, Barron, Bayfield, Burnett, Chippewa, Dane, Douglas, Florence, Fond du Lac, Forest, Iron, Juneau, Langlade, Lincoln, Marathon, Marinette, Marquette, Oconto, Oneida, Polk, Portage, Price, Rusk, St. Croix, Sawyer, Sheboygan, Taylor, and Vilas.

More information is available from the Wisconsin Department of Natural Resources, Box 7921, Madison, WI 53707.

Chapter 13

The Northeast

Half the sportsmen of America live in this small region, and not one with a fishing license is very far from fair bass-fishing waters. That is even true for residents of Long Island, Philadelphia, or Baltimore. Most waters of the East are heavily fished, of course, but a good bass fisherman can still stir up enough action to make a fishing trip worthwhile.

Not all waters of the East are heavily fished, though; remote waters still remain in parts of New York, Pennsylvania, and New England. A few streams, especially, are not subject to heavy pressure at all—and a serious bass angler should concentrate on these places.

Connecticut

Although it is extremely crowded, Connecticut does have bass-fishing opportunities. Pollution has hurt bass populations in some streams, however.

A fairly complete list of the best bass-fishing waters includes the following: Wood Creek Pond and Toby Pond, near Norfolk; Wononkapook Pond, South of Wononskopomuc, and Mudge Pond (for largemouths), below Wononkapook, in the Berkshires; Tyler Pond, west of Goshen; Spectacle Lakes and Hatch Pond, east of Kent; Lake Waramaug, near New Preston; Bantam Lake, between Bantam and Lakeside; Winnemaug Lake, near Watertown; Candlewood Lake (the largest in the state with over 5,000 acres), near Brookfield; Lake Zoar, at Sheldon; Trumbull Reservoir, near Bridgeport; Black Pond and Beseck Lake, near Meriden; Cedar Swamp Pond, south of Bristol; Highland Lake, southwest of Winsted; Shenipsit Lake, between Tolland and Ellington; Bolton Notch Pond and Willimantic Reservoir, near Bolton; Wamgumbaug Lake and Columbia Lake, near Willimantic; the group of ponds north of Colchester; Terramuggus and Pocotopaug Lakes, above East Hampton; Shaw Lake, Pickerel Lake, Bashan Lake, and Moodus Reservoir, near Hartford; Gardner's Lake, west of Norwich; Powers, Pataganset, and Rogers Lakes; Mashapaug, northeast of Stafford Springs; Roseland and Alexander Lakes, near Putnam; Quicksick Reservoir; and Long Pond, between Old Mystic and North Stonington.

More information is available from the Connecticut Bureau of Fisheries, 255 State Office Building, Hartford, CT 06106.

Delaware

Delaware has only a limited amount of bass fishing. The state owns twenty-eight public ponds that con-

Despite cold winters, good bass fishing can be found in the Northeast.

tain bass, and a number of privately owned ponds are open to varying degrees. Also worthwhile are the Nanticoke River, especially the upper reaches between Seaford and Woodland, for largemouths; Noxontown Pond near Middletown, where state record largemouth bass have been taken; and the Milford chain of lakes. The Maryland section of this chapter describes the ponds of the Delmarva Peninsula.

More information is available from the Delaware Division of Wildlife, 89 Kings Highway, P.O. Box 1401, Dover, DE 19903.

Maine

Half a century ago there were no bass in Maine, but smallmouths and largemouths are now well established in over five hundred lakes. They're more than established: Maine must rank with the best smallmouth fishing regions in America today. Not only are the bronzebacks plentiful, but also a few six-pounders are taken each year to add a flavor of trophy collecting. Maine's bass retain a large average size despite the state's northern climate.

Bass fishing here begins in June, is excellent all through the month, and, although it falls off, remains fairly good all through the summer. Those who enjoy casting bugs with a fly rod will find premium fishing in early June. Live bait and artificial lures work well throughout the season. In August, trolling is often very successful.

Sebago, the second largest lake in Maine, is the center of the Sebago Lake, Long Lake, and Oxford County region that encompasses a great part of southern Maine. During the summer there is fine bass fishing here.

To the north, connected to Sebago by the beautiful Songo River, is Long Lake. In the same region are Brandy Pond, Highland Lake, Woods Pond, Crystal Lake, Thomas Pond, Lake Pennesseewassee, and Moose Pond. A few miles to the west of Sebago is Peabody Pond and Hancock Pond. Toward the east lies Panther Pond and Little Sebago. Toward the northwest beautiful Lake Kezar, a jewel of a lake, nestles in the foothills of the White Mountains. South of Sebago, in York County, lie Bunganut, Crystal, Kennebunk, and Mousam Lakes.

The Kennebec lakes region furnishes excellent smallmouth-bass fishing in the spring. It includes Cobbosseecontee, Maranacook, Little Cobbosseecontee, and Annabessacook Lakes. Nearby, near Wayne, are Androscoggin and Pocasset Lakes. A long chain of smaller lakes affording very fine bass fishing extends through the towns of Readfield, Fayette, and Mount Vernon.

Big Lake, near Princeton; St. Croix River, also near Princeton; East Grand Lake, near Forrest City; Spednick Lake, also near Forrest City; and Pocimoonshine Lake, near Alexander, all have good smallmouth-bass fishing.

It cannot be overemphasized how well suited Maine is for handling the visiting bass fisherman. For example, there are over 3,000 skilled guides available, license fees are reasonable, and the country is very beautiful.

More information is available from the Maine Department of Inland Fisheries and Wildlife, 284 State Street, State House Station 41, Augusta, ME 04333.

Maryland

Maryland comes under great fishing pressure, but still contains fair bass waters. The Potomac, which flows from Hancock to Washington, D.C., is one of the premier smallmouth bass fisheries in the East, including the area from Cumberland to Great Falls near Washington, D.C. The following rivers also contain smallmouths: Casselman River, near Grantsville; Beaver Creek (lower section), near Hagerstown; Octoraro Creek, near Richardsmere; and Deer Creek, in Harford County.

Maryland's principal bass lakes include Liberty Reservoir, in north-central Maryland, which contains large bass but does not allow outboards. Deep Creek Lake, 3,900 acres near Thayersville, has a good bass population. So do Herrington Lake, near Oakland; Tridelphia Reservoir, near Brighton; Pretty Boy Reservoir, near Hereford; Loch Raven Reservoir, near Towson; Conowingo Dam, near Conowingo; Garland Lake, near Denton; Smithville Lake, near Smithville; Wye Pond, near Wye Mills; St. Mary's, near Calloway.

Also, on the Delmarva Peninsula (which separates Chesapeake Bay from the Atlantic and which includes parts of Delaware and Virginia as well as Maryland) are about fifty ponds, which can be public, semiprivate, or private. Most offer fair to good bass fishing in settings with a Southern accent. Motors are not allowed on most of these ponds, but boats are available for rent on a few.

Excellent largemouth fishing can be found in the freshwater portions of the tidal rivers that empty into Chesapeake Bay. The Potomac is consistently the best from Washington, D.C., on down, but the Susquehanna and Elk Rivers also have good fishing.

More information is available from the Maryland Department of Natural Resources, Recreational Fisheries Division, Tawes State Office Building, Annapolis, MD 21401.

Massachusetts

Massachusetts is another densely populated state. The best fishing often is in privately owned ponds, many of which can be entered by contacting the owner and/or paying a small fee. Most major rivers offer excellent bass fishing. The best bass lake with both largemouths and smallmouths is 25,000-acre Quabbin Reservoir, near Hardwick.

Berkshire County has much of the state's bass water. The best spots are Lake Potoosuc and Richmond Pond. Other bass waters include: Hoosac Reservoir; Garfield Lake, east of Great Barrington; Otis Reservoir and Big Pond, just to the north;

Lake Mahkeenac; Greenwater, Yokum, Center, and Goose Ponds, southeast of Lee; Ashmere Lake, near Dalton; Burnett Pond, east of Adams; Lake Wickapoag and other small ponds in Worcester County; Quinsigamond Lake, near Worcester; and the ponds of Myles Standish State Forest near Plymouth.

Also try Cheshire Reservoir, near Cheshire (largemouths); Mashpee-Wakeby Pond, near Mashpee (smallmouths); Congamond Lake, near Southwick (largemouths and smallmouths); Quaboag Pond, near Brookfield (largemouths); Concord River, between Concord and Billerica (largemouths); Monponsett Lakes, near Bridgewater (largemouths); and Long Pond, near Lakeville (smallmouths).

The Charles, Merrimack, and Connecticut Rivers are also highly regarded.

More information is available from the Massachusetts Division of Fisheries and Game, 100 Cambridge Street, Boston, MA 02202.

New Hampshire

Cool, green, and beautiful, New Hampshire's lofty mountains, rolling hills, valleys, and pasturelands form a scenic setting for a hundred lakes and bass ponds, plus miles of brooks and rivers. Deep forests of mixed conifers and hardwoods help to condition both air and water, maintaining good temperatures for fishing.

In the White Mountains zone, the Connecticut River along the western boundary has smallmouths. So do Armington Lake, near Piermont; Upper and Lower Baker Ponds, near Orford; Burns Pond, near Whitefield; and Tarleton Lake, near Piermont.

Stretching across the state, just south of the White Mountains, lies a belt of lakes and ponds from Sunapee and Mascoma on the west, to Ossipee and Province Lake on the east. The four largest lakes in this section—Winnisquam, Sunapee, Winnipesaukee, and Squam—all have bass.

The following bass waters lie in the central part of the state: Blaisdell Lake, Bradley Lake, Cooks Pond, Crescent Lake, Crystal Lake, Grafton Pond, Great East Lake, Guiena Pond, Halfmoon Lake, Highland Lake, Kanasatka Lake, Kezar Lake, Knights Pond, Knowles Pond, Kolemook Lake, Kusumpe Pond, Lovell Lake, Mirror Lake, Perkins Pond, Places Pond (Sunset Lake), Post Pond, Province Lake, Rust Pond, Silver Lake, Waukewan Lake, Webster Lake, Whitton Pond, Wickwas Pond, and Winona Lake.

Southern New Hampshire bass waters include: Ashuelot Pond, Ayers Pond, Beaver Lake, Bow Lake, Chesham Pond, Cole Pond (Crescent Lake), Connecticut River (lower part), Contoocook Lake, Contoocook River, Country Pond, Crooked Pond, Frost Pond, Gilmore Pond, Gould Pond, Gregg Lake, Halfmoon Pond, Harvey Lake, Haunted Lake, Highland Lake, Hubbard Pond, Hunts Pond, Island Pond (near Atkinson), Island Pond (near Washington), Jenness Pond, Massabesic Lake, Massasecum Lake, Mendums Pond, Merrimack River, North River Pond, Northwood Lake, Norway Pond, Otter Lake, Pawtuckaway Lake, Phillips Pond, Pleasant Pond, Robinson Pond, Shattuck Pond, Spofford Lake, Suncook Lakes, Thorndike Pond, Willard Pond, Willey Ponds, and Winnipocket Lake.

New waters include Baxter Lake in Rochester (for smallmouth and largemouth bass) and Forest Lake in Whitefield.

More information is available from the New Hampshire Fish and Game Department, 34 Bridge St., Concord, NH 03301.

New Jersey

Through the years, because of a high and always expanding population, New Jersey has been in the unenviable position of squeezing the most from every acre or foot of inland fishing water. Most of its ponds and lakes are likely to have as many fishermen as fish. Still, a good bass angler can find sport here by trying new methods and new lures, and often by fishing at night.

The largest natural lake in the state is Hopatcong, a few miles northwest of Dover. Cottages, resorts, and docks virtually consume its entire forty-mile shoreline. But several eight-pound bass have been taken, mostly after dark.

Most of Jersey's lakes and ponds are located in Sussex, Morris, Warren, and Passaic Counties, much of this land being state-owned. Some highly rated bass waters include Budd Lake in Morris County, Greenwood Lake near Browns in Passaic County, Allamuchy and Columbia Ponds in Warren County; and Lake Musconetcong, Hainesville Pond, Thunder Mountain Lake, and Swartwood, all in Sussex County.

Smallmouth bass are established in many New England lakes and furnish fast action in springtime.

Three major new reservoirs—Monksville Reservoir in Passaic County; Merrill Creek Reservoir in Warren County; and Manasquan Reservoir in Monmouth County—will be available for public angling in 1988, 1989, and 1992, respectively. All are expected to provide excellent bass fishing.

Smallmouth bass fishing in the Delaware River starts just upstream from Trenton and extends on up the river to New York State. There is also good smallmouth bass fishing in the Raritan River Drainage (North Branch of the Raritan, South Branch of the Raritan, Neshanic River, and the Millstone River).

In the southern half of the state, most of the rivers draining into the Atlantic Ocean do not contain bass. A wide area of southern Jersey, known as "the Pinelands," is characterized by naturally acidic waters which cannot support bass. Only when you get to the extreme southern portion of the state (from about Atlantic City south), or the western edge of the state, do you get out of the Pinelands and into suitable bass waters again. Some of the southern streams draining into the Delaware

Fishing the Hudson Tide

I wasn't sure what to expect when I launched my bass boat a few years ago on the Hudson River at Catskill, New York. I had never thought of New York as a bass fisherman's state, and certainly wouldn't have guessed that the Hudson River, which eventually cuts through the heart of grimy New York City, would be worth fishing. To complicate matters, the Hudson is a tidal river and the water level fluctuates daily about four feet. Weeds that would be submerged at high tide may be high and dry at low tide.

I was fortunate to have a navigation map marked out for me by a friend who knows the river, pointing out a number of spots where he had caught bass. All the places he marked had notations such as "fish during falling tide," "best on rising tide," and "good low tide spot." The key to fishing the Hudson, my friend had told me, is to be at the right spot during the right tide situation for that particular location.

I had obviously launched my boat during a falling tide, because a strong current was pushing downstream. I checked my map and found a "good falling tide spot" that in this case proved to be a nearby navigation light. The light stood on a mound about thirty feet in diameter which was composed of large riprap boulders. A shallow flat bordered one side of the mound, while the other side dropped into the deeper water of the main river channel. The falling tide rushed around the mound, creating an eddy of slack water behind it.

I cast a jig with a pork rind trailer into the current and let it wash into the eddy. I was sure that my lure would hang up in the rocks, but a two-pound smallmouth pounced on the jig before it hit bottom. I landed the bass and caught a three-pound largemouth on my next cast. I stayed in that one spot and caught eight bass, smallmouths and largemouths, almost as fast as I could hook and land them. Then the action stopped dead.

I tried other places my friend had marked, doing my best to hit them at the proper tide level. If I timed it right, I caught bass. If I was too early or late, I got little or no action. None of the spots produced as well as the first, but I did catch about twenty-five bass that day, including a few four-pound largemouths. When I returned to the launch ramp, I knew beyond a doubt that New York does offer good bass fishing.

—Mark Hicks

River and Delaware Bay do have bass populations, but none are well known for them.

More information is available from the New Jersey Division of Fish, Game, and Wildlife, CN-400, Trenton, NJ 08625.

New York

New York is a picturesque state for fishing, whether in the glens and tilled valleys of the Finger Lakes region, the green and blue Thousand Islands, or the cool and lonely Adirondacks. There is bass-fishing variety here, and an abundance of water, but competition for it is sometimes keen.

Close to New York City, there is some bass fishing in the Catskills. Smallmouths can be had in the Delaware River, from Deposit to Port Jervis. The lower east branch of the Delaware has bass, and so does the lower Neversink River. The Susquehanna River, a little west of the Catskills, is also very good for smallmouths, especially for float trips. The Hudson River has excellent fishing for largemouths and some smallmouths up to the Albany area as far as the Troy Dam. North of that, a section of the river is closed to fishing because of contamination.

The Adirondack highlands include some lakes and ponds containing bass. Lake Champlain has largemouths, in addition to better-than-average smallmouth fishing. Lake George is very good for smallmouths and has trophy bass. Above Riparius is Schroon Lake with smallmouths. There is scattered smallmouth fishing in the Saranac Lakes region.

The St. Lawrence Valley contains some of the best smallmouth waters in the East. Fishing is fastest in the Thousand Islands area and then westward into Lake Ontario beyond Cape Vincent. Watertown, Alexandria Bay, and Clayton are access points to the Thousand Islands. Good smallmouth and largemouth fishing exists in Black Lake. For smallmouths consider the Indian, Oswegatchie, Grass, and Raquette rivers, near Massena; the St. Regis, near Hogansburg; the Salmon, near Malone; and Chazy River, which flows into Lake Champlain.

Western New York has bass waters too. Lake Ontario and Lake Erie teem with smallmouths; the bass in Lake Erie generally run larger and receive less fishing pressure. Also good are the Finger Lakes: Skaneateles, Otisco, Owasco, Cayuga, Seneca, Keuka, Canadaigua, and Honeoye.

Lake Oneida near Oneida has excellent smallmouth fishing, and Delta Reservoir near Rome has bass. Otsego Lake at Cooperstown is good for smallmouths in late fall.

The Niagara River, from Buffalo past Niagara Falls to Lake Ontario, is good for smallmouths. Chautauqua Lake has both largemouths and smallmouths. River anglers in western New York frequent the Allegheny, near Olean and Salamanca; and the Tioga, Canisteo, and Cohocton, in the general vicinity of Corning. The Genesee is a good bass river in Allegheny County; float tripping is possible.

More information is available from the New York Division of Fish and Wildlife, 50 Wolf Road, Albany, NY 12233.

Pennsylvania

By any standards Pennsylvania is a fine bass-fishing state. Though suburban development, industrial expansion, and pollution have damaged or completely destroyed many waters, a bass fisherman can still find much pure water. And the pollution picture shows some signs of improvement.

Pennsylvania has picturesque bass rivers excellent for float tripping. Consider, for example, typical three-day floats on four rivers—the Allegheny, the Juniata, the North Branch of the Susquehanna, and the Delaware—which any basser can make.

The Allegheny trip begins at Warren, with a first night's camp at Tidioute. President is a good place to camp the second night. The trip ends at Franklin, about sixty-six miles downstream. There is good smallmouth fishing all the way.

The Juniata trip begins at Ryde, above Lewistown, and runs downstream to Granville for the first night's camp. Muskrat Springs near Mexico is fine for a second camp, and during the second day's run you will find some of the hottest bass fishing in the state. The float ends at Amity Hall.

The Susquehanna River winds alternately through fertile farm country and between high palisades that make it accessible for long stretches only by boat. A three-day North Branch trip can begin at Sayre, with a first-night stopover at Towanda. The second-night camp can be at Wyalusing. The trip concludes at Mehoopany.

A typical Delaware River float trip begins at Tighe's Boat Livery above Narrowsburg. The first and second night's camp can be made at Masthope and Pond Eddy. The trip ends near Milford.

Even in a lifetime of fishing, a fisherman couldn't adequately explore all the tributaries of these four float-trip rivers. In many cases, the tributaries have even better-looking bass waters than the main streams. One specific example is the Raystown Branch of the Juniata, which would excite any bass fisherman in the world. It's about fifty airline miles from Bedford (on the Pennsylvania Turnpike) to Huntington, but it must be at least three times that mileage because of stream meandering.

Pennsylvania's best bass lake is Raystown Lake, an 8,300-acre impoundment in Huntingdon County, which has an abundance of structure under the surface. Other worthwhile spots are Pymatuning and Allegheny Reservoirs, in the northwest; Beaver Run, Loyalhanna, and Conemaugh Reservoirs, east of Pittsburgh; and Shenango Reservoir, near Sharon.

More information is available from the Pennsylvania Fish Commission, Box 1673, Harrisburg, PA 17105-1673.

Rhode Island

Rhode Island has very limited bass fishing. The best is available in small ponds, where permission to fish must be obtained. There are a few "company" ponds and reservoirs built primarily for power- or water-supply purposes. Nearly all of these are open to fishing too.

One spot warrants special mention: 1,040-acre Worden Pond. It is a bowl-shaped natural lake no more than six and a half feet deep, often murky, devoid of the structures bass fishermen seek. But it can be a hot spot, especially in springtime.

More information is available from the Rhode Island Division of Fish and Wildlife, Government Center, Tower Hill Road, Wakefield, RI 02879.

Vermont

Scenically attractive Vermont contains good bass fishing in spite of its proximity to the eastern centers of population. In fact, thousands of out-of-state anglers invade it every year, and many of them have at least fair success. A bass fisherman's best bet is in early October, when the smallmouths seem to be most active. There is little fishing pressure then, and the color and atmosphere of autumn are magnificent.

Some of the best Vermont fishing is in border waters: Lake Champlain to the west and the Con-

necticut River to the east. Both have smallmouths. The Missisquoi River, from Richford to Swanton, has smallmouths, and below Swanton, largemouths begin to appear. Lake Carmi, east of Franklin, and Fairfield Pond, northeast of St. Albans, also have bass.

Also note these waters for bass, mostly smallmouths: the lower reaches of the Lamoille, White, Black, and Winooski Rivers; Hosmer Ponds, near Lowell; Seymour Lake, near Morgan; Moore Reservoir on the Connecticut River; Fairlee and Morey Lakes, near Ely; the West River, between West Dummerston and Brattleboro; and Little Otter Creek, near Lake Champlain. Bomoseen, Hortonia, and St. Catherine Lakes, in Rutland County, have mainly largemouths and some smallmouths.

More information is available from the Vermont Fish and Wildlife Department, 103 South Main Street, Waterbury, VT 05676.

Chapter 14

The Southwest

Traditionally an arid region, the southwest is impossible to drive very far through today without encountering an abundance of boats and trailers. There are two reasons: Many giant reservoirs were built during the past half century, and all of them have good fishing. And although nothing like these lakes ever existed in the original bass range, largemouths thrive in nearly all these waters. Bass fishing, in fact, is extremely good.

Arizona

Arizona's bass fishing is centered around two major areas: the Salt and Colorado River Lakes, and four individual lakes—Carl Pleasant, San Carlos, Bartlett, and Horseshoe.

The Salt River chain of lakes in east-central Arizona is formed by a series of dams on the Salt River. Starting at Phoenix and going east, the lakes are: Saguaro, Canyon, Apache, and Roosevelt. Boats and camping facilities are available at all of them. Roosevelt is considered to be the best producer of large bass, with Apache (a smallmouth lake) second. Canyon and Saguaro have become playgrounds for water-sports enthusiasts, but manage to produce a good many largemouths.

The Colorado River Lakes begin at the lower end of the Grand Canyon, where Hoover (Boulder) Dam forms the largest and most famous, Lake Mead, at Boulder City. The bass fishing at Lake Mead is well known. The next lake downstream, Lake Mohave, has the distinction of being excellent for both black bass and rainbow trout. Toward the lower end of the lake the water is not so cold, and boasts the best fishing for bass.

Between Lakes Mohave and Havasu is a swampy area where the river meanders and forms a large pool of shallow fishing water. Topock Swamp produces very good bass fishing, although the water supply to it is somewhat uncertain. Lake Havasu itself is an excellent bass producer.

Between Lake Havasu and Imperial Dam near Yuma a number of small lakes, not well known, furnish good bass fishing. These include Cibola, Ferguson, and Martinez Lakes. The final lake on the river is Mittry Lake, just outside Yuma.

Alamo Lake in western Arizona has produced many largemouths of modest size. Black River has fishing for small smallmouth bass.

The Verde River, which flows southward through central Arizona, connects two lakes: Horseshoe, to the north, and Bartlett. These two lakes furnish some fair to very good fishing. The Verde River, which joins the Salt below the dams, has smallmouth-bass fishing. The combined flow of

$1,000 a Pound

Professional bass angler Greg Hines is intimately familiar with Lake Mead and has enjoyed many exciting outings there. His most memorable experience took place while competing in the U.S. Open in 1981, the first bass tournament to award $50,000 to the winner.

A sweltering heat wave engulfed the region during the tournament, taking its toll on the competitors with midday temperatures climbing as high as 118°. The air already was warm and sticky at dawn as Hines sped forty miles across the lake on the first day of the tournament. His boat moved through the shadows of sheer canyon bluffs and past barren, rocky shorelines and old lava flows before he finally reached his destination, a series of long underwater points on an open area of the lake.

The points reached out nearly one hundred yards from shore, and Hines could see submerged trees, rock piles, and ledges through the crystalline green water more than thirty feet deep. He picked up a six-and-a-half-foot baitcasting rod and flung a Zara Spook far out over the point. The long rod and the heavy plug made for easy distance casting, which was necessary to prevent his alerting the bass.

Hines let the Spook set for a moment and then began the side-to-side sashay known as walking the dog. He would work the lure a few feet and then let it rest momentarily, giving the bass time to react.

Hines saw the first bass shoot up from a submerged tree twenty feet deep, and home in on his Spook like a torpedo. The fish blasted the plug at full tilt, knocking it clear out of the water, but failed to engulf the hooks. Hines continued fishing, his hands somewhat unsteady from the encounter.

The next bass also shot up from the depths, but was more leery than the first and stopped just short of the offering to inspect it. Hines coolly twitched the lure and the bass nailed it. By the end of the first day, Hines—fishing topwater—had caught twenty-five to thirty bass and had culled a tournament limit of five fish that weighed a total of nearly fifteen pounds. When the four-day event was over, Hines and his Spook had amassed nearly fifty pounds of bass—good enough for first place and $50,000.

Although the largest fish that Hines caught during the tournament was only about three and a half pounds, his topwater lures have hooked many bigger fish on Lake Mead, including bass of more than seven pounds.

—Mark Hicks

---

the Verde and Salt rivers furnishes several more miles of fishing. North and west of Phoenix lie Lake Carl Pleasant and Frog Tanks; the former produces some good largemouth fishing from time to time.

More information is available from the Arizona Game and Fish Department, 2222 West Greenway, Phoenix, AZ 85023.

Colorado

Although primarily a trout state, Colorado's bass fishing has increased in popularity and in quality over the past decade. Over 100,000 six-inch bass fingerlings are stocked within state waters each year, mainly east of the Rockies and in selected waters in southwest Colorado.

In the northeast region, Stalker Lake, near Wray, is good for big bass and produced the current state record of ten pounds, six ounces. Also try Bonny Reservoir in Yuma County. Four bass reservoirs near Lamar in the southeastern section include the Upper and Lower Queens, Nee Noshe, and John Martin Reservoirs. Other waters that offer quality bass fishing are Rifle Gap Reservoir in the northwest region; Chatfield Reservoir, near Denver; and Horseshoe Reservoir, near Fort Collins.

The top smallmouth bass lake in the state is Pueblo Reservoir, near Pueblo. McPhee Reservoir,

Cochiti Lake, north of Albuquerque, New Mexico, often produces large bass.

a new lake, should yield good smallmouth bass fishing north of Cortez.

More information is available from the Colorado Division of Wildlife, 6060 Broadway, Denver, CO 80216.

New Mexico

Bass fishing for largemouth and smallmouth is possible in New Mexico year-round.

Conchas, one of the biggest lakes, is stocked with bass, as are Alamogordo Lake and Elephant Butte Lake. Bear Canyon Lake has trout as well as bass. Bass live in the small, deep lakes near Santa Rosa, and in Red Bluff Lake. Other lakes for fair to good bass fishing are Avalon, Bitter, Bottomless, Caballo, Jackson, and Six-mile Lakes. Cochiti Lake, north of Albuquerque, and Navajo Lake often produce large bass.

The Pecos River contains bass from McMillan Dam south; the lower Pecos River is generally good. Berrendo and Hondo Creeks and Felix River, all in the Pecos Valley, have or have had bass.

The lower Rio Grande and the drainage canals near Las Cruces and Socorro and south of Belen have limited fishing.

Boats are available at Elephant Butte, Caballo, and Conchas Lakes and at several of the following bass waters: Alamogordo Lake, Avalon Lake, Bass Lake, Bitter Lake, Bottomless Lake, Caballo Lake, Calley Lake, Chain Lakes, Conchas Lake, Dosher Lake, Elephant Butte Lake, El Paso Lakes, Fin and Feather Lake, Harroun Dam, Harroun Lake, Hidden Lake, Pasamonte Lake, Power Dam Lake, Railroad Reservoirs, Red Bluff Lake, Red Lake (Navajo Reservation), Rio Grande Beach Lake, Zuni Reservoir, Belen-Riverside Drain (Los Lunas South), Belen-Riverside Drain (Los Lunas North), Berrendo Creek (tributary to Lower Pecos), Black River (tributary to Lower Pecos), Bosque del Apache Drains (tributary to Rio Grande), Conejo Creek (tributary to Pecos River), Del Rio Drain (tributary to Rio Grande), East Drain (tributary to Rio Grande), Felix River (tributary to Pecos River), Gila River (L) (tributary to Little Colorado), Isleta Drain (tributary to Rio Grande), La Mesa Drain (tributary to Pecos River), Mora River (tributary to Canadian River), Nemexas Drain (tributary to Rio Grande), Pecos River, and Penasco River (tributary to Pecos River).

The Navajo and Abiquiu Reservoirs are primarily smallmouth bass waters and offer excellent fishing.

Bass pro Joe Thomas hauls aboard a largemouth bass at a Texas impoundment.

The Gila River (lower) and Elephant Butte, Caballo, Cochiti, McMillan, Sumner, Conchas, Los Esteros, and Bear Canyon Lakes also contain fishable populations of smallmouth bass.

More information is available from the New Mexico Department of Fish and Game, Villagra Building, Santa Fe, NM 87503.

Texas

Texans like to brag about their great bass fishing, but they rarely agree on which bass waters are best. Although this also was a relatively waterless state originally, it now has fairly well scattered large reservoirs from border to border. More than likely there is more bass water here than anywhere else.

The biggest and probably the best bass lake is Toledo Bend, in the extreme east, with over 186,000 acres of flooded timber and other cover for largemouth bass. Quite possibly this is the best bass producer in the world. Vast, alligator-shaped Sam Rayburn Lake, not far away and similar, also offers splendid bass fishing in superstructure. Another of the giant reservoirs is Amistad, formed by Falcon Dam on the Rio Grande near Laredo. Although remotely located, it makes a red-hot bass lake year-round. A poll of Texas pro bass anglers reveals that in addition to the above three, the best bass lakes are Dow, near Freeport; Texoma, on the Oklahoma border; Lake of the Pines; Lake Belton; Mathis, near Corpus Christi; and Whitney, near Dallas.

Some river bass fishing exists in Texas, the best of it centered in the eastern part of the state. Bass are available in oxbows of the Red River and in the Sulphur River, west of Texarkana. Half of Caddo Lake rests in Texas, northeast of Marshall. Fully as good is Black Cypress Bayou, which meanders into the lake from near Jefferson.

Much fishing is found in the waters of Davy Crockett, Angelina, and Sam Houston Forests. The Big Thicket is a region of dense vegetation, lazy, interwoven bayous and sloughs. It makes good sense to go in with somebody who knows the region well. Largemouth bass there run to fair size. Attoyac Bayou and Angelina and Neches Rivers also furnish sport.

A series of dams has been built on Trinity River upstream from Fort Worth. Lake Worth is the oldest; others are Eagle Mountain Lake and Lake Bridgeport. Try three reservoirs near Wichita Falls: Lake Kemp, the largest; Diversion Lake, downstream; and Lake Wichita. All are good bass lakes.

Largemouths are numerous in picturesquely named Possum Kingdom Reservoir on the Brazos

near Mineral Wells. Below there you'll find fishing for bass in creeks and sloughs of the Brazos.

Cleburne fishermen visit Cleburne State Park, where there is a public lake. Bass can also be taken along Paluxy River southwest of Cleburne. Near Waco, fishermen have Lake Waco and the Leon River. Medina Lake, northwest of San Antonio, is a good possibility, as is the river above and below. The following lakes, widely scattered, also are excellent largemouth-bass prospects:

Lake Meredith, near Amarillo; Twin Butte Reservoir, near San Angelo; Belton Reservoir, near Belton; Benbrook Reservoir, near Fort Worth; Canyon Reservoir, near New Braunfels; Dam B Reservoir, near Town Bluff; Garza–Little Elm Reservoir, near Denton; Grapevine Reservoir, near Roanoke; Lavon Reservoir, near Lavon; Navarro Mills Reservoir, near Silver City; Texarkana Reservoir, near Texarkana; Whitney Reservoir, near Whitney; Lake Livingston, near Trinity; Lake Conroe in Montgomery County; Houston County Reservoir, near Crockett; Lake Travis, near Austin;

Fishing in Lake Powell, Utah. Once a dry desert, this is now an impoundment where good bass fishing can be found.

Lake Murval, near Carthage; Cedar Creek Reservoir, near Athens; Fairfield Lake, in Freestone County; Lake Casa Blanca, in Webb County; Lake Arrowhead, near Henrietta; Cypress Springs Lake, near Mount Vernon; and Dunlap Lake, near Daingerfield.

Other waters include Lake Monticello, near Mt. Pleasant, a power plant lake that routinely produces bass of over ten pounds. Another power plant lake, Gibbons Creek, near Bryan, yields large bass. Lake Fork, near Sulphur Springs, gave up the state record bass along with several others in excess of thirteen pounds each.

All of the waters in the state have benefited from the introduction of Florida bass. This program was initiated in the early 1970s and as a result the state record has been broken five times since 1980 and now stands at seventeen and three quarters pounds. Texas is currently refining its harvest regulations and stresses catch-and-release. Waters have minimum size limits or slot size limits.

Texas also has several bodies of water with significant smallmouth bass fisheries. The better lakes include Texoma, near Denton; Canyon Lake, between Austin and San Antonio; and Lake Meredith, near Amarillo. The current state record—six pounds, ten ounces—was caught at Lake Whitney, north of Waco.

More information is available from the Texas Parks and Wildlife Department, 4200 Smith School Road, Austin, TX 78744.

Utah

Utah has one good bass water, Lake Powell, formed by Glen Canyon Dam on the Colorado River in the southeastern part of the state. Largemouths strike especially well in spring, around Bullfrog Basin. Smallmouth bass are also coming on here and may eventually surpass the largemouths. Anglers at Powell often live and cruise on the lake in rented houseboats; narrow canyons and coves can be fished from trailed skiffs.

Otherwise, bass-fishing waters are scarce—extremely scarce, in fact. Deer Creek, below Salt Lake City, furnishes some bass fishing. Flaming Gorge Reservoir in northeastern Utah has good smallmouth bass fishing in May and early June.

More information is available from the Utah Division of Wildlife Resources, 1596 West North Temple, Salt Lake City, UT 84116.

Chapter 15
The West

Except for the Sacramento perch (a close cousin of the black bass), which inhabited the Sacramento River drainage in moderate numbers, no member of the black bass family lived on the West Coast until eighty years ago. Today the largemouth bass, at least, is an important game fish in every Pacific Coast state because it has been introduced into nearly every new reservoir built in modern times. What is more, as new reservoirs continue to be built to serve an exploding human population, bass will be released in still other waters.

Largemouths have adapted especially well to their new West Coast homes; at times and in places, the fishing for them rivals that found anywhere. In addition, the bass are attaining a size similar to that of southeastern bass.

California

No species of black bass are native to California, but today the state is on the verge of producing a new world's record, if such a fish is ever caught. While the San Diego County area receives the most press, due to fast growth rates and the introduction of Florida-strain largemouths, good bass fishing occurs throughout the state.

Still, San Diego County is the hot spot. Within

that area, Otay, Miramar, Murray, San Vicente, El Capitan, Henshaw, Wolford, and Cuyamaca Lakes all have produced bass beyond twelve pounds. In San Vicente, an eighteen-pound, nine-ounce largemouth was taken, and during one season (1978), anglers caught more than a hundred largemouths exceeding nine pounds apiece. That is astounding success, especially since the lake is relatively small, is opened only four days a week (Thursdays through Sundays) and for only nine months (October through June) each year. More information can be obtained from the San Diego City Lakes Department, Balboa Park, San Diego, CA 92101.

Probably the best largemouth bass lake in northern California (for numbers and size) is Clear Lake, north of San Francisco, the largest natural lake in the state. For smallmouths, Shasta Lake, formed by damming the Sacramento, rates as the best in terms of quantity. Trinity is best for trophy-sized smallmouths. Lake Casitas produced the second-largest bass known—twenty-one pounds, three ounces—taken in 1980.

Other worthwhile waters are: Castaic, Cachuma Reservoir, East Park Reservoir, Folsom Reservoir, Stony Gorge Reservoir, Pine Flat Reservoir, San Antonio Reservoir, Pardee Reservoir, New Hogan Reservoir (enlarged), New Melones Reservoir (enlarged), Tullock Reservoir, Tinemaha Reservoir,

Topwater Fishing at Lake Casitas

Rich Tauber, a noted professional bass angler from Woodland Hills, California, once enjoyed a remarkable day of topwater fishing at Lake Casitas, which is famous for producing trophy, Florida-strain largemouths. It was foggy on that June morning, due to the lake's close proximity to the ocean, and Tauber had to use his compass to guide him across the lake.

"I was heading out to a place called Station Canyon," he recalls. "It's a very popular place at that time of the year, and it's an excellent place to fish topwater baits."

When Tauber reached Station Canyon, he found that the stalky aquatic vegetation that grows there was just beneath the surface. Soon it would grow up and form a carpet on the surface, but until then it was perfect for topwater fishing. He tied on a Rebel Pop-R with a G finish and began casting to dark spots in the weeds. Because the water was exceptionally clear, Tauber made long casts to avoid spooking the bass.

His Pop-R landed several feet beyond one promising dark patch in the weeds, and he brought the plug to life with skillful twitches of his rod tip. *Chug-chug-chug*, pause; *chug-chug-chug*, pause. *Whoosh!*

The lure suddenly vanished in the midst of a violent strike. Tauber gingerly played the bass out before finally grasping its lower jaw and hoisting the eight-and-a-half-pounder aboard. It was the largest of twenty bass, over three pounds each, that he caught that day with the Pop-R.

"This is a lake," says Tauber, "that I've gone out on many times and never got a strike. It's probably one of the tougher lakes to fish, but if you hit it right, good things can happen. When the lake hasn't been receiving a lot of pressure, you'll find a large number of big fish."

—Mark Hicks

Exchequer Reservoir, Railroad Canyon Reservoir, Vail Reservoir, Barrett Reservoir, Lower Otay Reservoir, Hodges Reservoir, Nacimiento Reservoir, Anderson Reservoir, Coyote Reservoir, Woodward Reservoir, Turlock Reservoir, Don Pedro Reservoir, Piru Reservoir, Bullard's Bar Reservoir, and Salt Springs Valley Reservoir.

More information is available from the California Department of Fish and Game, 1416 9th Street, Sacramento, CA 95814.

Hawaii

Though not native to any of the Hawaiian Islands, bass today are well established in a few waters there. Public fishing for bass is possible at Wahiawa Reservoir on the island of Oahu. There are also several privately controlled bass fishing waters. You'll need permission to fish on them.

More information is available from the Hawaii Division of Aquatic Resources, 1151 Punchbowl Street, Room 330, Honolulu, HI 96813.

Idaho

Bass fishing in Idaho ranges from good to excellent in those lowland lakes and reservoirs where it occurs. Because fishing pressure on bass has increased tremendously in the last ten years, a twelve-inch minimum size limit has been imposed statewide. Larger size limits and shortened seasons on select reservoirs promote higher-quality populations.

Two areas offer excellent largemouth bass fishing. Area 1, or the Panhandle region, provides good largemouth fishing in nearly all of the lakes. Area 4, in the southwestern part of the state, offers good largemouth fishing in most of the lowland lakes and reservoirs. The best smallmouth fishing is found in the Snake River, particularly in the Brownlee, Oxbow, and Hells Canyon impoundments. Inland reservoirs that offer good smallmouth fishing include Hayden Reservoir and Ririe Reservoir, which has a newly established but expanding smallmouth population.

More information is available from Idaho Fish and Game, 600 South Walnut, Box 25, Boise, ID 83707.

Montana

Although Montana is best known for its trout fishing, it also provides opportunities for bass. Interest in warm-water fishing has increased greatly in recent years, and the Montana Department of Fish, Wildlife, and Parks has responded with a management plan that should improve bass fishing in the years ahead.

The best bass fishing occurs in lakes in the Clark Fork, Flathead, and Kootenai River drainages. All these lakes have largemouths; in addition, smallmouths swim in Noxon, Horseshoe (Ferndale), Loon (Ferndale), Little Loon (Highway 2), and Loon (Highway 2). The state record largemouth—three pounds, two and a half ounces—was caught in 1984 from Milnor Lake in northwest Montana. The state record smallmouth, 5.11 pounds, was caught in the fall of 1987 from the huge 230,000-acre Fort Peck Reservoir in eastern Montana.

More information is available from the Montana Department of Fish, Wildlife, and Parks, Region One, P.O. Box 67, Kalispell, MT 59903.

Nevada

All waters of the Colorado River reservoirs (see entry for neighboring Arizona) provide good largemouth bass angling. The next best bet is Ruby Lake National Wildlife Refuge, near Elko. This 38,000-acre marsh often has fast largemouth fishing early in the season. Not all of the marsh is open during waterfowl nesting, though, and you'll need a small boat.

Other good largemouth waters include Fort Churchill Pond, Lahontan Reservoir, Indian Lakes, Mason Valley WMA, Ruby Marsh, and Rye Patch Reservoir, which also has smallmouths. Dry Creek is another good bet for smallmouths.

More information is available from the Nevada Department of Wildlife, Box 10678, Reno, NV 89510.

Oregon

Primarily a trout-fishing state, Oregon has a surprising number of first-rate bass waters. On the north coast lie Sunset and Cullaby Lakes in Clatsop County and Devils Lake in Lincoln County. Farther south on the coast are Sutton, Mercer, Cleawox, Siltcoos, and Tahkenitch. The latter two produce high catch rates and are considered the best in the state. Still farther south lie the Tenmile lakes in Coos County and Garrison Lake in Curry County. Fishing for bass goes on year-round, with the most productive period from May to October.

Owyhee Reservoir, Malheur County, in the southeastern corner of the state has good bass fishing, but is not an easy lake to reach and even launching a boat there can be a chore. In the spring, especially, the fishing should be worth the trouble. Klamath and Lake Counties contain several lakes, including Lake of the Woods, with fair bass fishing. Cottage Grove Reservoir in the Willamette drainage produces nice largemouths.

A great number of very small bass ponds—including sloughs of the Columbia River—contain good bass populations. Most of them are concentrated in Multnomah (especially Sturgeon Lake), Columbia, and Clatsop Counties. At times excellent bass fishing exists in the Willamette River above tidewater and within sight of downtown Portland.

Smallmouth bass fishing in the John Day River of central Oregon compares with any river-fishing for the species in America. The best areas are reached by float-tripping, although at times (after early summer) the water level may be low enough to make this difficult.

More information is available from the Oregon Department of Fish and Wildlife, 506 Southwest Mill St., P.O. Box 59, Portland, OR 97207.

Washington

Washington has good bass fishing in widely scattered waters that receive relatively little pressure. The best in terms of catch rate is 28,000-acre Potholes Reservoir, southwest of Moses Lake in central Washington, which also has bass. Equalizing Reservoir (known as Banks Lake), below Grand Coulee, has both largemouths and smallmouths. Silver Lake is another top bass producer.

Cowlitz, Grant, Douglass, Spokane, and Stevens Counties each contain a number of public bass fishing lakes. Many are not heavily fished, often making for fast action, especially when the water temperatures are ideal for the species.

Casting in the weedy fringes of a typical bass lake in western Oregon.

More information is available from the Washington Department of Wildlife, 600 North Capital Way, Olympia, WA 98504.

Wyoming

Except for Alaska, where no bass exist at all, Wyoming is the poorest bass state. Flaming Gorge Reservoir has the best smallmouth fishing, and Keyhole Reservoir in the northeast part of the state also has good smallmouths. Grayrocks Reservoir near Wheatland has both largemouth and smallmouth. Lake Cameahwait near Riverton has largemouths. Probably the best largemouth fishing in the state is at Hawk Springs Reservoir south of Torrington.

More information is available from the Wyoming Game and Fish Department, Cheyenne, WY 82002.

Chapter 16

Beyond U.S. Borders

Canada

No country other than Canada contains such a high ratio of clear, cool, sweet waters to dry land. Much of this water, in the southern parts of the eastern provinces, is good to excellent for bass. Many lakes contain either largemouths, smallmouths, or both.

Canada is not a promised land for an angler with a record bass on his mind because the shorter summer season in the north precludes their reaching great size. Still, bass fishing in Canada has an attraction all its own. Usually it means casting in an evergreen setting scented and air-conditioned by nature. The smallmouths in particular are terrific performers in waters chilled year-round.

No fisherman will have any trouble finding accommodations or facilities to fit his budget, no matter what it is, in any corner of Canada where bass fishing exists. He can enjoy his fishing from a plush American-plan resort or he can camp for a few dollars in a national or provincial park. There are cottages and cabins of every description. The more adventurous fishermen can plan a canoe trip deep into a wilderness area.

Ontario

Ontario can honestly claim to be a whole continent's favorite fishing ground, with a lake-and-river-surface area estimated at 80,000 square miles—one fifth the total extent of the province. In addition to the Great Lakes, all but one of which touch Ontario, there are numerous large bodies of water—such as Lake of the Woods and Rainy Lake on the international border; and Nipissing, Nipigon, and Simcoe—completely contained within the province. Many other well-known waters average nearly one hundred square miles in area (for instance, the Rideaus, the Muskokas, and the Temagami chains of lakes). To these add countless smaller lakes that lie in an endless chain across the Precambrian Shield of northern Ontario—the count is well over 100,000. (According to expert geographers, only 40,000—less than half the total—are named.) And bass inhabit many of these waters. No Canadian province has more parks, camp grounds, or public facilities for visiting fishermen than Ontario.

There are five major fishing "regions" in Ontario where you can bass-fish from canoe, rowboat, motor launch or cruiser, or by wading. Usually the farther you go from the beaten track, the better are your chances of getting fish. However, some of the best bass fishing awaits you right off Long Point, on the north shore of Lake Erie—an hour's drive from Buffalo, two hours from Detroit.

Southeastern Ontario includes such famous waters as the St. Lawrence River, Lake St. Francis,

Fishermen trolling, during springtime, for smallmouth bass along a rocky shoreline in Ontario.

the Rideau lakes, and Lake Ontario around the Isle of Quinte, plus hundreds of streams and pools lying north of the St. Lawrence from Belleville to Pembroke.

Lake St. Francis and the St. Lawrence River provide the best trolling or casting for bass. Farther west, in Lake Ontario, around the Bay of Quinte, is smallmouth bass territory. Less than fifty miles north of Belleville and Kingston begins the "Land O' Lakes" district, with many bass lakes and streams. There are fishing camps and resorts around Napanee, Tweed, Madoc, Kaladar, Carleton Place, and Renfrew. Just east are the Rideau lakes, accessible from Kingston, with good fishing for largemouth and smallmouth bass early in the season.

Central Ontario covers the populated and industrial areas around Toronto and such vacation districts as Muskoka, Georgian Bay, and the Kawartha Lakes, with Bruce Peninsula on the west and the Haliburton Highlands on the east.

North and west of Lake Simcoe (fair bass) lies the Georgian Bay–Bruce Peninsula area with its good bass fishing. Simcoe is not an easy lake to fish, but with the right combination, it produces fine catches of largemouths and smallmouths. Midland, Penetanguishene, Honey Harbour, Go Home Bay, and the whole rocky shore of Georgian Bay through Parry Sound to French River are good for smallmouths. This whole area, west of Orillia and covering the length of Georgian Bay, makes good bass-fishing territory.

Huntsville marks the entrance to Algonquin Park, which contains numerous bass lakes. In this natural park the canoe is the ideal means of transportation. Any of the resorts or camps in the park, or around Dwight, will outfit you and provide bass guides.

East of Toronto are the seventy-five Kawartha lakes. At Rice Lake, Young's Point, Burleigh Falls, Fenelon Falls, and Bobcaygeon there's good fishing for bass. Lake Scugog is also good for largemouths.

In southwestern Ontario an angler will discover fine bass fishing along the reefs off Nanticoke, Port

A Thousand Fish in the Thousand Islands

A few years ago, I pulled into a large shallow bay off Lake Ontario in the Thousand Islands region of the St. Lawrence River. I was fishing in Ontario waters just after the June opener for bass, and hoped the smallmouths would still be in the shallows after spawning.

I idled into the middle of the bay, watching my depthfinder and keeping my eyes open for boulders that could damage my outboard. When the water reached a depth of about seven feet, I moved up to the bow of my bass boat and continued with the electric motor. The water was so clear that I could see the scattered boulders and sparse weeds on the bottom as though I were looking into an aquarium.

As I worked my way toward the back of the bay, I began casting a tube jig (a Gitzit) with a light-action spinning outfit. I would let the lure sink to the bottom, and then swim it back by slowly cranking the reel handle. The jig skimmed just over the bottom, making occasional contact with a weed or boulder.

I had made only a few casts when my line straightened and I felt the weight of a fish. I pulled back on the rod and a two-pound smallmouth suddenly leaped out of the water. Playing the spunky bass on light line was sheer exhilaration, and it took several minutes to wear the bass down enough so I could land it.

I released that fish and proceeded to catch six more smallmouths on the next six casts. I don't know how many bass I caught that evening; there were very few slow periods between strikes. The bass averaged about two pounds apiece, and I had a few that weighed four pounds. It was the kind of action that all bass anglers dream about, but that few are lucky enough to experience.

—Mark Hicks

Dover, and Port Ryerse. At Rondeau Provincial Park, a forest area and game preserve, there are camping grounds as well as the usual good bass fishing associated with the Lake Erie region, as at Erieau Beach.

Northern Ontario begins at a line drawn from Mattawa to Georgian Bay. In Lake Nipissing plenty of bass swim, especially in the west arm, Trout Lake, and the French River. Eastward from North Bay, the waters connecting Lake Nipissing and the Ottawa River combine bass fishing with historic interest, for this is the time-honored route of Indians and *voyageurs*, the path Champlain took on his first trip into the Northland.

West of North Bay is Sudbury and Aiginawassi, Wanapitei, Ashigami, Kookagaming, Metagamasine, Oden, Thor, and Ivanhoe Lakes, all containing bass. Farther north, in the Chapleau District, Onaping, Metagama, and Biscotasing Lakes are good. On the road to Manitoulin Island, Lake Penage has good smallmouth bass.

Manitoulin Island, the largest freshwater island in the world, is surrounded by Lake Huron, with its excellent summertime bass fishing. Also good are North Channel, Manitowaning Bay, South Bay, Honora Bay, Bayfield Sound, and Meldrum Bay.

Northwestern Ontario from east of Lake Nipigon to the Manitoba border includes Lake of the Woods, a vast lake with thousands of miles of irregular shoreline, making it ideal for fishing camps. South to Fort Frances and Rainy River lies more good smallmouth water.

More information is available from the Ontario Ministry of Tourism, 900 Bay Street, Toronto, Ont. M7A 2E5, Canada.

Quebec

Thanks to widespread stocking during the past sixty years, smallmouth bass are now established in countless Quebec waters. A large percentage were closed to public fishing in the past, due to private clubs that controlled vast areas of backwoods real estate, but all territories now are accessible to all anglers. Some territories may require small daily fees from those who want to fish. The best small-

Angler Dick Kotis grasps a good bass at Treasure Lake, Cuba.

mouth lakes are concentrated in the southwest region of Quebec between Montreal and Hull (Ottawa).

The most important bass water in Quebec is the St. Lawrence River in the Montreal area, including Lake St. Francis, Lake St. Louis (especially at the mouth of the Chateaugay River), Lake St. Pierre, and Lake Two Mountains. Quebec's biggest largemouths probably come from the Missisquoi Bay of Lake Champlain. All the above also have smallmouths. Some good bets for smallmouths alone are Blue Sea and Bitobi Lakes, near Gracefield; Wolf Lake, at Gatineau Provincial Park; and Ottawa Lake, north of Quyon. More than half of the lakes in the Outaouais region contain some smallmouth bass.

More information is available from the Quebec Department of Recreation, Fish, and Game, Place de la Capitale 150 East, ST-Cyrille Blvd., Quebec City, Que. G1R 2B2, Canada.

Manitoba

Smallmouths have been stocked in a few Manitoba lakes, most in the southeast, and in the Whiteshell Forest Reserve. The best fishing is in the Crow Duck (very good), Caddy, and Falcon Lakes, and in the Winnipeg River. Spring and summer are by far the best periods. Two Loon Lake, north of The

Pax, is a catch-and-release lake that produces trophy-sized smallmouths.

New Brunswick

Smallmouth bass aren't widely spread through New Brunswick, but in waters where the fish have become established the fishing is excellent. These are confined to the southwestern part of the province, along or close to the Maine border. They include waters of the Chiputneticook Chain, the beautiful St. Croix River (float-tripping is a good possibility here), Utopia, Palfrey, Magaguadavic, and Little Magaguadavic lakes.

The greatest fishing of all occurs in early June, when smallmouths are in very shallow water. At that time the bass bugging is unbelievably good. Decent fishing occurs throughout the summer and conditions often peak again briefly in September.

Saskatchewan

There is no important bass fishing in Saskatchewan. Largemouth bass are presently being managed at Boundary Reservoir, near Estevan, and smallmouth bass have been stocked into Oyama Reservoir, near Regina.

More information is available from Saskatchewan Parks Recreation and Culture, Fisheries Branch, Box 3003, Prince Albert, SK, S6V 6G1, Canada.

Cuba

Because the United States has cut off diplomatic relations with Cuba, Americans who travel there risk fines and prison terms. If the two countries establish friendlier relations in the future and allow travel, some of the best bass fishing in the world may once again be available to American sportsmen.

Bass from the United States were stocked in Zapata Swamp in the 1920s and have thrived there as in few other places. While a world-record bass has never materialized there, as some predicted, bass have been taken weighing over fifteen pounds, and eight to ten-pound bass are relatively common.

Treasure Lake is well known for producing many big bass, but there is no such thing as a bad bass lake in Cuba, which has 117 major lakes, 700 minidams, and 33 lakes under construction. Some of the top bass lakes now include Redonda, Por Venir, Cuayaguateje, Najasa, Leonardo, and Nipe.

A fifteen-pound bass from Lake Zaza, Cuba, where even larger bass may someday be taken.

Mexico and Central America

Mexico offers much good bass fishing, and some of the better waters close to the United States border include Guerrero Lake and Obregon Lake, near Cuidad Obregon. Nearer the border lies Angostura Reservoir, just south of Douglas, Arizona. You can charter a small plane or go by group-package charter to most of these places from points in the southwestern United States.

A complete list of all Mexican bass-fishing waters has never been compiled, but the following lakes have excellent bass fishing: Don Martin Dam, The Republic of Espanol, Lake Lavaderos, San Lorenzo, Lake Nivillo, Diminguez, Hidalgo, Cero-prieto, Pedro J. Mendez, Baccarrac, Adolfo Lopez Mateos, Lopez Portillo, Guadalupe Victoria, Yosocuto, and Ocoroni, a new lake.

Anglers interested in fishing in Mexico would do well to contact Dan Snow, Bass Research International, P.O. Box 5481, Kingwood, TX 77325. Telephone: (713) 358-2262.

During the early 1970s, some very large (at least fourteen-pound) bass were taken in beautiful Lago Yojoa in Honduras. Some fish just as large may still exist, despite much subsistence fishing by locals. Lake Atitlan in the Guatemala highlands has largemouth bass, but very little sport fishing has been done there for the species.

Appendixes

APPENDIX I

Fishing Information

All American Poor Boy
7611 S. Quebec Place
Tulsa, OK 74136
(918) 494-0032

American Fishing Institute
Indiana State University
Instructional Services
Terre Haute, IN 47809
(812) 237-2345

Bass Anglers Sportsman Society
P.O. Box 17900
Montgomery, AL 36117
(205) 272-9530

Bassing America Corp.
4660 Sunbelt
Dallas, TX 75248
(214) 380-2656

Bass 'N Gal
P.O. Box 13929
Arlington, TX 76013
(817) 265-6214

Bass Research Foundation
P.O. Box 99
Starkville, MS 39759
(601) 323-3131

Bass World Sports Tournament Assoc.
1159 North Hwy. 67
Florissant, MO 63031
(314) 839-2433

Budweiser Bass Series
37201 Beech Hills Dr.
Willoughby Hills, OH 44094
(216) 942-4470

Budweiser Pro Bass League
P.O. Box 702292
Tulsa, OK 74170
(918) 494-0032

Fish America Foundation
1010 Massachusetts Ave. N.W.
Washington, D.C. 20001
(202) 898-0869

Fishing Facts
P.O. Box 609
Menomonee Falls, WI 53051

Fishing Hall of Fame
Box 33, Hall of Fame Drive
Hayward, WI 54843
(715) 634-4440

Guys and Gals Bass Assoc.
1215 Southeast 44th
Oklahoma City, OK 73129
(405) 672-FISH

Hardee's Tarheel Team Tournaments
2002 Knightdale Drive
Wilson, NC 27893
(919) 237-3380

Hungry Fisherman
Route 2, Box 262
Denver, NC 28037
(704) 483-1143

In Fisherman
P.O. Box 999
Brainerd, MN 56401

International Game Fish Assoc.
3000 E. Las Olas Blvd.
Ft. Lauderdale, FL 33316
(305) 467-0161

Lady Bass
P.O. Box 1939
Winter Haven, FL 33883
(813) 293-3129

Match Bass Fishing
600 Texas Commerce Bank
Amarillo, TX 79109
(806) 376-9900

Military Bass Anglers Assoc.
P.O. Box 796908
Dallas, TX 75379
(214) 380-2656

National Cartographic Information Center
U.S. Geological Survey
507 National Center
Reston, VA 22092
(703) 860-6045

Northwest American Bass
P.O. Box 9037
Nampa, ID 83652
(208) 466-8557

Operation Bass/Red Man
Route 2, Box 74B
Gilbertsville, KY 42044
(503) 362-4880

Pro-Am Teams, Inc.
11647 Jefferson Davis Hwy.
Chester, VA 23831
(804) 748-8972

Professional Bass Anglers Assoc.
P.O. Box 23958
Tempe, AZ 85282
(602) 831-6419

Smallmouth Magazine
P.O. Box 670
Edgefield, SC 29824
(803) 637-5722

Specialty Bass Tournament
334 Lollipop
Franston, TX 75763
(214) 876-4288

Sport Fishing Institute
608 13th Street NW
Washington, DC 20005
(202) 898-0770

Sun Country Bass Assoc.
P.O. Box 337
Alamogordo, NM 88310
(505) 437-6340

Suzuki Scholarship Tournaments
P.O. Box 971
Madison, IN 47250
(812) 273-2799

Texas Black Bass
7880 Carr Street
Dallas, TX 75227
(214) 388-4724

Tournament Fisherman Unlimited Inc.
P.O. Box 37100
Tallahassee, FL 32315
(904) 576-7169

U.S. Army Corps of Engineers
536 South Clark St.
Chicago, IL 60605

U.S. Bass
P.O. Box 696
Mesa, AZ 85201
(602) 834-5045

West Coast Bass
7956 California Ave.
Fair Oaks, CA 95628
(916) 962-BASS

World Bass Assoc.
P.O. Box 6389
Deltona, FL 32728
(305) 574-9393

APPENDIX II

Manufacturers

Abu-Garcia Inc.
21 Law Dr.
Fairfield, NJ 07006
(201) 227-7666

Acme Tackle Co., Inc.
69 Bucklin St.
Providence, RI 02907
(401) 331-6437

All Star Graphite Rods
10235 W. Little York, Suite 150
Houston, TX 77040
(713) 939-7188

Fred Arbogast Co., Inc.
313 W. North St.
Akron, OH 44303
(216) 253-2177

Arkie Lures Inc.
P.O. Box 1460
Springdale, AR 72764
(501) 751-7891

Jim Bagley Bait Co., Inc.
P.O. Drawer 110
Winter Haven, FL 33880
(813) 294-4271

Bass-Hawg Baits
P.O. Box 547
Middleton, ID 83644
(208) 585-2583

Bass Hunter Lures Inc.
RR #1 Box 193
Yorktown, IN 47396
(317) 286-4020

Bass Unlimited Lure Co., Inc.
620 Monroe St.
Beatrice, NE 68310
(402) 228-FISH

Bass Pro Shops
P.O. Box 4046
Springfield, MO 65808
(417) 883-4960

Berkley & Co., Inc.
Hwy 9 & 71
Spirit Lake, IA 51360
(712) 336-1520

Blakemore Sales Corp.
P.O. Box 1149
Branson, MO 65616
(417) 334-5340

Blue Fox Tackle Co.
645 N. Emerson
Cambridge, MN 55008

Bomber Bait Co.
Box 1058
Gainesville, TX 76240
(817) 665-5505

Boone Bait Co., Inc.
Box 4009
Winter Park, FL 32793
(305) 671-2930

Brother's Bait Co.
P.O. Box 24078
Lexington, KY 24078
(606) 278-4277

Browning Co.
Route 1
Morgan, UT 84050
(801) 876-2711

Bumble Bee Baits
P.O. Box 1169
Mountain Home, AR 72653
(501) 425-7868

Burke-Flexo Products Co.
1969 S. Airport Rd.
Traverse City, MI 49684
(616) 947-5010

Canyon Lures
2465 Northern Ave.
Kingman, AZ 86401

Lew Childre & Sons, Inc.
110 E. Azalea St.
Foley, AL 36535
(205) 943-5041

Cordell Tackle Inc.
Box 1452, 3601 Jenny Lind
Fort Smith, AR 72902
(501) 782-1607

Cortland Line Co.
Kellog Rd.
Cortland, NY 13045
(607) 756-2851

Crankbait/Anglers Pride
Division of Highland Group
9300 Midwest Ave.
Garfield Heights, OH 44125
(216) 475-9300

Creme Lure Co.
Box 87
Tyler, TX 75701
(214) 593-7371

Daiwa Corp.
7421 Chapman Ave.
Garden Grove, CA 92641
(714) 895-6645

Eppinger Mfg. Co.
6340 Schaefer Hwy.
Dearborn, MI 48126
(313) 582-3202

Fenwick
Division of Woodstream Corp.
14799 Chestnut St.
Westminster, CA 92683
(714) 897-1066

The Fishin' Worm Company
5512 S. Florida Ave.
Lakeland, FL 33803
(813) 644-1149

Fishmaster Mfg. Co.
825 N. Portland
Oklahoma City, OK 73107
(405) 946-3371

Flambeau Products Corp.
Valplast Rd.
Middlefield, OH 44062
(216) 632-1631

Fleck Lure Co.
P.O. Box 715
Marlboro, MA 01752
(617) 481-4408

Gladding Corp.
Box 164
S. Otselic, NY 13155
(315) 653-7211

Gudebrod Bros. Silk Co., Inc.
P.O. Box 357
Pottstown, PA 19464
(215) 327-4050

James Heddons Sons
P.O. Box 167
Ft. Smith, AR 72902
(616) 782-5123

Hopkins Fishing Lures Co., Inc.
1130 Boissevain Ave.
Norfolk, VA 23507
(804) 622-0977

Johnson Fishing Inc.
P.O. Box 3129
Mankato, MN 56001
(507) 345-4623

Johnson Fishing Inc.
P.O. Box 118
Amsterdam, MO 64723
(816) 267-3217

Knight Mfg. Co., Inc.
Box 6162
Tyler, TX 75711
(214) 561-0522

La Cross Rubber Mills Inc.
Box 1328
La Crosse, WI 54601
(608) 782-3020

Lazy Ike Corp.
Box 3410
Sioux City, IA 51102
(402) 494-2013

Bill Lewis Lures
P.O. Box 4062
Alexandria, LA 71301
(318) 487-0352

Lindy-Little Joe Inc.
P.O. Box C
Brainerd, MN 54601
(218) 829-1714

Luhr Jensen & Sons
P.O. Box 297
Hood River, OR 97031
(503) 386-3811

Mann's Bait Mfg. Co.
P.O. Box 604
State Docks Rd.
Eufaula, AL 36027
(205) 687-5716

Marathon Rubber Products
510 Sherman St.
Wausau, WI 54401
(715) 845-6255

Martin Reel Co., Inc.
30 E. Main St.
Mohawk, NY 13407
(315) 866-1690

Maxima Fishing Lines
5 Chrysler St.
Irvine, CA 92718-2009
(213) 515-2543

Mister Twister Inc.
P.O. Drawer 996
Minden, LA 71055
(318) 377-8818

O. Mustad & Son (U.S.A.), Inc.
P.O. Box 838
Auburn, NY 13021
(315) 253-2793

Norman Mfg. Co., Inc.
P.O. Box 580
Greenwood, AR 72936
(501) 996-2125

Normark Corp.
1200 E. 79th St.
Bloomington, MN 55420

The Orvis Co., Inc.
10 River Rd.
Manchester, VT 05254
(802) 362-3622

Penn Fishing Tackle Mfg. Co.
3028 W. Hunting Park Ave.
Philadelphia, PA 19132
(215) 229-9415

Pflueger Sporting Goods Div.
P.O. Drawer P
Columbia, SC 29260
(803) 754-7540

Plano Molding Co.
113 S. Center
Plano, IL 60545
(312) 552-3111

Plastics Research and Development Corp.
3601 Jenny Lind Rd.
Ft. Smith, AR 72902
(501) 782-8971

Producto Lure Co., Inc.
590 Rinehart Rd.
Lake Mary, FL 32746
(305) 323-3060

Rabble Rouser Lures
P.O. Box 644
New Philadelphia, OH 44663
(216) 339-7511

Red Ball Outdoor Products
Benson Rd.
Middlebury, CT 06749
(203) 573-2000

Scientific Anglers/3M
3M Center 223 3S
St. Paul, MN 55144
(612) 733-6066

Shakespeare Co.
P.O. Drawer S
Columbia, SC 29260

Sheldon's Inc.
CS 508
Antigo, WI 54409
(715) 623-2382

Shimano American Corp.
205 Jefferson Rd.
Parsippany, NJ 07054
(201) 884-2300

Silstar Corp. of America
P.O. Box 6505
West Columbia, SC 29171
(803) 794-8521

Smithwick Lures Inc.
P.O. Box 1205, 5935 N. Market
Shreveport, LA 71163
(318) 929-2318

Shagproof Mfg., Inc.
4153 E. Galbraith
Cincinnati, OH 45236
(513) 489-6483

South Bend Sporting Goods Inc.
1950 Stanley
Northbrook, IL 60062
(312) 564-1900

Stanley Jigs Inc.
P.O. Box 722
Huntington, TX 75949
(409) 876-5901

Storm Mfg. Co.
Box 265
Norman, OK 73070
(405) 329-5894

Strike King Lure Co., Inc.
174 Hwy. 72 W.
Collierville, TN 38017

System Lures
P.O. Box 1225
Athens, OH 45701

Tru-Turn Inc.
P.O. Box 767
Wetumpka, AL 36092

Uncle Josh Bait Co.
P.O. Box 130
Fort Atkinson, WI 53538
(414) 563-2491

Whizkers—The Fishing Systems
World Wide Outdoor Mktg.
1601 Shreveport Rd.
Minden, LA 71055
(318) 371-2151

Whopper Stopper/Fliptail
Box 1111
Sherman, TX 75090
(214) 893-6557

The Worth Company
P.O. Box 88
Stevens Point, WI 54481
(715) 344-6081

Yakima Bait Co.
P.O. Box 310
Granger, WA 98932
(509) 854-1311

Zebco
Div. of Brunswick Corp.
P.O. Box 270
Tulsa, OK 74101
(918) 836-5581

Appendix III

Electronic Devices

Eagle Electronics
P.O. Box 669
Catoosa, OK 74105
(918) 266-5373

Fish Hawk Electronics Corp.
Box 340
Crystal Lake, IL 60014
(815) 459-6510

Impulse
329 Railroad Ave.
Pittsburg, CA 94565
(415) 439-2072

King Marine Radio Corp.
5320 140th Ave.
N. Clearwater, FL 33520
(813) 530-3411

Lowrance Electronics
12000 E. Skelly
Tulsa, OK 74128
(918) 437-6881

Ray Jefferson
Main and Cotton Streets
Philadelphia, PA 19127
(215) 487-2800

Si-Tex Marine Electronics Inc.
P.O. Box 6700
Clearwater, FL 33518
(813) 535-4681

Techsonic Industries Inc.
1 Humminbird Lane
Eufaula, AL 36027
(205) 687-6615

Vexilar Inc.
9252 Grand Ave. S.
Minneapolis, MN 55420
(612) 884-5291

APPENDIX IV

Trolling Motors

Byrd Industries
P.O. Box 278
Shelbyville, KY 40065
(502) 633-1338

Evinrude Motors Div. Outboard Marine Corp.
4143 N. 27th St.
Milwaukee, WI 53216

Johnson Outboards
200 Seahorse Dr.
Waukegan, IL 60085
(312) 689-6200

Mariner Outboard Motors
1939 Pioneer Rd.
Fond du Lac, WI 54935
(414) 929-5107

Mercury Marine
1939 Pioneer Rd.
Fond du Lac, WI 54935
(414) 929-5997

Minn Kota
Johnson Fishing, Inc.
1531 Madison Ave.
Mankato, MN 56001
(507) 345-4623

MotorGuide
Zebco Corp.
A Brunswick Company
Box 270
Tulsa, OK 74101

Pflueger Sporting Goods Div.
P.O. Drawer P
Columbia, SC 29260
(803) 754-7540

Shakespeare Co.
P.O. Drawer S
Columbia, SC 29260

APPENDIX V

A Directory of Conservation Bureaus and Other Sources of Fishing Information in the United States and Canada

(Fishing seasons, license costs, and up-to-date information are available from state and provincial addresses listed here.)

United States

Alabama Department of Conservation and Natural
    Resources
64 North Union Street
Montgomery, AL 36130

Alaska Department of Fish and Game
P.O. Box 3-2000
Juneau, AK 99802

Arizona Game and Fish Department
I and E Division
2222 West Greenway Road
Phoenix, AZ 85023

Arkansas Game and Fish Commission
No. 2 Natural Resources Drive
Little Rock, AR 72205

California Department of Fish and Game
1416 Ninth Street
Sacramento, CA 95814

Colorado Division of Wildlife
6060 Broadway
Denver, CO 80216

Connecticut Department of Environmental
    Protection
State Office Building
165 Capitol Avenue
Hartford, CT 06106

Delaware Division of Fish and Wildlife
P.O. Box 1401
Dover, DE 19903

Florida Game and Fresh Water Fish Commission
620 South Meridian Street
Tallahassee, FL 32399-1600

Georgia Department of Natural Resources
205 Butler St.
Atlanta, GA 30334

Hawaii Department of Land and Natural Resources
1151 Punchbowl Street
Honolulu, HI 96813

Idaho Fish and Game Department
P.O. Box 25
600 South Walnut Street
Boise, ID 83707

Illinois Department of Conservation
Lincoln Tower Plaza
524 S. Second St.
Springfield, IL 62706

Indiana Department of Natural Resources
608 State Office Building
Indianapolis, IN 46204

Iowa Department of Natural Resources
E. Ninth and Grand Ave.
Wallace Bldg.
Des Moines, IA 50319

Kansas Department of Wildlife and Parks
900 Jackson St., Suite 502
Topeka, KS 66612-1220

Kentucky Department of Fish and Wildlife
   Resources
#1 Game Farm Road
Frankfort, KY 40601

Louisiana Department of Wildlife and Fisheries
P.O. Box 15570
Baton Rouge, LA 70895

Maine Department of Inland Fisheries and
   Wildlife
State St., Station #41
Augusta, ME 04333

Maryland Department of Natural Resources
Tawes State Office Building
Annapolis, MD 21401

Massachusetts Division of Fisheries and Wildlife
100 Cambridge Street
Boston, MA 02202

Michigan Department of Natural Resources
P.O. Box 30028
Lansing, MI 48909

Minnesota Department of Natural Resources
500 Lafayette Road
St. Paul, MN 55155

Mississippi Department of Wildlife Conservation
Box 451
Jackson, MS 39205

Missouri Department of Conservation
P.O. Box 180
Jefferson City, MO 65102

Montana Department of Fish, Wildlife, and Parks
1420 E. Sixth
Helena, MT 59620

Nebraska Game and Parks Commission
2200 N. 33rd St.
P.O. Box 30370
Lincoln, NE 68503

Nevada Department of Wildlife
P.O. Box 10678
Reno, NV 89520

New Hampshire Fish and Game Department
34 Bridge Street
Concord, NH 03301

New Jersey Department of Environmental
   Protection
Division of Fish, Game, and Shell Fisheries
401 E. State St., CN 402
Trenton, NJ 08625

New Mexico Game and Fish Department
Villagra Bldg.
Santa Fe, NM 87503

New York State Environmental Conservation
   Department
Division of Fish and Wildlife
50 Wolf Road
Albany, NY 12233

North Carolina Wildlife Resources Commission
Archdale Bldg.
512 N. Salisbury St.
Raleigh, NC 27611

North Dakota State Game and Fish Department
100 North Bismarck
Bismarck, ND 58501

Ohio Fish and Game Division
Department of Natural Resources
Fountain Square
Columbus, OH 43224

Oklahoma Department of Wildlife Conservation
Box 53465
Oklahoma City, OK 73152

Oregon Department of Fish and Wildlife
107 20th St.
La Grande, OR 97850

Pennsylvania Fish Commission
P.O. Box 1673
Harrisburg, PA 17105

Rhode Island Division of Fish and Wildlife
Washington County Government Center
Wakefield, RI 02879

South Carolina Wildlife and Marine Resources
    Department
Rembert C. Dennis Bldg.
P.O. Box 167
Columbia, SC 29202

South Dakota Game, Fish, and Parks Department
445 East Capitol
Pierre, SD 57501-3185

Tennessee Wildlife Resources Agency
P.O. Box 40747
Ellington Agricultural Center
Nashville, TN 37204

Texas Parks and Wildlife Department
4200 Smith School Road
Austin, TX 78744

Utah Division of Wildlife Resources
1596 West North Temple
Salt Lake City, UT 84116

Vermont Department of Fish and Wildlife
Waterbury Complex 10
Montpelier, VT 05602

Virginia Department of Game and Inland Fisheries
P.O. Box 11104
Richmond, VA 23230

Washington Department of Wildlife
600 North Capitol Way
Olympia, WA 98504

West Virginia Department of Natural Resources
1800 Washington Street
East Charleston, WV 25305

Wisconsin Department of Natural Resources
P.O. Box 7921
Madison, WI 53707

Wyoming Game and Fish Department
Cheyenne, WY 82002

Canada

Manitoba Department of Natural Resources
Fisheries Branch
Box 20
1495 St. James Street
Winnipeg, Man. R3H 0W9
Canada

Ontario Ministry of Natural Resources
Fisheries Branch
Toronto, Ont. M7A 1W3
Canada

Prince Edward Island Fish and Wildlife Division
P.O. Box 2000
Charlottetown, PEI C1A 7N8
Canada

Quebec Department of Tourism, Fish, and Game
Tourist Branch
Place de la Capitale
150 East, St. Cyrille Blvd.
Quebec City, Que. G1R 2B2
Canada

Saskatchewan Department of Tourism and
    Renewable Resources
Fisheries Branch
3211 Albert St.
Regina, Sask. S4S 5W6
Canada

About the Authors

ERWIN BAUER is a full-time outdoor writer and photographer whose articles have appeared in many magazines, including *Sports Illustrated, Outdoor Life, National Geographic,* and *Audubon.* With his wife, Peggy, he has written numerous books on outdoor sports and nature, including *The Waterfowler's Bible* and *The Saltwater Fisherman's Bible,* also in this series. The Bauers live in Jackson Hole, Wyoming.

MARK HICKS is an award-winning outdoor writer and photographer who specializes in bass fishing. He has fished for bass extensively across the United States, and his articles have appeared in many publications, including *Bassmaster, Bass Fishing, Field & Stream, Outdoor Life, Sports Afield, Fishing Facts,* and others. Hicks currently writes the fishing column for *Fur-Fish-Game.*

He has also been a consistently high finisher in state and regional bass fishing tournaments and is now competing on the professional B.A.S.S. circuit. The professional tour has taken him west to Lake Mead, Nevada, east to the Thousand Islands region of the St. Lawrence River, to Lake Okeechobee in southern Florida, and to many bass waters between these points. He has fished with many of the top professional bass anglers in the country and has learned their most productive tactics firsthand.

A frequent lecturer at fishing seminars, Hicks resides with his wife, Debbi, and daughter, Valerie, in Millfield, Ohio.